Hiram Francis Fairbanks

A visit to Europe and the Holy Land

Hiram Francis Fairbanks

A visit to Europe and the Holy Land

ISBN/EAN: 9783337280062

Printed in Europe, USA, Canada, Australia, Japan

Cover: Foto ©Andreas Hilbeck / pixelio.de

More available books at **www.hansebooks.com**

A VISIT TO EUROPE

AND THE

HOLY LAND

BY

REV. H. F. FAIRBANKS

NEW YORK
THE CATHOLIC PUBLICATION SOCIETY CO.
9 Barclay Street

London : BURNS & OATES, Limited
28 Orchard Street

1888

DEDICATION.

TO THE

HOLY FAMILY OF NAZARETH,

JESUS, MARY, AND JOSEPH,

THIS BOOK IS

MOST HUMBLY DEDICATED

BY

THEIR UNWORTHY SERVANT,

THE AUTHOR.

PREFACE.

In the following pages I have endeavored to describe what I saw, and the impressions received, during a visit to some of the most interesting countries of the Old World, from the point of view of an honest and unprejudiced American. The time that I was abroad might be considered by some as insufficient to obtain an intelligent understanding of the matters about which I write. My answer to this is, that I have not attempted the impossible, and I am well aware that few men are able to write a thoroughly philosophical treatise on the historical, political, and social life of even their own native land. I am also cognizant of the fact that many foreigners, after a brief sojourn in other countries, attempt to discuss them intelligently, a work which they oftentimes would not be able to accomplish if they had lived in them their whole lives. Yet it must be admitted by all that previous thorough preparation and honesty of purpose will enable the traveller to make more correct observations, and to understand better the customs, character, and condition of the people whom he visits, than would be possible for those less honest or less intelligent, who might take up their residence among them many months, or even years.

The book which I now present to the public does not pretend to high things, but is a simple narrative of the travels of one who never before had been out of America, where his ancestors have lived for nearly two and one-half centuries.

I did not go abroad with the idea that everything American is right and everything in Europe wrong. I tried to look on all that I saw in an honest and truthful light. I was willing to learn, and to conform myself to the manners and way of life of those with whom I came in contact. I did not expect that Europe would adopt American customs for my particular benefit; in fact, I am glad that it did not, for by so doing my journey would have been much less agreeable. While I may have doubts whether I would prefer to live in Europe or America, I am certain that I would prefer to travel in Europe.

I am aware of the fact that many books have been written on European and Palestine travel; but it is well known that hardly any of them have been written by Catholic Americans. Our people, both Catholics and non-Catholics, have read too many books of travel written by dishonest writers, or else by those who are so narrow in their views and so ill-informed with reference to the countries through which they passed that their statements and "facts" have been a mere travesty of truth. I am convinced that there has been in America a long-existing need, but a poor supply, of books of travel written by travellers who are able to see with honest eyes, and who do not go abroad with preconceived prejudices, which they are determined to confirm by perverted facts and short-sighted observations.

Being conscious of this need, I have endeavored to do my share to remedy the deficiency by presenting this book to my co-religionists and countrymen, with the hope that they will find it entertaining and instructive.

H. F. FAIRBANKS.

Milwaukee, 1887.

CONTENTS.

CHAPTER I.
The Atlantic Voyage and the Emerald Isle................. 11

CHAPTER II.
Wales and England............................... 28

CHAPTER III.
La Belle France................................ 38

CHAPTER IV.
Northern Italy and Rome................................. 56

CHAPTER V.
Southern Italy and the Voyage to Egypt.................. 66

CHAPTER VI.
The Land of the Pharaos and of the Pyramids............. 79

CHAPTER VII.
The Pyramids—Refuge of the Holy Family in Egypt—Our Voyage to Palestine......................... 97

CHAPTER VIII.
Jaffa and the Road to Jerusalem....... 110

CHAPTER IX.
The Holy City, Jerusalem.............................. 122

CHAPTER X.
Some Sacred Places near Jerusalem..................... 146

CHAPTER XI.
The Jewish Temple on Mount Moria, and the First Christian Church on Mount Sion................................. 157

CHAPTER XII.
Bethlehem.. 172

CHAPTER XIII.
Jericho and the Dead Sea................................. 182

CHAPTER XIV.
A Morning and Day in Palestine......................... 194

CHAPTER XV.
The "Hill-Country of Judea" and House of the Visitation.. 200

CHAPTER XVI.
"Nobis Donet in Patria"................................. 207

CHAPTER XVII.
Mount Carmel—The Mountain of the Prophets and of the Blessed Virgin Mary.................................... 210

CHAPTER XVIII.
The Light of Nazareth................................... 216

CHAPTER XIX.
"His Own Country".................................. 226

CHAPTER XX.
Departure from the Holy Land........................ 238

CHAPTER XXI.
From Alexandria to Naples........................... 244

CHAPTER XXII.
"See Naples and then Die"........................... 252

CHAPTER XXIII.
The Eternal City.................................... 263

CHAPTER XXIV.
The Holy Father—Education, Religion, and Art........ 283

CHAPTER XXV.
Sacred and Historic Places of Pagan and Christian Rome... 293

CHAPTER XXVI.
From Rome to Loretto................................ 320

CHAPTER XXVII.
Bologna, Padua, and Venice.......................... 329

CHAPTER XXVIII.
Northern Italy and Southern Switzerland............. 346

CHAPTER XXIX.

The Home of William Tell and the Four Forest Cantons.... 360

CHAPTER XXX.

From Lake Constance to the City of the Apostle of Germany, by way of Munich.................................. 367

CHAPTER XXXI.

From Mainz to Cologne—The Vine-clad and Castle-crowned Rhine... 379

CHAPTER XXXII.

From the Banks of the Rhine to Belgium's and Holland's Capitals.. 388

CHAPTER XXXIII.

Return to England, and a Trip to Scotland................ 402

CHAPTER XXXIV.

The Emerald Gem of the Ocean........................... 422

CHAPTER XXXV.

Cashel of the Kings and the Lakes of Killarney........... 453

A VISIT TO
Europe and the Holy Land.

CHAPTER I.

THE ATLANTIC VOYAGE AND THE EMERALD ISLE.

The afternoon of a bright day in the early part of the month of May, in the year 1884, found us aboard one of the large Atlantic steamers, which had thrown off her lines and was gradually floating out of New York harbor towards the broad ocean.

It was our first trip to the Old World, and the varied sensations as we steamed down the bay, past the various objects of interest, towards the vast Atlantic were new and strange to us. Our eyes lingered lovingly on the receding shores of our native land, and as we bid them adieu memory dwelt fondly on the friends and loved ones whom we had left at home.

There were three of us: Rev. Thomas Fagan, of Bay View; Rev. Joseph Keenan, of Fond du Lac—two clerical friends—and myself, all of the

Archdiocese of Milwaukee. A few weeks before we had decided that the time had come to make a visit to Europe and the Orient. Our passage and rooms had been secured, and at last we were leaving America; and, although the time for our travels was limited, perhaps we should never return, or, returning, what changes might take place during our absence!

Darkness at length settled down over the waters of the deep, and the morning only revealed to us a leaden sky and an expanse of black, gloomy waves. The record of one day was the repetition of another, except that some days were sunshiny and others were dismal with a dense fog or dark, threatening weather; and sometimes the ever-restless ocean was less restless, and sometimes wilder and more angry. Some of the passengers enjoyed themselves, and considered the voyage a most pleasant affair. I disliked it very much. I was not sea-sick, but my entire surroundings had a most depressing effect on my spirits. If ever again I cross the Atlantic it will be on the fastest steamer that sails the sea. Too much imagination is very disagreeable when you are a thousand miles from land, and your steamer, with its living cargo, is only a speck on the immensity of waters. I looked out upon the dark and troubled sea, and sometimes not even a white-winged ship was in sight during the entire day. Neither did the sportive finny tribes nor monsters of the deep display themselves. A few sea-gulls here and there were seen enjoying themselves over the waves, many hundred miles from their rocky homes. Or have they a home? Is the ocean their home, or the rocky crag where they build their nests?

My only real recreation was reading. I read the principal poems of two or three volumes of poetry; but I enjoyed myself best in reading and taking notes from a work entitled *Walks in Rome*. Our steamer—like all those of all lines sailing from New York to Liverpool, so far as I know—was thoroughly English. And as many of the passengers lived in some portion of the British Isles, for the last two days of the voyage there was a cheerful air about nearly every one in anticipation of home. Even we ourselves began to get animated at the thought that, if not approaching our own homes, we were drawing near the land of our ancestors.

Early in the forenoon of the ninth day from New York old voyagers said that land was visible, and aided the less experienced travellers to get sight of it; but a thin haze very much impeded their and our effort. It was not long, however, before the dim outlines of the Great Skellig Rock could be distinguished from the clouds and water by the more inexperienced eye. Then other rocks appeared, and, finally, the blue line of the southern mainland of Ireland, and farther in the interior, rising higher, could be seen the mountains of Kerry.

This was our first sight of the Old World, and the indistinctness with which we saw it lent a wonderful enchantment to the view. There, not far away, lay ancient Erin, the beautiful Emerald Isle, which even in modern times possesses such a magic influence over the hearts of all her children. We were approaching nearer and nearer to grand, faithful, Catholic Ireland, the "Island of Saints and Scholars." It was not the land of my ancestors, but it was the home of the fathers and mothers and the birthplace of a large number of those who are among the nearest and dearest to me of any in this life. With my mind filled with memories of her past glories and sanctity, of her centuries of sorrow and martyrdom, and with the thought of her present hopes, with the affection I hold for many to whom the welfare of that island is dearer than life, I could not help being stirred with deep emotion, so that I hardly dared speak a single sentence lest the fulness of my heart might become too manifest.

The southern coast looked brown, bleak, and barren, and the waves could be seen dashing into white foam against it. A number of sails were seen, indicating the near approach to busy life. The waters of the ocean gradually changed from their dark color into the most beautiful green that I have ever seen. We passed Fastnet Light and Old Head of Kinsale, while the coast became more settled and cultivated. We could see houses and villages, and, with the aid of a glass, trees and hedge rows, and green fields which, to the unaided eye, had appeared brown.

About the middle of the afternoon on Saturday we arrived in the Cove of Cork, or harbor of Queenstown. Our steamer came to a stop, and we were transferred to a tender which would convey us to the land. The harbor is very fine, and the shores were covered with the typical emerald green. As we started towards the shore we gave a farewell cheer to the great ship that had borne us safely across the Atlantic, and waved "adieu" to those companions of our voyage who did not land. Everything about us was now Irish. The voices, the laughter, the countenances, and the scene were all Irish. The sights and surroundings were thoroughly Irish, and I fully enjoyed them. At the landing we were met by a good-sized crowd of "Hibernian gems," old men with donkey-carts drawn by sleepy-looking donkeys, and boys of every size, with good-natured, smiling faces, ready to offer their services to carry our luggage to the hotel. Having chosen several as our escort, we walked with the procession to the nearest hotel, where we registered and were soon resting, thankful that we were once more on dry land, and in the Old World, where the day-dreams of our life were about to be realized. But let no one imagine that in the midst of strange and attractive surroundings we did not think of our far-off home and friends. Into my heart gradually and silently stole a frequent and unwelcome companion of my entire journey—homesickness —which tinged the bright green scenes around me with a sombre hue.

After a brief rest we started out for a walk. It does not take long to see Queenstown, but as it was the first place that we had visited in Ireland everything seemed most interesting. We visited the new cathedral, and wandered through the streets and pleasure-grounds looking at everything. I began thus early to gather leaves and flowers as mementoes, and bought some shamrocks to send home in letters which I would write in the evening. In the morning we attended Mass at the cathedral. Two of our number did not usually say Mass, except in places of special devotion, as we knew that it was often inconvenient for the pastors of churches to have foreign priests saying Mass at irregular hours, especially on Sundays.

After Mass we started for Cork by boat, as we wished to behold with our own eyes the far-famed beauties of the river Lee. They are not overestimated. It was a fine Sunday morning in the month of May, and the ever-changing picturesqueness of the scenery was all that the heart could desire./

We arrived in Cork before noon, and, having chosen a hotel and learned the hour of dinner, we hired a jaunting-car for a trip to Blarney. It was our first ride on a jaunting-car, and from the accounts of some travellers we expected that it would be difficult to keep our seat. Nothing is farther from the truth, as they are very easy and safe vehicles on which to ride./

Cork was in its Sunday attire, and we saw it at its best. The inhabitants, who are good specimens of the southern Celt, were well dressed and respectable-looking, and seemed to be thoroughly enjoying themselves. Crowds of people who had attended late Masses were coming out of the churches, and, like those who attend High Mass in nearly all countries, were among the most genuinely respectable of the population of the city. To realize that we were in a real Irish city we had only to read the signs on the different places of business. The smallest as well as the largest had on it the name of an Irishman. This fact produced in us a new feeling never before experienced: that all around us, the worst and the best, the poorest and the richest, the most humble and the highest of the land, were Irish. This same peculiar feeling, changing according to circumstances, was to a certain extent produced by the thought of race or nationality in other countries, but its novelty gradually wore away. We passed by many fine pleasure-grounds and through several fine streets, one of which was particularly broad and attractive, with grand shade-trees on either side.

The country was fresh and flowery in spring-time and the ride was full of interest. We passed neat, whitewashed cottages and green fields surrounded by bright hedges; and the grass land was frequently ornamented by sleek-looking cows and contented-looking sheep. Sometimes a mild-looking donkey of gentle manners added variety to the appearance of the neighborhood. Pleasant groups of merry children completed the attractiveness of rural scenes. We often saw a house in ruins, with walls crumbling and roof gone, and sometimes only a few piles of stones marked the site of a former home, to which perhaps the family love of centuries clings. When we asked the question about their former occupants, the driver answered : "They have gone to America" ; and the quiet stillness of the day added sadness to our reflections./

But there, at length, lay Blarney before us, with the far-famed groves, lake, and castle of Blarney. Passing through meadows and groves, we came to the castle. It is a very solid, romantic ruin, built by Cormac MacCarthy about the middle of the fifteenth century. We climbed up the heavy stone stairs until we were near the top, and in the vicinity of the celebrated blarney-stone. I would not attempt to kiss it for all the blarney possessed by the entire human race from the beginning of time until now. For most persons it is a most foolhardy thing to do. One of our number did not even see it except from the ground below. The other member made up for this lack by a most gallant attempt to acquire the gift, which he already sufficiently possessed. He claims that he succeeded. I can testify that several men held him by the heels while he threw himself over the wide opening that looks down from the dizzy height of a hundred feet; that he grasped the irons, by which he let himself down towards the stone, and made several frantic efforts to press his lips and tongue against it; but whether he actually succeeded will never be exactly known to anybody but himself. As we returned through the grounds I loitered behind to hear the sweet notes of the feathered songsters that enlivened those romantic groves. If there is such a thing as blarney in music, they possessed it of the most bewitching kind. But why should they not possess it? They breathe the pure air of that magic locality, and drink the clear water of that mysterious lake, and live and love and sing out their souls in the charming retreats of those mystic groves.

We returned to Cork by the middle of the afternoon, in time for dinner. After dinner we started out to visit the city. Almost the first sounds that greeted our ears were

>"The bells of Shandon,
>That sound so grand on
>The pleasant waters of the river Lee."

We visited every church in the city but one, and all in which there were afternoon services were filled with worshippers. The congregations appeared devout and the services were stately and solemn, according to the rubrics, and breathing the spirit of the church. Cork was one of the largest British or European cities which I remember to have seen having no street-cars; but her people know how to observe a Christian Sunday./

On Monday morning we left Cork for Dublin. It was our first experience on European railway-trains. From all the American criticisms I had heard about the compartment-cars, I did not expect to like them; but I was mistaken. They are not so finely built as ours, but, excepting the Pullman and similar coaches, in many respects I prefer them. On American trains I usually get a headache, but rarely did I get it on those of Europe./

During our two visits to Ireland we passed through thirteen counties, and obtained a very good idea of the country. We now again saw Blarney Castle in the distance, and also obtained a fine and extended view of the Galtee mountains. Soon after noon we arrived in Thurles, county of Tipperary, and concluded to stop over until the evening train. The Archbishop of Cashel, who resides here, was making a visitation of his diocese, and therefore was not at home; but we were kindly received by one of the priests attached to the cathedral, who showed us everything of interest connected with the ecclesiastical buildings of the place. The cathedral is the finest, and I should judge the largest, church that I saw in Ireland. It possesses a magnificent high altar of marble, and an exquisite tabernacle made of rare and antique marbles obtained in Rome and other places by the late archbishop. The grand chime of bells was set ringing for our benefit, and played several of the national airs of Ireland.

After leaving our kind entertainer we took a leisurely stroll through the town, passing some interesting ruins of the middle ages; but we were more interested in the streets, houses, and people than in anything else, for this was our first visit to an Irish country town. Some ballad-singers—an aged man and his wife and daughter—were moving slowly down the street, singing a ballad with sad air and words, recounting the sorrows and hopes, and the patriotism and faith of the people. And, after all, a very strange people they are—a people to whom sorrow has become an inheritance which they treasure and love almost equally with their innocent joys. And why should they not love the memory of their sorrows? For sorrow is their mother. Joy may be their pure, smiling sister; and even she, with her face wreathed in smiles, has the features and sad eyes of her mother. But the sorrowful Irish mother, who has nourished them on her breast and directed their eyes to heaven, has always had faithful children. Why then should they not sing in sweet and plaintive notes the story of their fidelity ? /

Leaving Thurles, we continued our journey towards Dublin, passing up through the Golden Vale of ancient Erin, past the Devil's Bit and Slieve Bloom Mountains, and past villages and towns of historical associations and ruins. Before the shadows of evening had rested upon the earth, but after the sun was already set, the train made quite a long delay at Kildare, which gave us a good opportunity of viewing its round-tower and ecclesiastical ruins in the twilight. Kildare was a pleasing picture as it appeared in the mellow light of departing day, and it seemed even now beautified and hallowed by the Christian learning and sanctity of a glorious past, when St. Bridget and her great monastic establishments blessed Ireland. We arrived in Dublin rather late in the evening, and at once took a carriage to the Imperial Hotel, on O'Connell Street, formerly Lower

Sackville Street. On our return to Dublin we stayed at both the Imperial and Morrison's hotels. /

The next morning we hired a jaunting-car and drove through the principal parts of the city. We saw the old Parliament House, Trinity College, Dublin Castle, the Four Courts, the Custom-house, and other important buildings. On our return to Dublin the noted and historic buildings of the city became to us more familiar objects, and made a more lasting impression on our memory. We went to the Zoölogical Gardens, where I was most interested in a very cross Irish raven, and a fine specimen of the Irish wolf-dog. The keeper informed us that it is now the only one in existence; certainly there are but two or three living specimens of this symbolical Irish dog. We drove through Phœnix Park, which is one of the finest in the British Isles. It comprises 1,760 acres, is seven miles in circumference, and enjoys many delightful views. The spot where the assassination of the late chief-secretary and under-secretary took place was pointed out, which was marked by a cross in the ground. It was one of the most public places of the park, with a wide, unobstructed view in every direction, not even a tree or shrub near it; an altogether more public place than I had supposed. We next drôve to Glasnevin, and as we wandered through the silent, shaded streets of the city of the dead we saw the tombs of many celebrated men, of which the grandest, that of O'Connell, rises in form and height like an ancient Irish round-tower. We finished the ride by driving to St. Patrick's Cathedral. It is in the hands of Protestants, but possesses great interest for Catholics, who earnestly pray that one day it may be restored to its rightful owners and service. It was founded by St. Patrick in the year 448 over a well where he had baptized the king of Dublin. This well was seen during the recent repairs made on the church. The present edifice was built by Archbishop Comyn in 1192, and is a grand and chaste specimen of Gothic architecture. So strong and devotional is the hope of Catholic Dublin that this cathedral will again be the dwelling-place of the Incarnate God on our altars, and that its magnificent organ and sweet and powerful chimes of "joy-bells" will ring out their joyful peals of praise to God on that welcome day, that no other church has ever been dedicated to St. Patrick in Dublin./

Later in the day each of us started out on

the particular excursion that most took his fancy. I took the tramway for Clontarf, to look over the ancient battle field of Brian Boru, to wander around in the neighborhood, to look out upon the beauties of the bay and its surroundings, and meditate and dream on the great events of the past and make them seem real in the present. It was a clear, beautiful afternoon, and that quiet suburb of Dublin was in an almost ideal state of repose. The few persons whom I met had such modest ways and quiet manners, the leaves fluttering in the faint breeze, and the birds singing in the trees were so gentle, that neither act of theirs nor unkind breath of nature disturbed the calm surface of my soul, which, like a placid lake under a summer sky, mirrored scenes of beauty and peace, while its more sensitive depths felt the touch of the spirit of joy. To the north of the bay the black, bleak-looking Hill of Howth raised its historic head; over the bay to the south the Dublin mountains calmly lay, three peaks more noble than the rest standing against the southern sky. I wandered out into the country under old, magnificent trees and through large and well-kept pleasure-grounds. In this walk in the suburbs I met but few persons, among them a beggar-woman with her child who asked for alms—the only time I was asked for charity during my visits to Dublin. It seems to me that I must have got out into that quiet neighborhood where Brian Boru prayed while his army fought the invaders. And in the realms of imagination, in which I walked almost as much as in those of reality, I do not know that I should have been surprised if I had heard the sounds of battle breaking upon the stillness of the day, and had seen in the distance towards Dublin the standards of ancient Erin waving in Tomar's Wood, or had seen the ancient monarch of Ireland praying in his tent while others fought. While his sons and countrymen fought he prayed, but by prayer he fought with the golden sword of Jeremias given to Judas Machabeus, and, like him, gained the victory. But he who prayed for those who fought sealed the victory with his life's blood. On my way back I saw an ancient well with the inscription: "Well of Brian Boru."

CHAPTER II.

WALES AND ENGLAND.

The next morning we took passage on the *Shamrock*, a packet, for Holyhead, where we should arrive in five hours. After a few months we would return and make a longer stay in Ireland, but now we wanted to hasten on towards the East.

Dublin Bay was so brightly reflected in the morning sun and my eyes were so dazzled that I did not appreciate it so well as I did the day before, which led me to suspect, perhaps incorrectly, that it is seen to best advantage from the land.

In less than five hours of a not unpleasant passage we were drawing near to the Welsh coast. At Holyhead we connected with a fast train for London. On the train we passed across the Holy Isle, and isle of Anglesea, and the whole northern part of rugged, mountainous Wales. The scenery is very romantic, with its fine views of bays and sea on one side, and its picturesque mountains on the other, and its forests, its fields, and excellent houses.

Its houses, even in the country, are well built and of good material, and, judging from a hasty look, equal to those of any country through which we passed. The quick succession of wild and beautiful scenes stirred within me a poetical feeling which manifested itself in the beginning of a poem :

> When brave Llewellyn led his host,
>   When Wales was proud and free,
> Where mountain cliffs and rock-bound coast
>   O'erlook a stormy sea,
>
> No people ever fought more brave
>   Than they on mountain heights
> For freedom or an honored grave,
>   Their country and their rights. /

Over the borders in England we passed through the city of Chester, whose Gothic cathedral was built in the eleventh century for the Benedictines by Hugh, Earl of Chester, assisted by St. Anselm. During the remainder of the afternoon we whirled through the beautiful farm country of England, where between gently-rising hills lay many smiling vales. We rushed past green meadows and pastures surrounded by well-trimmed hedges with gateways, on either side of which stood fine shade-trees, which, with frequent groves dotting the landscape, made up a repetition of rural scenes to captivate the hearts of lovers of the peaceful and beautiful in nature. The large-eyed, contented-looking cows no longer looked in wonderment at passing trains, but grazed quietly or hardly raised their heads to see us, while others rested sleepily in the shade of some noble old oak or stately elm.

Among the other towns which we passed was Rugby, and I took in every object of interest in it or its surroundings that came within the range of my vision. Not that I remembered much about the place, but faint glimpses of the school days of "Tom Brown" stole across my memory; and although the events recorded in a book read in my college days, when but sixteen years of age, were not very clear to my mind, I remembered that there was near the town a pleasant stream running through green fields, where the young student enjoyed his sports, and the scenes new to my eyes were brightened by the memories of years ago. Such scenes always remain green in the hearts of old boys.

During the afternoon we sometimes glided quickly along by the side of a river, whose grassy banks, sylvan shades, and sparkling waters commingled to form a pleasing succession of bright pictures. It was near sunset when we passed Rugby; and some time before we reached the end of our day's journey night came, and we rushed on through the darkness towards London. On our arrival we put up at the Euston Hotel, which belongs to the railroad company, in which the accommodations were good; but on our return we preferred a more central place, and took rooms at the Golden Cross Hotel, near Charing Cross. All London seems to centre at Charing Cross.

The next morning we rose early and looked out of our windows at great, smoky London. Long before our rising we were unable to sleep on account of the noise for which London is noted. It was a holyday of obligation, and our first interest was to find a church where we could attend Mass. After some inquiry and search we found a church of rather humble pretensions in the neighborhood. Having assisted at Mass and returned to the hotel for our breakfast, we started out to see the city. Our first objective point was the City Bank of London, in Threadneedle Street, on which we had letters of credit. We took an omnibus to Charing Cross, and from there found our way to the bank. On this and our return visit we became quite well acquainted with this latter route. In fact, the only part of London that I got to know in any kind of familiar way was that leading from Cheapside, past St. Paul's

Cathedral and Ludgate, down Fleet Street and the Strand, past Trafalgar Square and Charing Cross, through Whitehall and Parliament Street to Westminster Abbey and the Houses of Parliament. In almost any other part of London quite probably I should lose my way. My only course when I wanted to go elsewhere was to take a hansom, which is a quick and pleasant means of conveyance. After leaving the bank we returned to St. Paul's, where ten o'clock service was progressing. Perhaps two hundred persons were present, some of whom, like ourselves, were drawn thither by curiosity. The service was "higher" than I had expected to find in St. Paul's. Catholic vestments were not used, but the officiating minister and his two assistants—like deacon and subdeacon—stood with their backs to the people, and the minister sang the preface in nearly the same tone used by us. We left, after sufficiently viewing the church, which, although large, was cold-looking and did not very much impress me. I then hired a hansom by the hour, and first went to the British Museum. After a brief look at some of the curiosities, I became interested in the library, where I remained for about three hours, entirely forgetting the hansom. On going out I found that the driver was looking for me, thinking he had lost his pay. I then went to Westminster Abbey, where one of my companions met me. Afternoon services were in progress, at the close of which we were at liberty to walk through the different parts of this grand and interesting old edifice. It was founded by St. Mellitus, Bishop of London, in the sixth century, and as the cathedral church of London was dedicated to St. Paul, this church was dedicated to St. Peter. After various vicissitudes of fortune it was rebuilt by St. Edward the Confessor in the eleventh century, and again rebuilt by Henry III. in the thirteenth century, and to which Henry VII. made many elegant additions. As we walked through the corridors of the ancient abbey we read many inscriptions in the pavement nearly obliterated by the footsteps of centuries, which told us that these were the last resting-places of the old abbots who once ruled here to the honor of God. If they could arise from their graves they would stand in wonderment at the change that has been effected in their cloister. Instead of meek-eyed monks in modest habit, engaged in study, prayer, and contemplation, they would see groups of gaily-dressed ladies invading these holy precincts, chatting about all the vanities of life, hardly dreaming of the religious life once lived within these walls. Affrighted, they would hasten back to the enclosure of the tomb and the silence of death. All the kings and queens of England, from Edward the Confessor to the present time, have been crowned and many of them buried within the sacred precincts of Westminster. The chair of coronation is a dilapidated thing, having a rough stone for a seat. This stone is believed by many to be the celebrated stone of destiny upon which the head of the patriarch Jacob rested when he saw the vision of the ladder reaching unto heaven: "And Jacob, arising in the morning, took the stone, which he had laid under his head, and set it up for a title, pouring oil upon the top of it." It is related that it was afterwards taken by Jacob and his sons into Egypt, whence, in course of time, it was carried to Spain and afterwards to Ireland, B.C. 700, on which the ancient kings of Tara were crowned. It was then sent to Scotland, where it remained for centuries. In the ninth century it was placed in the gilded throne of the Royal Abbey of Scone; where the coronation of the Scottish kings took place. In the latter part of the thirteenth century it was transferred to Westminster by Edward I. of the Norman line. The tomb of St. Edward the Confessor is near by, and is the most noteworthy of any in the Abbey. We wandered out around the exterior of the building, and in a short time seemed to live in many different centuries, communing with the many generations of priests and prelates, statesmen and kings, poets and saints, to whom Westminster Abbey and its neighborhood had been holy ground, within whose contemplative limits inspired thoughts have been born and quickened. The new palace of Westminster, which comprises the two houses of Parliament, stands near by, and is an immense structure, covering eleven acres. We walked through its grounds and its halls, which are accessible to the public without special permission. We were not very anxious to enter the legislative halls, more especially as those who had tickets were subjected to a tiresome delay in waiting for their turn.

We now separated, and each one strolled through the streets according to his inclination. In my rambles I saw many familiar names of streets and public-houses, some of them exceedingly insignificant in their appearance, but rendered famous by the poets and literary men who at different times frequented London. A strange feeling steals into the heart of the Catholic traveller when he sees on every side so many reminders of the ancient faith of England. Besides many streets and a vast number of churches—once Catholic, now Protestant—that bear the diversified names of saints of the Roman calendar, there still remain such names as Whitefriars Street and Blackfriars Bridge and Road, Paternoster Row, Ave Maria Lane, and others similar.

On my return to the hotel, although I rode in an omnibus the greater part of the distance, I lost my way, and it took me nearly two hours of walking and inquiring of policemen before I found it. The faculty of quickly noting the cardinal points seems never to have been well developed in my mind. I must first become quite accustomed to my surroundings before different directions are clear to me. As several of my relatives and ancestors have been surveyors, they either must have absorbed this faculty of the family intellect, or else have too much accustomed it to instrumental guidance. I had therefore to be always on my guard in European cities to mark mentally my route, unless accompanied by one of my companions whose sensitive faculty in this matter was the exact reverse of mine.

The next day we went to the Brompton church

of the Oratorians, which was undergoing the process of renovation at great expense, which was making it exceedingly fine. Afterwards we went to the South Kensington Museum, which contains a vast number of curiosities and productions of art. On our return trip we visited the Natural History Museum near by; and, although I took due interest in its great animal and other skeletons, what pleased me most was the skilful arrangement of stuffed birds, showing the nests, eggs, and habits of the different species in the British Isles. On our way back to Charing Cross we rode in the omnibus with a very respectable, aristocratic-looking gentleman, who, seeing that we were strangers, with great politeness and kindness pointed out to us all the chief places of interest along the route, among them the residences of some of the chief noblemen and statesmen of England. Each day we spent some considerable time in the enjoyment of the different views and street scenes of the great metropolis. On our return they seemed less strange and more pleasing to us./

The next morning we left the station at Charing Cross for Paris by way of Dover and Calais. We first passed through several miles of streets and houses out into the smiling country, going through Kent from one extremity of the county to the other. Our journey was made enjoyable by a succession of old-looking towns, often made more interesting by an ancient, picturesque church, beautiful farms and comfortable-looking farm-houses, and rural scenes like those which had greeted our eyes on our first introduction to England—scenes which we found to be characteristic of the country wherever we went, except in certain limited portions. Towards Dover we came in sight of the chalk cliffs which line the coast, between which we caught occasional glimpses of the blue sea.

CHAPTER III.

LA BELLE FRANCE.

At Dover we took the boat for Calais. It was a bright, still day, and the Strait of Dover was as calm as a "summer's sea." Nearly all the passengers spoke French instead of English, when I had expected the reverse. We approached France with the French tongue sounding in our ears, with French breezes cooling our cheeks, and the gayety and animation of French life surrounding us. The shores of

Albion receded from our view and the shores of France drew nearer. It is a pleasurable event in one's life to approach for the first time a strange and interesting country. Gentle but joyous excitement quickens the pulse and the flow of life through the heart. Images form in the mind of a long list of the achievements and glories of that land in the midst of historic and poetic scenes. The coast-line, the hills and plains, the old towns, the very sea and sky seem to belong to the realms where the spirit of dying heroes and undying deeds continues to dwell. The spirits of the great past seem yet to live in the places to which they gave renown, and to pervade the very air with their mysterious presence.

The smiling fields of bright, beautiful France lay before us, which, with all its faults and deep, disgraceful stains which blot its fair name, still retains much of the chivalry and devotion of the Catholic ages of faith. At Calais we went from the steamer directly to the train for Paris. The language of France was everywhere heard, and the ways and manners of the people, including the railway employees in their plain blue blouses, were distinctively French. During the afternoon we passed many famous old towns, among them Amiens, possessing, in the judgment of many, one of the most perfect Gothic cathedrals in the world. But to me the most pleasing part of the ride was through the country districts. The highways which we frequently crossed, and beside which we sometimes rode for miles, were, like those of nearly all Europe, smooth and hard, running between hedges and trees and green fields and over picturesque stone bridges. The peasants of northern France appear to be a hardy and industrious race, many of whom, in their plain, simple attire, were working in the fields or journeying along the roads to and from their quaint little villages. On our arrival in Paris, not knowing much about the hotels, we took rooms at the Grand Hotel, on the Boulevard des Capucines. We found it grander than we really desired; yet it was central and convenient to the famous portions of the city.

Street life in Paris is animated and possessed of numerous attractions; yet, from glimpses of the mode and character of thousands of the inhabitants of this great French city, I ceased to wonder at the irreligious policy of its rulers and scandalous and sacrilegious acts of its communistic and revolutionary mobs. On the broader boulevards the evening scenes were gay and bright. The tables of the various restaurants extended out on the broad sidewalks, and surrounding them, seated in the open air, were hundreds of stylish ladies and gentlemen enjoying the happy sounds and sights and polite and easy companionship especially characteristic of the streets of Paris in early evening in the month of May. The great majority of the French people are polite, and I believe that their politeness comes from the heart. In restaurants and *bouillons* and similar places we were served with a grace that possessed a genuine charm, and among all there seemed to be a real regard and delicacy for the feelings of others, except with those where the spirit of irreligion has penetrated. These last mentioned may yet keep on the mask and outward manners of old-time French politeness, but it does not reach the heart or come from it, and their brutality is often manifest. With the French people, unlike some other nations, religion and gentle manners go hand-in hand.

The next day was Sunday. We inquired the way to the Madeleine, which was not far distant. It is the grandest and most perfect reproduction in existence, according to pure antique forms, of the ancient Grecian temple. Between eight and half-past nine o'clock we attended one Mass and portions of two others. On account of the statements of some travellers with reference to the attendance of Parisians at Sunday Masses, I took particular notice of the exact facts. At each of these three Masses the church was emptied and again filled, and I judged that fully half of those present were men. Some eyes cannot see truthfully, or else since some authors wrote Paris has very much changed in this respect for the better. After breakfast we wandered through the streets to the Place de la Concorde, which has witnessed so many strange scenes. Here the guillotine was set up during the Reign of Terror, and here the German army encamped after its triumphal entry in 1871. We wandered through the gardens of the Tuileries, and afterwards through the Champs Élysées to the Arch of Triumph, begun by Napoleon and finished by Louis Philippe, and which is considered the grandest existing structure of the kind in the world. The people on the streets were not quite so gay, but for the most part they were of a more retiring and respectable class than the ostentatious frequenters of public places whom we saw the previous evening.

Sometimes we spent an hour in walking, another hour in the tram-cars, and another hour in a carriage. In this way we passed through retired and quiet streets, through streets where the great body of the people live, and through grand, broad boulevards. We also saw many of the vast public buildings of Paris; and when the day was over we had become settled in the conclusion, which we had partly formed on our first entrance to the city, that it is by far the most magnificent city of Europe and the world. We arrived at the cathedral of Notre Dame at near sunset, but the doors were closed, and we had to be content to take a good view of its exterior.

The next day each one of us had different objects of interest in his mind, and so we agreed to separate. As for myself, when we entered Paris I desired rather to see the Madeleine, Notre Dame, and La Sainte Chapelle than all the other buildings of the city. I therefore took the route, rather indirect, to Notre Dame. On the way I entered an ancient-looking church, where a large class of schoolboys were being prepared for First Communion. They appeared very attentive and devout. The interior of the church was old and venerable, and attractive to devotion. I soon after arrived at Notre Dame, the church which I would prefer to all others in Paris. The present noble structure was founded in the twelfth century, and was situated on the "Isle of the City," one of the two islands in the Seine near each other, around which, as the ancient nucleus, Paris was built. It is not my intention to give detailed descriptions of the churches and public buildings visited during my travels, as they only serve to weary the reader, and can be found more accurately given in guide-books.

Like the other great cathedrals of the middle ages, Notre Dame is an immense edifice, and is built in the pointed style of Gothic architecture, possessing those rich treasures and decorations which were lavished by the hands of monarchs, and those enduring qualities and that artistic excellence which come only from the mind and hand of genius. When I entered the church the canons were reciting the Divine Office. The divine harmony of prayer sounding through the sacred edifice and re-echoed in heaven, united with the ever-abiding presence of the "Lamb that was slain," made the material temple seem possessed of life and soul. Like living realities the historic scenes of centuries passed before my eyes. Monarchs were crowned amid grandest solemnities, and I seemed to hear outside the walls the voice of cheering multitudes; they were brought back uncrowned, and I seemed to hear the slow footsteps of men in procession, the beat of muffled drum, and the sad, musical dirge of death, and within the intervals the low sobs and sighs of weeping mourners. And then the scenes were changed and the hell-fired fiends of revolution raised their hoarse shouts of blood and lust, and desecrated the sacred temple, and even the altar of Jesus in the Holy Sacrament, and a harlot was worshipped by men base enough to make her—whose life exemplifies one of their most brutal passions—their typical god. O abomination of desolation in the Holy of Holies! But prayer and sacrifice are ever the same, and Notre Dame is still their consecrated abode; and, as in days gone by, she consoles the living and mourns for the dead, but not as those who have no hope. In the highest aspirations of life and in the dread realities of eternity, how far separated are Notre Dame and Westminster!\

After wandering about and taking a brief and reverential view of everything, and saying a few prayers and mentally joining the canons in their office, I returned towards the entrance, where a woman was selling wax-candles to be burned before a statue of the Blessed Virgin. I bought one, which she lighted and gave to our dear Mother as a votive-offering for me, while I knelt and prayed that she might obtain for my companions and myself a safe journey and safe return to homes unchanged by sickness or death. I then went forth again into the busy streets of Paris, but they seemed changed. The busy, frivolous world appeared to talk in a subdued tone, and to have put on a more modest demeanor. It was the influence of the holy Presence which I had just left, and in some sense that Presence was still with me, changing the appearance of men and the face of nature. \

I was desirous of seeing more of the quiet life of the people. Back of the cathedral is a park, in which, raised on a high column, is a statue of Mary Immaculate. In the park, which is of fair size, well supplied with rustic seats beneath the shade, were congregated old and middle-aged men, staid and comfortable-looking dames, many of whom brought with them their knitting or sewing, young people in their teens, and pleasant, playful children, whose playground was usually in the immediate vicinity of their mothers. I sat a long time on a bench in the shade of one of the trees, enjoying the most peaceful and pleasant scene of quiet happiness that I saw during my stay in Paris. It was all the more attractive because it was almost in the shadow of that great church where probably most of those present attended their week-day Masses and offered their daily devotions.

Not far distant was La Sainte Chapelle, which is one of the finest and most complete gems of Gothic architecture of the thirteenth century. It was built by St. Louis of France to receive the crown of thorns, which was deposited in it, together with a portion of the true cross, the iron point of the lance which opened our Saviour's side, and part of the sponge which bore vinegar and gall to His dying lips. A portion of these relics are still in Notre Dame, and a part of the crown of thorns is exposed to the veneration of the faithful on Good Friday. I obtained permission to enter, and was conducted through the chapel by one of the custodians. Notwithstanding the beauty of its architecture, it looked to me desolate, for Mass is but rarely celebrated at its altars. If St. Louis were now to visit his royal chapel, or even his royal city, he would find many changes to bring grief to his soul. Towards evening we had all returned from our wanderings, and had to hurry to get ready to take the train for Marseilles, which started about an hour before dark.

We had hardly passed through the environs of Paris before the shadows of evening began to dim the landscape, and things seen might as well have been conjured up in day-dreams, so indistinct were they and full of romance. We had taken a first-class carriage, and, as the only other occupants of the compartment were a French gentleman and his lady, we passed the night in comparative comfort.

On European railways one is inclined to awaken early; but all the better, for by so doing I enjoyed a number of beautiful European sunrises and mornings, where country, hamlets and towns, winding streams, extended plains, and gray old mountains renewed their gladness and vigor in the light and life of a new-born day. During the night we had passed through several important cities—among them Lyons—and the morning found us speeding down the valley of the Rhone, of which we often caught glimpses. Low mountain ranges, at some distance away, lined the valley on either side. As strange as it may seem, the sources of the Rhone and Rhine are near together; and while, after many windings, one flows to the south and the other to the north of Europe, a certain similarity accompanies them. Both flow through regions having some of the finest vineyards in the world, and the rugged banks of both are crowned with grand old castles and historic cities. Although in portions of the valley of the Rhone the rainfall is abundant, the country through which we passed during the forenoon appeared to be somewhat arid, and the goddess of perpetual summer seemed to rule; but it is a land rich in fruits and wine.

Early in the day we had entered the boundaries of ancient Provence, which is the land where sunshine ever loves to dwell, and leaving which it is homesick and quickly returns. No wonder that it is the region of romance and of the troubadours. We passed through strange-looking towns, where we could look down old-fashioned streets and into quaint old stone houses surrounded by flower-gardens and orchards and overhung with trellised vines. At length, not far distant to the right, on the majestic heights that overlook the river, rose the lofty towers, battlements, and spires of Avignon, the residence of seven popes for more than half a century. Those vast piles of buildings, rising in stately grandeur and distinguished above the others, are the cathedral and palace of the pontiffs who once ruled here and made Avignon a second Rome. In a cave in the great rock on which the cathedral is built once lived St. Martha of Bethany, where she had come after the ascension of our Saviour into heaven; and St. Rufus, son of Simon the Cyrenean, who carried the cross for our Lord, was first bishop of the city. O Avignon! thou hast for a brief period worn the imperial robes of Rome, the mistress of the earth; and such has been the efficacy of their virtue that, like her, thou hast become immortal. A brief half hour was all we saw of Avignon, but the city of St. Martha and St. Rufus, the city of the popes and the city of bells, the city of devotion to the Blessed Sacrament, rising grandly on the banks of the Rhone and reflecting the warm, bright sun of Provence, will remain an ineffaceable picture in our memories.

Within less than an hour after quitting Avignon we left the Rhone behind us at the ancient city of Arles, twenty-five miles from its mouth. Having skirted the shores of the inland lake of Berre, and having passed through the longest tunnel in France, we soon came into a region of high, barren, rocky peaks. Occasionally, far above us on rocky heights, appeared some old castle or monastery, once the stronghold of family pride or power, or of faith and devotion. Finally the blue Mediterranean appeared, on which our eyes rested with a strange, quiet, fascinating pleasure. It is no wonder; for it is the great sea on whose borders have existed and still exist most of the historic nations of the earth. Its waters have washed the shores of ancient kingdoms and empires until the proud monuments and cities of their glory have crumbled into dust. Carthaginian, Grecian, and Roman galleys, bearing the armies of hostile nations to death or victory, have danced lightly upon its glistening waves, and on its wide waters have contended with wild storms and fierce foes. The nations on its shores were the first in the history of the human race, and one succeeded another on the grand historic stage of Western Asia. Its bright waters have reflected the majesty and glory of Egypt, Greece, and Rome, the grandest nations of the pagan world; and their sons most gifted by genius, and even the psalmists and prophets whom God himself inspired, have sung its praises. In our own modern history some of the foremost nations of the epoch hold the proud pre-eminence of a place on its historic shores, and all of them lay claim to its vantage-grounds and strongholds, and uphold their position and influence by fleets of iron monsters that thunder their warning or their challenge and hurl their missiles of death and destruction over its calm surface. This beautiful blue sea, upon whose peaceful bosom I seem to see the white-winged carriers of the heroes and saints of centuries sailing before the favored breezes of heaven, is to me utterly unlike the vast, black, dread ocean with its dark, unfathomed caverns, where dwell its horrid, unknown monsters. In the following weeks we were to see much more of this great sea which we now viewed for the first time. We never grew weary of it, but, leaving it for a time, we longed to rest our eyes once again on its blue, watery expanse—on the one side melting into the azure sky, and on the other lined by its gray and green and purple shores.

Before noon we were in Marseilles. It is the chief seaport of France, and was founded by the Greeks six hundred years B.C. After taking our dinner at a restaurant we hired a carriage to convey us to the principal places of interest in the city. We cannot claim to have made a very thorough inspection of Marseilles in the three hours' visit that we made, but we saw all that could be seen in that length of time. Now, after more than two years, only four things have left an impression on my memory: the cathedral, the tramways, the harbor, and the cosmopolitan appearance of the people thronging the docks. How different is busy Marseilles from peaceful Bethany; yet here Lazarus, Mary, and Martha landed, and in Provence passed the remainder of their days; and St. Lazarus was the first bishop of the city. Often did the contemplative Mary, from the high cliffs where she spent her solitary life, look out over the sea to the distant land where she had loved her Lord so faithfully. We visited the new cathedral which was being built, and which was not only under roof, but much substantial ornamentation already adorned it. When finished it will be one of the finest modern churches of Europe. The docks and shipping afford a pleasant sight to those who can endure their dirt and smell; but they are not much different in these and other respects from those of New York and Liverpool, except that the port of Marseilles has more intimate connections with the Levant, and oriental costumes were frequently seen. Two Eastern gentlemen in their peculiar dress, wearing crooked swords at their sides, accompanied us some distance on the train. In our inexperience we took them for Turks, although afterwards we could anywhere readily recognize them as Greeks.\

We saw many pleasant streets in Marseilles, notwithstanding the general business character of the town; but what struck us as peculiar was that several street or tramway cars were passing along smooth streets without any special track on which to run, and turning here and there at their convenience. The white cornet and gray dress of the Sisters of Charity, which I saw on the streets here as in other French cities, as well as in some towns of the East, reminded me of home—where I attend St. Vincent's Asylum—and gave me a slight twinge of homesickness.

Early in the afternoon we entered the train for Genoa. It runs along the southern coast of France and northern coast of Italy, and passes through some of the most romantic scenery of the world: Especially from Nice to Genoa we enjoyed beautiful and magnificent views of the Mediterranean, and grand and sublime views of mountain-heights approaching to the very waters of the sea, all uniting in one glorious panorama of nature. After riding more than an hour we passed through Toulon, one of the great war-harbors of France, and formidable-looking with the many forts surrounding it and its great war-ships at anchor. Little did we think that in five weeks' time these two cities—Marseilles and Toulon—would be smitten by the terrible scourge of cholera. Little did they then suspect the near approach of the destroying angel. With outstretched wings, that cast their shadows on the earth, he even now hovered over them. Before reaching Nice we passed through several fine towns surrounded by pleasant villas; for not only Nice and vicinity but the cities and country on either side are the winter resorts of a large number of people of more northern and rigorous Europe.

We passed the night at Nice, but early the following forenoon we resumed our journey. This day was one of the most pleasant of our entire European travels. Nothing more in nature or in outward evidences of religion could be desired. We passed through interesting cities, each one possessing such striking features of beauty and grandeur that all the others would be forgotten. On the one hand great, rocky heights overlooked the sea, which, on the other hand, reflected all the beauties of the sky, now colored with its azure blue, now bathed in its golden light. And in the midst of numerous groves of lemon, orange, cypress, myrtle, oleander, olive, and palm-trees appeared lovely villas and pure white churches with their shining crosses. Beautiful flowers and flowering vines were almost everywhere, and among them quite remarkable, wide-spreading vines of purple flowers, and climbing roses frequently covered the entire sides of houses.

CHAPTER IV.

NORTHERN ITALY AND ROME.

We passed over the border into sunny Italy. In Italy the scenes gradually changed. We entered the region called the Riviera, the ancient Liguria. Small villages and towns were nearer together—in fact, we seemed hardly to lose sight of one before another came in view; and the number of convents and churches surpassed anything that I ever saw before or expect to see outside of cities. Every village possessed several, and the hillsides and valleys between were dotted over with them. The crosses on one or the other were continually in sight. Rustic wayside shrines frequently met our eyes to remind us, if we needed it, that we were in a land where Mary and the Crucified dwell in the hearts of the people. Nearly all the convents and churches were picturesque in appearance and venerable in age, and many occupied sites which nature seemed to have created for them, so skilfully were they selected. At nearly every station we saw one or more of the clergy in clerical habit—cassock, hat, and ferraiolo. At one place a bishop with nearly a dozen priests came on the train. The church seemed to be entirely at home in this region.

About the middle of the afternoon we arrived in Genoa. As our train left for Rome at midnight we did not go to a hotel, but immediately hired a carriage to drive until dark through different parts of the city. We did not yet possess the faculty, which we afterwards acquired, of seeing a town to advantage in a few hours. Perhaps it was well; for, while we did not enter even the churches, except one or two, we obtained a number of fine natural views, and saw Genoa the Superb as if exhibited to us in panoramic pictures, although the forms and figures were living and the scenes realities fashioned by the hand of the great Artist. On the streets we saw the people, young and old, rich and poor—a new revelation to us of another species of national character and customs. Picturesque Italy thronged the streets and enlivened life. Genoa is noted for its palaces, and in some streets palaces and palace-like buildings came in quick succession. The city was founded before Rome, it is said, by "Janus, grandson of Noe," and has always been the seaport centre of a large commercial trade. In the middle ages it was one of the great Italian republics, like Pisa and Venice, and extended its possessions both in the Occident and Orient. During my travels I could not help feel considerable pride in these ancient republics, as well as in the more modern republic of Switzerland, which were brought into being by Catholic peoples, and which, by their brave, industrious, and independent spirit, became prosperous and renowned. In the strict sense of the word, I am neither a republican nor a monarchist. It is quite probable that one or other of these forms of government is more congenial to the habits and character of different nationalities; but the fact that I was born and reared under the flag of a republic adds a new interest with me to the great republics of the past. A constitutional monarchy is, without doubt, a very attractive form of government. It not only gives a voice to the popular will, but it serves as a check to sudden changes and fanaticisms, and it rewards those who deserve well of their country by reason of marked patriotism or genius in a manner that republics are incapable of doing: by granting to them and those of their blood an inheritance of title and position that will be permanent in their country's roll of honor. And however much we may admire our own country's youthful life and vigor, its condition does not appear to us entirely satisfactory. But it would be hardly just to judge our government by itself, and from its brief existence, without considering what the old-time republics were able to accomplish. If there is anything that a country needs, it is respect for home and family. And without doubt it conduces to a people's welfare that virtuous and respectable families shall be built up that in time can trace an unsullied and honorable lineage back through the centuries, and which will have a standing and influence in communities according to their merits. The history of the old republics proves that this was possible under their systems of government; and if in our country the family does not occupy the place that it should, the educational and moral principles of the people are at fault, and not the form of government.

We took the midnight train for Rome. The early morning found us leaving Pisa and Pisa's wonderful leaning tower behind, and speeding over the Maremme, an unhealthy expanse of forest, swamp, and pasture-land that extends a good portion of the way to Rome. The railway coincides with the ancient Aurelian Way built 109 B.C. Frequent herds of large, fine white cows with long horns served to bring to our minds the fact that we had entered the land of the Latin classic poets, which yet retains many striking reminders of their times. Farther on we saw numerous herds of a more mixed breed of cattle, and between Civita Vecchia and Rome, mingled with the others, great mouse-colored oxen. Civita Vecchia, the seaport of Rome, was finally reached. We then passed down the sea-coast, getting a pleasant view of the Mediterranean, and when its bright waves had disappeared we soon came in sight of the yellow waters of "Father Tiber," about which we had read so much in our school-boy days.

At length we neared Rome, the Eternal City of the Cæsars and the Popes. I will not attempt to describe my thoughts and feelings as I was about to realize the longings of a lifetime. We were now passing over the famous Campagna, while in the distance, the former to the right and the latter to the left, were the Alban and the Sabine hills, which I had so often imagined in my day-dreams to be before my eyes; and Rome, seated on her seven hills, appeared before us, with her churches and her palaces, her walls and her ruins, the city of St. Peter. It is unlike any other city in the world; but, after all, is this Rome? A spirit of disappointment hovered over me, although it did not fully enter my breast. But when I knew the city better it seemed changed, and now no city on earth could fill my life so full of grand realizations of my ideal as Rome, except a few of the sacred towns and cities of the Holy Land; and in many respects we know that even the Holy City, Jerusalem, is far inferior to the Eternal City, Rome. For centuries Jerusalem has been under Moslem control, while Rome has been under Christian rulers. The train passed over the Tiber and skirted for some distance the ancient walls, built more than sixteen hundred years ago, crossed the celebrated Appian Way, passed through the city walls, and we were in Rome.

Having arrived at the station, we entered the omnibus of the Hotel Minerva, where we took rooms. It is situated in that part of Rome which was the ancient Campus Martius, and opposite the site of the temple of Minerva, occupied by the Church of the Minerva, dedicated to the Blessed Virgin. It is also in the immediate vicinity of the Pantheon. As the warmer season of summer was near at hand, we determined at this time to remain in Rome only two days and hasten on towards the East, reserving the principal Roman visit for our return. We arrived in Rome about noon, and, strange as it may seem, it was one of my homesick days; but on our return Rome was the place where I always felt least a heaviness of spirits.

The sun shone brightly, but its rays did not penetrate my heart. Home, and home only, dwelt there. I hope that but few know what it really is to be homesick. You feel a weight on and in the heart that would seem to rend it from its place and tear it asunder, and you can hardly tell whether you are going to live or die. God help exiled and homesick hearts! Later in the day we took a carriage, and, having first driven to the bank in the Piazza di Spagna, on which we had letters of credit, and to the post-office, we visited some of the principal churches.

As one approaches Rome, although it may not be for the first time, the first object he will endeavor to behold is St. Peter's and St. Peter's dome, the marvellous productions of the genius

INTERIOR OF ST. PETER'S, ROME.

of Michael Angelo. To write the name of Michael Angelo recalls to our minds one of the great master-intellects of the world. His genius was not confined to one particular line, but in painting, in sculpture, and in architecture his works are among the highest masterpieces. St. Peter's wonderful dome, the admirable "Pietà" in St. Peter's, the grand and severe "Moses" in the church of St. Peter ad Vincula, and the "Last Judgment" in the Sistine Chapel, stand among the grandest works of Christian genius. We turned first towards St. Peter's, not alone to admire the wonders of the edifice, but to pray at the tomb of the holy apostles...

It is a well-known fact that at first sight either of the exterior or interior of St. Peter's it hardly comes up to one's expectations; but it grows on you by repeated visits. At each visit new beauties and new grandeur spring into being, and finally, when one gets a conception of what the church really is, the soul expands with wonder and admiration. We now had the joyous privilege of kneeling beneath that wondrous dome and before the tomb of the holy apostles. As afterwards we made more ex-

INTERIOR OF ST. PETER'S, ROME.

of Michael Angelo. To write the name of Michael Angelo recalls to our minds one of the great master-intellects of the world. His genius was not confined to one particular line, but in painting, in sculpture, and in architecture his works are among the highest masterpieces. St. Peter's wonderful dome, the admirable "Pietà" in St. Peter's, the grand and severe "Moses" in the church of St. Peter ad Vincula, and the "Last Judgment" in the Sistine Chapel, stand among the grandest works of Christian genius. We turned first towards St. Peter's, not alone to admire the wonders of the edifice, but to pray at the tomb of the holy apostles St. Peter and St. Paul, over which this church was raised by the Christian world as an enduring monument.

It is a well-known fact that at first sight either of the exterior or interior of St. Peter's it hardly comes up to one's expectations; but it grows on you by repeated visits. At each visit new beauties and new grandeur spring into being, and finally, when one gets a conception of what the church really is, the soul expands with wonder and admiration. We now had the joyous privilege of kneeling beneath that wondrous dome and before the tomb of the holy apostles. As afterwards we made more extended and systematic visits to this cathedral of the world, our first observations, except those already given, are hardly worthy of record. During this and the following day we made visits to the churches of St. John Lateran, the Minerva, the Pantheon, and several others, on our way passing the ancient church of St. Clement and the mighty Coliseum. Inasmuch as on our return we visited all these with more care and attention, anything I may have to write about them will be deferred until the account of our second visit.\

Near the church of St. John Lateran are the Scala Santa, or Holy Stairs, taken from the palace of Pilate in Jerusalem, consecrated by the sacred feet and sprinkled with the Precious Blood of Jesus Christ. The stains of His blood are even now seen beneath the covering of glass, fastened to the stairs, which the pious kiss. We went up these stairs on our knees, praying as we went; and the tears flowed from my eyes as I remembered our Saviour's sorrows, that calmed my heart, troubled by homesickness, which almost entirely left it.\

About the middle of the afternoon of the following day we were at the railway station to take the train for Naples. In a little while after we were speeding over the Campagna, past

Frascati and Albano, and past Castel Gandolfo, the pope's former country residence, with the Sabine and Alban hills in view, and for a considerable distance the Volscian Mountains. The scenery for a good portion of the journey, until the darkness of night settled down, was really fine. We passed down through what appeared to be a succession of beautiful valleys with mountain ranges on either side. At first the valleys were wide and expanding, and we passed through country scenes where picturesque-looking peasants, retaining much of the old-style dress of Italy, journeyed over their splendid but countrified-appearing roads. As we advanced the mountains drew nearer together until they fairly looked down upon us, and the valleys grew proportionately more beautiful. Dead and seemingly fossilized old cities stood on mountain-sides, and we wondered whether they were inhabited by bats and owls or by human beings. Others appeared differently and gave no room for such doubts. Towards evening we passed Aquino, the birthplace of St. Thomas of Aquin; and when the dimness of evening began to obscure all things, we saw, resting grandly on an eminence of the mountain, the great monastery of Monte Casino. We obtained a much better view of it on our return, and intended stopping over to see its sacred precincts and numerous treasures, but were unable to do so for want of time. Taken all in all, it is the most remarkable monastery in the world. In some respects others may surpass it, like that which stands on Carmel's heights overlooking Galilee and the Mediterranean. But, with due respect and reverence for all other religious orders, none of them stand side by side in the fore rank with the Order of St. Benedict; for, under God and the Holy See, it has been one of the greatest influences in the civilization and Christianization of Europe. Monte Casino was the mother-house of the Benedictines, and the religious home of St. Benedict more than thirteen hundred years ago; and from its foundation until now it has always been a great monastery.

CHAPTER V.

SOUTHERN ITALY AND THE VOYAGE TO EGYPT.

NEAR midnight we arrived in Naples. Although the hotel which we chose was first-class, we did not take a fancy to it, and on our return trip we selected the Hôtel de Rome, next to the parish church of St. Lucy, which was found in every way satisfactory. The next morning, after wandering awhile through the streets to observe the people, we hired a carriage to drive to some of the principal places of interest. The visit on our return from the East was more pleasant and was made with a better acquaintance with the city, but the order of narrative will require a brief description of our present sight-seeing. On this occasion we first went to the cathedral church of St. Januarius. This saint is patron of the city, which, it is claimed, was his native place, to which his relics were undoubtedly transferred. His head and body, and vials containing his blood, which liquefies on being brought near the relics of his head, all rest in this church. We were shown the casket containing his body, a relic-case containing his finger, and a fac-simile of the vial of blood when liquefied. The church contains the tombs of noted princes and ecclesiastics, and the old chapel of St. Restituta, attributed to Constantine. We also entered a beautiful church across the street where the exposition of the Blessed Sacrament was taking place.

We afterwards visited several other churches,

among them the fine church of St. Francis de
Paulo, and then the royal palace. As we
strolled through its grand rooms and gorgeous
apartments, and viewed the beauties of the
bay and its surroundings from the garden-like
balconies, and saw the empty royal throne,
the vanity of earthly power and glory was
brought forcibly to our minds. They for whom
it was built, and who once dwelt here and enjoyed its regal pleasures and splendors, were
either lying in narrow coffins or passing the
few remaining years of their life in exile.

We went to the aquarium—which is one of
the finest in the world—and there saw the
living curiosities of the mighty deep from a
place of observation similar to being side by
side with them in the depths of the sea. Leaving there, we passed the tomb of Virgil, who
for many years made Naples his home, and
we then drove through the grotto of Posilippo,
mentioned by writers nineteen hundred years
ago.

We closed a day of sight-seeing by ascending the heights below the castle of St. Elmo
and the monastery of San Marino, where we
obtained a grand and far-reaching view of the
city and bay. In the distance, at the mouth
of the bay, rose the islands of Capri and Ischia,

and on its high, rugged shores on either side gleamed the white walls of ancient towns whose foundations date back more than a score of centuries. Towards the north old Vesuvius belched forth his cloud-like column of smoke. Although the conditions were favorable, the scene before us could not at all compare with that presented to our eyes on our return, entering the bay from the sea a little before sunset.

In the evening about dark we started on the train for Brindisi by way of Foggia. The lights shone brightly over the city. Naples is always animated; it is the most lively city that we saw in Italy. I have often heard it called "lazy Naples," but I saw nothing lazy in it except the climate. I had been led to believe that the lazzaroni of Naples—who are not necessarily beggars—were the most indolent class of persons in the world. In all my travels I have never elsewhere met such lively and active beggars. The only fault I could find with Naples is that it is altogether too full of life; it does not seem consistent with its paradisal climate. Everybody is either in continual motion or eagerly awaiting the opportunity to bring into exercise his native potential activities.

For some time the only other occupant of our railway compartment was a captain of the Italian army. Although we had taken a compartment in which smoking was forbidden, the officer soon began to make preparations for a smoke—a proceeding which the smoker of our party viewed with evident signs of satisfaction. Whenever we two non-smokers were alone with him in a railway carriage he respected the rights of the majority; but the slightest encouragement of bad example would lead him in a moment to cast to the winds all rules and railway regulations in regard to smoking. For the next two hours they enjoyed themselves amidst clouds of smoke in the lofty regions of fancy. As for ourselves, we could hardly distinguish the thick smoke rolling out of the crater of Vesuvius.

During the night our feverish sleep was interrupted at frequent intervals by the noisy shouts of the men at stations, in which the names Napoli and Foggia were always mingled, and for days afterwards at odd times those two names were ringing in our ears. As the next day would be Pentecost Sunday, we intended to stop over for Mass at the latter episcopal town, situated on the great plain of Apulia, where we arrived early in the morning.

The streets were already filled with people from the country, who appeared to belong mostly to the poorest and most rustic class—shepherds and workingmen on farms, with their wives and daughters. Many of them wore clothes so patched and old that they must have been the Sunday suits of their grandfathers in their courting-days. One of our number obtained permission to say Mass in the cathedral. The bells were rung and the church was quickly filled with people. A few were well dressed, but, taken all in all, it was one of the most motley crowds I have ever seen. At later Masses a higher social grade would probably have been present. The sanctuary was filled with women of middle age, who were plainly but cleanly dressed, and sat in rows, seemingly some privileged confraternity. If I had known exactly who they were they would probably have appeared to me more interesting. Of those in the main body of the church some stood during almost the entire Mass, some knelt a portion of the time, while others—some of them young men in ragged raiment, with great, heavy shoes with large nails thickly driven in their soles—knelt on the hard stone pavement from the beginning to the end of Mass, in deep and earnest prayer and adoration. True devotion is not dependent on rank in society, respectable dress, or even on education. Among the most impoverished and illiterate classes, while some from lack of proper dispositions, and others, with good dispositions, from lack of instruction, fail in that outward respect which is due to the solemn sacrifice, some, poorest of God's poor, most scanty in their store of knowledge, most humble of God's lowly ones, kneel before the altar like the rapt cherubim and seraphim before God's throne.\

After Mass the rain began to pour down, and Foggia looked dreary. I am afraid that our impressions of the town were not such as they could have been under more favorable circumstances. We saw many respectable-appearing people, both in the town and at the station, and the priests whom we met were a very respectable and priestly-looking clergy.

Before noon we were again on the train, moving quickly through the country. At first we passed over a level plain where often, in shepherd's hat and cloak and with shepherd's staff, tending their flocks and herds, we saw the brothers in likeness of those who had attended early Mass in Foggia. Passing over the country roads in all styles of vehicles, drawn by teams of variegated kinds, large numbers of people were going to or returning from the churches in neighboring towns and villages. In the early afternoon we came in sight of the Adriatic, and until near evening passed down its queenly shores. This is the region of ancient Apulia in classic times, and in the early Christian centuries belonged to the patriarchate of Constantinople, and Greek was the language of its liturgy. We passed through numerous olive-groves, getting frequent views of the blue waters of the Adriatic, and passed many fair cities on its shores, whose walls and spires and towers shone with a white brightness towards the land and cast their majestic shadows o'er the sea.

Towards evening we arrived in Brindisi, the ancient Brundusium, which was settled at a very early time in history by the Cretans, and for many centuries was an independent city ruled by its own princes. In the year 267 B.C. it was taken by the Romans, who made it one of the most renowned harbors of the world. It was the chief naval station whence they set sail on all their great expeditions to Greece and the East. It was the scene of some of the exploits of Cæsar, and was visited by Cicero, Horace, and Virgil, where the last named died. It was the end of the Appian Way from Rome, and contains a vast number of Roman ruins. Of late years its harbor has been greatly improved, which has brought about a corresponding revival in the business and importance of the town. On our arrival we immediately bought tickets for Alexandria, on the Peninsular and Oriental line of steamers, owned by an English company. As one of the boats was lying at the dock, we went on board without delay, although she would not sail until the next afternoon. In the evening we took a stroll through the city. Some kind of a noisy demonstration was taking place in honor of some event of Italian unity. An uncouth crowd of boys, from eighteen to twenty years of age, seemed to be the principal agents of the farce. Some sympathy might be felt for a people in their efforts for national unity, if they had not consummated their iniquity by drawing down on themselves the curse of God by smiting the anointed Vicar of Jesus Christ. When they shall have repaired that wrong, crying to Heaven for vengeance, some of their other victims, who have been cast under the national car of Juggernaut, may ask the pardoning prayer of mercy for the guilty ones, or rather for those of them who have not already appeared, unabsolved or unrepentant, before the judgment-seat of God.

The following morning we were able to get a better view of our surroundings. Brindisi rose by rather steep incline to its dignified eminence overlooking the bay. Standing above us, not far distant, was the stately column that marked the end of the Appian Way. Just across an alley from it we could see the roof and upper portion of Virgil's house. At a little distance was the cathedral, built in Norman times on the highest elevation of the city, with a square tower on one corner and opposite to it a pointed round tower surmounted by the cross. On the other side of the vessel appeared the beautiful bay, with a narrow but fair opening to the sea, whose blue expanse could be seen beyond. On the shores of the bay on either side were groves of the principal trees of South Italy—olive, lemon, orange, and palm. And towering over the bay with its immense round towers frowned the old castle, built by successive sovereigns in the middle ages. After breakfast I climbed the hill to make a closer inspection of the column and Virgil's house. Sometimes in Italy the most historic buildings are occupied by the poorest and most humble families, which was also true in the case of the house of the great Latin poet. I chose a good position on a large stone near the base of the column, and gave myself to musing on the marvellous power, the grand highways, the extensive dominions, and the poets, orators, and warriors of ancient Rome. Afterwards I entered the cathedral, where they were just commencing a solemn High Mass. The canons were present, and here, as elsewhere in Italy, I was very favorably impressed by the priestly look and bearing of the clergy.

About the middle of the afternoon we got under way and steamed out of the harbor and down the eastern coast of Italy, beholding in the distance the land of Otranto, the ancient Calabria of the Romans, passing cities and towns upon its shores which appeared to us more like a mirage than a reality, until night closed down upon the waters.\

When we came on deck the next morning the island of Cephalonia was in sight not far distant, which is the largest of the Ionian Islands and frequently mentioned by Homer. It was named after the mythological Cephalus, and is separated from ancient Ithaca by only a narrow channel. Ithaca is another of the Ionian Islands, and the "kingdom of Ulysses" in Homeric poems. In a short time Zante, the most productive of the Ionian Islands, rose above the horizon. It is only ten miles south of Cephalonia, between which two islands ships can sail into the Gulf of Lepanto, celebrated for its victorious battle in defence of Christendom. Passing by Zante, we sailed all the afternoon down the shores of fair Greece, where delightful breezes kissed the most lovely blue waters that I have ever seen. All of the country to the north and northeast of us was the ancient Peloponnesus, whose chief city, Sparta, so celebrated in history, was only twenty miles inland from that rocky coast, among those blue mountains on which our eyes now rested.

The day was beautiful, the air was delicious, the sky was like the pure dome of heaven, the sea was an image of the sky in deeper colors, and the spirit of historic centuries not only hovered over us but had already alighted in our hearts. Greece in ancient times must have been to its refined inhabitants a fascinating country, an earthly paradise. Captivated by my surroundings, I began to compose a poem, of which I wrote only two stanzas, but which reflect my feelings at the time:

> O Greece! if thou hadst been my home,
>   On shores of thy blue sea,
> In golden vales though I might roam,
>   My heart would cling to thee.

> Though fairer skies might smile on me
> In realms of goddess queens,
> My homesick heart would turn to thee
> And languish for thy scenes.

The next morning we were sailing near the shores of Crete, which, veiled in a thin, light haze, and its mountain-tops shining like silver crests, seemed to us a fairy island of romance. An island of romantic history it truly is; for on majestic Mount Ida, one of those highest mountains seen rising from its centre, Zeus, chief god of the Greeks, and Jupiter of the Romans, supreme ruler of mortals and immortals, was said to have been born. Homer, who lived nearly three thousand years ago, spoke of Crete as the island "of a hundred cities." How often have the pennants of Greece and Rome fluttered in sight of its shores as their galleys flashed past, under the quick stroke of banks of gleaming oars, on their way to conquest or dominion! How many of the apostles of Christ and the early Church have sailed along those shores and seen the same bright vision that we saw, and lovingly, with apostolic eye and zeal, have looked on those bays and cities, with ardent longing to bring the blind worshippers of mythical deities to a knowledge of Christ, the true God! In the afternoon the blue waters of the Mediterranean alone were visible on every side.

The next day soon after noon we came in sight of the shores of Egypt. As we approached them a dark, sultry atmosphere overhung the coast and the city of Alexandria. Everything was typical of Egypt, and no country that we had yet visited was more like what we had conceived it to be than the one before us.

CHAPTER VI.

THE LAND OF THE PHARAOS AND OF THE PYRAMIDS.

The kingdom of Egypt is more than four thousand years old, its first king having been Misraim, or Menes, a grandson of Noe. It is said that Cham, son of Noe, settled in Egypt, and after his death was worshipped under the title of Jupiter Ammon. Egypt is certainly a very extraordinary country, and one of the most wonderful nations of pagan times. A stable government, wise laws, and a fertile soil combined to procure for her a long era of prosperity, during which great cities rose on the banks of the Nile, whose imperishable ruins evidence their elegance, grandeur, and magnificence. The history, ruins, and monuments of ancient Egypt prove her advanced knowledge and culture in the arts and sciences. When we consider where the human race had its origin, and where a good portion of it continues to dwell, we see that she is situated in one of the most favored centres of the earth.

.We soon entered the harbor of Alexandria, and the scenes which surrounded us were full of dreamy excitement. Vessels of nearly all the chief nations of the world were riding at anchor, from the ancient Egyptian barque with its single tall lateen sail to the great iron monsters of modern warfare; and their flags floating from their masts represented a large portion of the history, sentiments, and principles of the world for more than a thousand years. But we looked in vain for a vessel flying the stars and stripes.\

Alexandria was founded by Alexander the Great more than twenty-two hundred years ago, and was once a city of great magnificence. It is on the great highway between the East and West. Although in many respects distinctively oriental, it is one of the most cosmopolitan cities of the world. The different nationalities comprising its population are an evidence of this. In 1870 its entire population was about 240,000. Of these there were 25,000 Greeks, 20,000 Italians, 15,000 French, 12,000 English Maltese, 12,000 Levantines of miscellaneous European descent, 8,000 Germans, and 8,000 other foreigners, besides Arabs, Copts, Turks, Armenians, and Persians. On account of the English occupation of Egypt, since that time the number of English residents in Alexandria must have greatly increased. Nearly one thousand passengers, on an average, daily enter and leave its port.

Various buildings and ruins stand prominent on the shores on either side; but among them all the eye seeks for the famous Pompey's Pillar, about which there has been much discussion as to its origin and in whose honor erected; but it was probably built by an Egyptian governor named Pompey, in honor of Diocletian. Far out at sea its majestic form is visible.\

Having come to anchor, a fleet of small boats immediately surrounded us, whose commanders and rowers were decked out in all the innumerable styles of the Orient. Fez and turban, flowing robes and wide breeches gathered below the knee, rich dress and scarcely any dress at all, distinguished the men in the boats below the gangways of the steamer who contended for place and passengers. A passenger gained at the port often means service for a tour through Egypt and up the Nile. We selected an Egyptian dragoman who, with the exception of a Turkish fez, wore the usual dress of Europeans. From the landing, where we had no difficulty, not even our passports being required, we drove to the Hotel Abbat, accompanied by our guide. Having taken rooms, being yet inexperienced in the East, we placed the entire excursion for the day, carriages, fees, and all, in his hands, for which he was to receive a stated amount. Alexandria is a very interesting city, and although there are not a large number of existing monuments of historical renown, there are many ruins which mark the sites where pride of power has crumbled into dust, where the fanes of learning, sacred and secular, have become smoke and ashes, and where the Christian religion once shone with a new splendor and left an immortal name. But the people and street scenes were a constant source of pleasure to us. When one considers the many diversified oriental races and nationalities that throng the streets of the city, and the varieties and combinations in the cut and colors of their costumes, he can readily conceive how strangely new those Eastern faces and old fashions seemed to us. Our guide could tell us to what people or race, and usually to what trade or profession, the different persons that we met belonged. He pretended to like the Americans and to dislike the English, not because they were English, but because of their continued occupation of his country. He took great pride in the Egyptians and frequently told their superiority over the Turks and Arabs. He seemed to bear a special hatred against the Greeks, and would never speak of them with respect.

On our way to Pompey's Pillar we met wagon-loads of women coming from the cemeteries. They wore a kind of thick veil reaching from below the eyes, and partly kept from the face by a sort of spiral spool above the nose. They appeared to me as the Egyptian women might have looked three thousand years ago. Pompey's Pillar is constructed of red granite and is one hundred and fourteen feet high. Surrounding it were many large blocks of stone half-buried in the sand, and near by was a Mohammedan cemetery. Although now deserted, this was once a busy place on the most magnificent street of the city.

In the evening we wandered through the

streets to see the city after nightfall. Two of us, realizing that the ornamental part of our education had been neglected, and knowing that it would soon become a necessity and that the practice which makes perfect usually appears more graceful in the dark, concluded to take a donkey-ride. About twenty boys and donkeys immediately surrounded us—for they seemed to get a knowledge by instinct of our half-formed resolution—and amid much confusion of names and qualities of donkeys we got astride of those which we thought would suit us; but to this day I cannot tell whether my donkey was the "Prince of Wales," "Yankee Doodle," or the "Emperor of China." Let it be well understood that one must stand pretty high in the public esteem of Egypt and the world before he can have an Egyptian donkey named after him. The ride was pleasant. I afterwards got to love the sound of the quick clatter of donkey-hoofs on the streets, and to see the donkey-boy running behind, urging on his favorite. It is a picturesque sight. Our friend who did not care for a ride, in fact who thought it was rather undignified, returned nearly the entire distance to the hotel accompanied and surrounded by the remaining eighteen boys and donkeys. He did not take an undignified ride, but his march was triumphal. We enjoyed his situation then better than he did, but I believe that he enjoys it better now when he looks back at it. Afterwards in Palestine he got to prefer those innocent, long-eared, useful little pets to any other means of conveyance.

The next day we took the train for Cairo. In a short time we came in sight of and passed Lake Mareotis, which, with the low-built, brown Egyptian villages with small white domes or minarets rising in their midst, and the green groves of palm-trees on its banks, presented a perfect picture of oriental scenery. The route led across the famous Delta of the Nile. The valley of the Nile and the Delta constitute one of the most fertile countries of the world and one of the most impoverished. It is enough to make the heart bleed to see the poor, industrious people of Egypt, working hard the whole year, bringing forth abundant harvests from a rich soil, and at the same time living on the verge of starvation. Are not the so-called Christian nations of Europe guilty of the crime of allowing it ? Who but God hears the cry of the oppressed ?

On our journey we saw many curious and

instructive sights. However attractive the low mud villages of the country might appear at some other season, under the burning heat of the sun in June, without the proximity of a cooling body of water, they looked quite the opposite. Nearly the whole way the tillers of the soil were engaged in artificial irrigation. A waterwheel with a number of buckets surrounding it served the purpose. Sometimes a mule, more frequently a buffalo, often a cow, was hitched to a pole and moved around in a circle to turn the water-wheel, sending down empty buckets into an opening at the side of the canal, and bringing up full ones, which were emptied out over the fields on the other side. I noticed that these wheels were always placed under the grateful shade of a tree. Irrigation in a somewhat similar manner was seen practised in southern Italy, and it occurred to me that some such plan might be successfully adopted in our country in case of continued drought. Along the way we often saw herds of cattle lying in the water, with only their heads and necks uncovered, to protect them from the hot rays of the sun.\

Men and women were frequently seen reclining under the cool shadows of the trees. In such a land trees are a great blessing, well *and the Holy Land.*

enjoyed and appreciated. Their graceful forms, and verdant colors seem endowed with a new and more ethereal beauty to the heated dwellers in tropical and sub-tropical climes. Many of the country people were travelling over the roads, going to and from villages on foot or on horses, asses, and camels. Sometimes long trains of camels, bearing burdens, were seen, perhaps caravans from distant places; and sometimes a band of Bedouins would come upon the scene with their wild and warlike appearance. Once we saw approaching a village a party of horsemen, dressed in rich and showy costumes, riding fine blooded, high-spirited steeds gaily caparisoned with silk sparkling with gold. The leader of the party, who rode at its head, was a venerable man with a long gray beard, a royal-looking man, of such dignity and appearance as one would imagine were the ancient Egyptian kings. It was the finest Eastern cavalcade that we saw in our travels, and any which we saw in Europe could not compare with it. At another time I saw a tall man in white turban and black flowing robes, with a full black beard, walking on the road beside a donkey on whose back was a woman in blue dress, bearing in her arms an infant child. Seen from the distance it was a faithful representation of the Holy Family in Egypt nearly nineteen hundred years ago. In both Egypt and Palestine one frequently meets such living reminders of holy scenes.

We crossed on our way both the Eastern and Western Nile, and at length saw that we were approaching the vicinity of Cairo; for there, away in the distance on the sands of the desert, distinct and clear-cut standing against the sky, were three forms that had been familiar to us in pictures from our youth. There were many buildings and monuments in Europe and the East which, as soon as we saw them, so well known was their appearance, seemed to us like old acquaintances; but the pyramids could never be mistaken for anything elsewhere on the face of the earth.

Having arrived at the station, we intended to go to Shepherd's Hotel, but on leaving the train we saw its omnibus driving away, and so took the one for the Hôtel d'Orient, which we found very satisfactory. It was only a little after midday when we were settled down in our rooms. A blast of air was blowing from the desert, as heated as if coming from the furnace of Nabuchodonosor, King of Babylon. We concluded that it was not safe to venture out, so we saw what we could from the windows. We were opposite a square where many donkey-boys and carriages were waiting for a job. For a time we witnessed the antics of the boys and drivers, and their untiring readiness to catch sight of a stranger or acquaintance who might wish to employ them. But nearer by, across a narrow street, was a domestic scene that pleased me more: A young Egyptian of the humbler class, in a long, coarse blue robe, with a white turban on his head, was tending a little stall in which were boiled eggs, cakes, crockery, and similar cheap articles for sale. With him was his wife, dressed in the same poor material, and veiled. She had with her a little curly-haired boy, not yet weaned. In a little while his father took him in his arms and fondled and caressed him in a way to show, by unmistakable signs that brought tears to my eyes, a father's tender love. A father's and a mother's love is about the same everywhere, and to witness its manifestation brings all of us back to our childhood once more.

For several hours I had heard a solemn, monotonous music not far away, and now it seemed to be moving; so I determined, notwithstanding the heat, to start out alone and gratify my curiosity. I went around several blocks and met what proved to be a funeral procession of a young married man of wealthy family. At its head was a camel covered with rich trappings, on which rode a fantastic-looking man. These were followed by musicians and hired mourners, who in musical tones bewailed the departed. A carriage in the procession evidently belonged to the young wife. A lady richly dressed, whom I took to be her, frantically left the carriage and endeavored to seize the bridles of the horses to prevent them going further. I suppose this also was one of the customary manifestations of grief. Taken all in all, to our Western eyes it was a funeral procession most remarkable for show and as an exhibition of outward sorrow, which probably was the exterior of a truer and deeper sorrow in the hearts of the afflicted wife and relatives.

Later in the afternoon we took a carriage for a drive through the city. Cairo is a true Egyptian and oriental city, and possesses all the charms of orientalism, partaking much more of the Eastern character than Alexandria. In Alexandria one sees much more of the whole world; in Cairo much more of the East. Cairo is a great emporium of trade between Europe, Asia, and Africa, receiving their treasures by railways, boats on the Nile, and caravans of the desert. Her merchants deal in the silks, jewelry, and gold and silver trimmings of Damascus, the products of India and the East, and ostrich plumes, ivory, and slaves of the Upper Nile region and Central Africa. It is also one of the great marts for precious stones. People from all the different lands with which Cairo is connected by trade crowd her streets in dresses peculiar to their race and regions, and with complexions in all the shades from pure white to jet black. A large number of well-dressed ladies are met, heavily veiled; and from head to foot, covering their dresses of rich material, falls a black silk mantle. Every kind of four-footed animal used for pleasure or bearing burdens is seen in its thoroughfares: the donkey for riding or heavy loads, horses for quicker or more aristocratic conveyance, the pure-blooded Arabian studs of the Bedouins or of those with wealth to afford them, and camels, singly or in long lines—"stately ships of the desert," as they are often called.

We drove to the citadel to get a good view of the city and to see the mosque of Mehemet Ali. The citadel is in the hands of the British troops, and the mosque in the hands of a crowd of beggars as persistent as the world affords. From the heights of the citadel Cairo lay before us, with its walls and battlements, its store-houses, its palaces, its harems, and its four hundred mosques with their tapering minarets shining in the glaring sun of an almost perpetually cloudless sky. The eye wandered up and down the Nile for thirty miles, and beheld the sites and monuments of some of the oldest cities of antiquity: the sands of the far-famed Libyan desert, on whose borders the everlasting pyramids raise their mighty forms; Old Cairo with its granaries of Joseph and refuge of the Holy Family in Egypt; Memphis, ten miles towards the south, founded by Menes forty-two hundred years ago, and one of the grandest cities of ancient Egypt; Heliopolis, a few miles toward the northeast, the ancient On, the oldest ecclesiastical city of Egypt and the chief centre of the worship of the sun, the daughter of one of whose priests the Hebrew Joseph married: This great city with its grand temples has been a city of ruins for two thousand years. Some of its most magnificent temples reflected their new-born splendors in the morning sun of four thousand years ago. An obelisk, covered with hieroglyphics, alone marks the site of the ancient city. It is the oldest of its kind and has been in existence from thirty-seven to thirty-nine centuries. We were standing in the centre of one of the oldest populated regions of the earth, where one of the first and most ancient streams of history had its origin; and having admired with expansion of soul this grand scene, where the monuments of the long-sleeping dead look down serenely on the activities and vanities of life, we turned to our more modern surroundings.

The mosque of Mehemet Ali was near at hand. It is built in great part of yellow oriental alabaster. At the door of the court before the mosque slippers were put on over our shoes. In the East they cover the head and uncover the feet as a mark of respect. Of late, however, instead of uncovering the feet, it does as well to cover the boots or shoes with a pair of slippers. It takes several able-bodied men to manage one pair of slippers, all of whom expect backsheesh. As well as I could understand the arrangement, one man puts them on your feet, another looks out for them when they slip off, as they are very loose, and another owns them. They are a source of revenue for all. It requires less capital to enter into business partnership in a Mohammedan mosque than in any other place in the world. A man with a dollar as capital will take three partners to help him conduct the business. I think there were about ten men who managed us. As we found out afterwards, the affair could have been better arranged; but at that time we were inexperienced in mosque visits, and had been misled by writers who had travelled in Eastern countries, but who had not learned much by experience. Dark looks and fierce frowns of fanaticism were not cast on us, although we lost considerable backsheesh. If it had been the Grand Turk himself, he would hardly have been treated with greater respect and deference than we were by all the officials, devotees, and hangers-on of the mosque. One intelligent young fellow acted as guide and told us to whom to give backsheesh. At this date I cannot remember any exceptions that he made, except a devotee who was prostrating himself in prayer near a fountain in the outer court. No one who has not once entered a Mohammedan mosque under favorable conditions, when business was slack, will ever be able to understand how many men it requires to conduct you through the entrance, to take your umbrella and return it, to care for your slippers, to keep you from losing yourself, to manifest a kind interest in you, to get you out safely, and finally to assure you, as it were, of your personal identity, that you are actually the same person you were when you entered. Of course we emerged with empty pockets but high in the esteem of a portion of our fellow-men.

One of my friends is a person who is not perfectly satisfied with the smooth flow of any stream; he usually wants to cause at least a ripple on the surface. Looking at a very beautiful alabaster mosque and giving backsheesh were too monotonous. As he had very large slippers, he could easily let one slip off and still push his foot along the floor, as if the fact were unnoticed. With large slippers one moves along as if skating; in his case the slipper was about two feet behind him, held to his ankle by strings, and the attendant made frantic attempts to catch hold of it and attract his attention, which he of course innocently considered was an effort to show him some new beauty in the mosque. The mosque was certainly beautiful, but not nearly so fine as the mosque of Omar in Jerusalem, and was almost colder to the spiritual nature of man than St. Paul's Cathedral in London. No edifice of worship that I have ever seen can even approach, in the spiritual warmth and beauty of heaven's sunlight, to the temples of the Catholic Church.

We would have visited other mosques, but our change was exhausted, and somehow our experience had not been sufficiently pleasant to induce us to do so, at least for some time, unless there was something more attractive than costly material and clever architecture. In this way we missed the most elegant mosque in Cairo, that of Sultan Hassan, which is considered the finest structure in modern Egypt. We returned to the hotel by a circuitous route in order to see more of the city.

In the evening a pretty little girl seven or eight years of age came in front of the hotel, where a number of guests were sitting, and performed some very skilful tricks of jugglery. She then wanted backsheesh; and when one of the party jocosely asked her to continue, she quickly replied: "No backsheesh, no juggle." She was a bright, clever little Egyptian, spoke English well, and succeeded in getting backsheesh.

CHAPTER VII.

THE PYRAMIDS—REFUGE OF THE HOLY FAMILY IN EGYPT—OUR VOYAGE TO PALESTINE.

WE retired to our rooms early, as at daybreak the next morning we were to start for the pyramids. It was so warm that I did not sleep well and wakened at frequent intervals, and each time I heard that sad, monotonous, funereal music. I must have heard it in my sleep, for it seemed continuous in my ears until dawn, when it ceased. At early dawn we were ready, the driver having slept in his carriage in front of the hotel. We employed a guide whom we did not need, and who understood just enough English to misunderstand everything said to him.

Cairo appeared much more charming in the mild light of early morning than in the fierce glare of the sun when his red, angry countenance looked down from the higher heavens. We passed over the wondrous Nile, crossing on a bridge six hundred feet in length, built on six spans, and having at each of its four corners an enormous lion in repose carved in stone. The pyramids are from six to eight miles from the city. The smooth road is lined on either side with fine trees, which interlaced their branches above us and gave a refreshing shade; and thus, the road being not only well made but cool, the ride was very pleasant./

From the time we crossed the bridge until some distance in the country the way was thronged with camels, asses, and horses, and their drivers and riders. Numbers seemed to have been encamped by the roadside, and were just awakening from their slumbers or preparing to move; others seemed to have come some distance and to have started in the night in order to arrive with their loads in the city early in the morning. Some were Bedouins, but the large number were country people bringing the produce of their farms and gardens to the city market. We passed some fine grounds and villas in the suburbs, among them a royal harem, and further in the country several villages some distance from the wayside. Near one or two of these villages were large ponds, into which a dozen or score of women and girls with jars were wading to procure water. About a mile from the pyramids several Arabs met us, and ran behind the carriage the whole distance, frequently repeating their offers of service.\

At the pyramids a dozen others who were

waiting for us joined them, all anxious to render any service in their power. The day had already begun to grow very warm, and the rays of the sun, reflected on the white sands of the desert and the great stones of the pyramids, acquired a new intensity of heat. My companions concluded that they would not make the ascent of the pyramid of Cheops, which so many undertake. As for myself, I never intended to run the risk of any such experiment. To say nothing of the heat, I believe that I could hardly stand on such a height without dizziness, unless the pyramid was steadied with its base up with a railing around it.

When we approached the pyramids they seemed disappointingly small; but when we got near them, and looked up at the great pyramid of Cheops, and saw the size and number of the stones of which it was constructed, and hired an Arab to ascend it in our place, and had seen him go up, up, stone after stone, until he was only a white speck, we concluded that after all they were very large. The greatest of the number is the pyramid built by King Cheops four thousand years ago. At the present time it is 460 feet in height, and its slope 610 feet, and it covers an area of about twelve acres. Its size is not so large as formerly, as great quantities of stone have been taken from it to Cairo for building purposes; its surface was formerly smooth, but is now rough for the same reason that it has diminished in size. Leaving the pyramids, we went to see the Sphinx, accompanied by the entire crowd of Arabs and our "guide," who had come with us to protect us from the ravages of the Bedouins. He sometimes did scold them for their excessive forwardness, but with no apparent success. The truth is, he had got into "bad company," for we rather encouraged them in all their enterprises. We really enjoyed their company. They were more like the same number of children than anything else. We had to choose first and second assistants to help us through the sand, into the underground apartments, and over the walls of the temple of the Sphinx. We could have accomplished everything as well without them; but their transitory friendship—for our silver pieces—was worth something. One of our party even purchased specimens of the "antique,". found near the pyramids, and probably manufactured in Europe, perhaps in Cairo. My chief young man told me when I ridiculed the other's purchase:

"You know better, but many English people do not know." Then he got confidential and told me that they bought them from the manufacturers and sold them again. Perhaps he told me that to please me, for he was trying by all reasonable means to make himself agreeable. We all bought a few specimens of a beautiful stone from the temple of the Sphinx, which I think we preserved until we got back to Cairo; they certainly are not yet lost to Egypt. The venerable Sphinx was an old acquaintance of ours, and had not changed any since we last saw him in school-books. He is a stone lion 146 feet long, with a man's face 28 feet in length. But different authors give the measurement differently, and I do not pretend that I actually measured him. The paws are extended about fifty feet in front. The Sphinx was a deity among the ancient Egyptians—the "god of the setting sun"; they worshipped the sun under the different appellations of "morning," "noonday," and "setting sun." It is quite probable, from inscriptions which have been found, that this Sphinx was chiselled out of the solid rock of the desert before the time of Cheops, who built the first pyramid. In former times an altar stood before this huge image, where the incense and odors of sacrifice ascended into his nostrils. He then wore the royal helmet of Egypt, which has since been broken off. Near the Sphinx is his temple, which has been excavated from beneath the sand, over which it once raised its costly walls. It was built of polished red granite and marble in tiers of great square blocks, over which and under which we passed in curious admiration.

On our return to the carriage near the great pyramid, as we approached it, my chief young man said to me: "It is finished." I had intended to give him his backsheesh as a parting token of my regard, so that he would not further annoy me by future requests for more. In a short time he again told me: "It is finished." His meaning began to dawn on my mind. I said that I supposed those were the chief attractions, but that we would look at them awhile longer. He still insisted: "It is finished; would you please give me my backsheesh before the others come up to us? I do not want them to see what I receive; give me what you please." I yielded to his reasonable request; and I must give him, and the boy with him, the credit of not asking for any more. Amid the clamor of voices we rode away, and by the same pleasant route by which we came returned to Cairo.

A short time after our return we took another carriage for a visit to Old Cairo, to see the place where the Holy Family dwelt during their sojourn in Egypt. Old Cairo is a peculiar-looking place, without much external grandeur; in fact, it looks like the dwelling-place of the poor and neglected. We soon found the place we were seeking. It is in the hands of the schismatic Copts. The Copts are probably the only descendants of the ancient Egyptians. Some congregations among them are united to the Catholic Church, including about one-third of the Christians of that rite. The remaining two-thirds are schismatics, in union with whom are the Abyssinians, who receive whatever orders they have from the Copts. The Copts are the only schismatic body in the East whose ordination is doubted by Rome, and it seems that both their clergy and laity are to a great extent men of loose morals and principles. Yet, in common with all the Christians of the Orient, they hold the sacred places in great veneration.

We were met by a young Coptic priest, who was very ready to show us the places we sought. We first entered an ancient and rather attractive church possessing several fine paintings and carvings in wood. We descended still lower to what is now a subterranean chapel. Our clerical guide pointed out to us the places where the divine Infant Jesus was laid by His parents, and where the Blessed Virgin and St. Joseph sat to rest themselves and gaze in silent rapture on the face of the Holy Child. We knelt and said short prayers to each of the Holy Family.

O mysterious Egyptian land! the refuge thou didst give to the Holy Infant, even though unknown to thyself, brought down upon thee for centuries the choicest blessings of faith and sanctity, so that thou didst become the garden of Christ, and even thy deserts were peopled with the saints of God. What hast thou done, O sorrowful and oppressed land, that thou hast lost thy heritage?

When our priest guide saw us kneel and kiss those sacred places, he asked us if we were Latin priests. When we told him that we were he showed us much more respect and attention than before, although he had already been sufficiently attentive. All over the East, although they may sometimes possess considerable bigotry and bitterness, the schismatic priests usually manifest a genuine respect, not unlike a deep feeling of brotherly kindness, towards their Western brethren who acknowledge the supremacy of the great Patriarch of Rome. No wonder that Leo XIII. has manifested an admirable sympathy and love for these mistaken Christians of the East. Their return to the fold of Peter should not by any means be considered an unlooked-for event. I was pleased to see, while in Rome, that any information pertaining to the present condition of the Orient was listened to with deepest attention ; and in fact, judging from appearances, the authorities of the Church are at present more interested in the return of the Eastern schismatics than in the labors for the conversion of any Western people.

The places once occupied by the Holy Family are now small altars in the form of niches cut in the rock. Under certain conditions, and by permission easily obtained, Catholic priests are allowed to say Mass in this holy chapel. The church above, which we first entered, was probably built by St. Helena, mother of Constantine ; and even before her time the house of the Holy Family had been converted into a church by the primitive Christians. We were then shown the well which was miraculously produced for the use of the Holy Family ; and having given fees to the priest, and to some attendants who had furnished tapers and had otherwise been of service to us, we returned to Cairo./

Later that afternoon we were again in the railway train, which was moving out of Cairo towards Alexandria. A number of the passengers on this return trip were officers and soldiers of the English army, some of whom, having brought along a good supply of beer, were enjoying themselves. We arrived in Alexandria after dark and immediately drove to our hotel. The next day was Sunday, and we attended Mass in the cathedral church of St. Catharine of Alexandria, built over the spot where this holy virgin received the crown of martyrdom. St. Catharine is the patron saint of the city, but her body is preserved in the Greek monastery on Mt. Sinai. On our return we all celebrated Mass in this church, around whose altars from early morning until late in the afternoon gather the various nationalities and races that compose the population of Alexandria, from the fair-haired Saxon of the northern German-land to the jet-black native of Central Africa. The Orientals retain many of their old customs, and assist at Mass in fez and turban without uncovering their heads. As already remarked, this is in accordance with their ideas of reverence—to uncover their feet rather than their heads—and is in harmony with the sanctioned customs of olden times; for when the Lord appeared to Moses in "a flame of fire out of the midst of a bush," He said to him: "Come not nigh hither, put off the shoes from thy feet; for the place whereon thou standest is holy ground" (Exodus iii. 5). In Alexandria similarity of customs was sometimes manifest among people of different races who are very dissimilar in appearance: black mantillas covered the heads and hung low from the shoulders of Spanish ladies whose intelligent faces and clear complexions indicated the pure blood of Castile; a white mantle over the head and falling to the feet, enveloping the entire body, was the usual covering of a very different race of females, who, when they turned their faces towards us, revealed the dark skin and black, glittering eyes of the Nubian negress. The Catholics of Alexandria and Cairo together number about sixty-three thousand.

That same day we took passage on a Russian steamer for Jaffa. Everything on board was according to the Russian style, and we found the first cabin very pleasant, the officers of the boat very kind and polite, the beds clean, and an excellent table, with its white cloth and napkins, its neat, shining silver service, and its many courses of food well cooked according to the Russian mode.

Early the next morning we arrived in Port Said, where we remained until the middle of the afternoon. The town itself was not interesting, but the harbor was filled with vessels, among them some of the finest war-ships of different nations which I have ever seen. Until then I had never realized the beauty and finish, combined with strength and power, of the best class of Italian, English, and French war-vessels. That some of the other powerful nations of Europe have ships of equal excellence is probable, but I do not remember to have seen them. As a patriotic American I grieve to say that our American naval arks are shabby-looking hulks, with the only things of beauty about them the flag that floats over them and the thought that they bear upon their shaky decks men with hearts true to their colors. We hired a row-boat with rowers and took a ride up the harbor, hoping to get a better view of the now famous Suez Canal. On our return to the steamer we spent the remainder of the listless day watching half-naked men at work, who, like a great many others who only half work, made up the deficiency by a generous amount of noise. We also tried to amuse ourselves looking at the huge porpoises, of which the harbor seemed full, disporting themselves, rising partly out of the water, skimming along its surface, and then diving again into its depths.

About the middle of the afternoon we moved slowly out of the harbor to the open sea. The land gradually disappeared; we had left successively America, Europe, and Africa, and now the great continent of Asia was before us. The next country which we shall see is the land of promise, not alone to the chosen people of God, but in a wider sense to all the nations of the earth. Oh! is it possible that in to-morrow's light our eyes shall rest upon that favored country? The night and sleep will intervene, but in to-morrow's rising sun we shall look upon that land. To-day is the dark Egypt of this life, to-night will come the sleep of death, and to-morrow will appear the bright, beautiful shores of the heavenly country and the haven of eternal rest. The city of the living God is enclosed in those emerald hills beyond, and before our eyes its jewelled walls and golden splendors will flash in the celestial light of to-morrow's eternal day.

THE HOLY LAND.

CHAPTER VIII.

JAFFA AND THE ROAD TO JERUSALEM.

At an early hour the next morning we stood on the deck of the steamer, waiting anxiously for the first glimpse of land, which we knew lay not far away before us. We had been deeply interested in the lands which we had already seen; and before our return home we expected to visit other countries, cities, and shrines of the Old World; but none of them, not even the Eternal City itself, could compare in interest with the land which we were now approaching. It is the Holy Land, the cradle of the human race and of Christianity. It is the very soil that has been impressed with the sacred footprints of our Lord. It was the earthly home of St. Joseph and the Blessed Virgin Mary and the Divine Child Jesus. And as the land is so dear, and everything that pertains to it so interesting to every Christian, I will try to describe, in a simple way, our too brief visit there. I will be strictly truthful in describing what I saw, as it is possible that sometimes imagination has run away with veracity. Truth cannot do harm, even when told of the most sacred places. In many other countries you will find longer rivers, higher mountains and more extended plains, more beautiful and sublime scenery, a more fertile soil and more salubrious climate. Palestine evidently is not what it once was; but even in ancient times, in the days of Naaman, there were more magnificent rivers than the Jordan, but none so sacred. A mother's grave may not be the brightest spot on earth, but it is often the dearest. So with the land to which, with every stroke of the wheel and every beat of our ardent hearts, we drew nearer.

There at length, lying before us, appeared the hills of Palestine—the mountains of Ephraim to the north, and the "hill country of Judea" to the south—and a little later the white and colored walls and houses of Jaffa were plainly visible. In the distance, seen from the sea, Jaffa, rising in terraced heights on a conically-shaped promontory, surrounded by its numerous palm, cypress, and orange groves, is certainly beautiful; and when you are once within the town, although you will find many things to shock your taste, you will also come upon many fine views from which you will find it difficult to draw yourself away.

Our steamer came to anchor about half a mile from the shore, as all vessels of fair size do; and the water was soon covered with a multitude of small boats, making to us as quickly as possible. We had already become used to Oriental costumes, Oriental ways, and the East in general, but never before had we seen a Jaffa boatman. There may be other mortals in the world like him—we know there are in Haifa—but we never expect to look upon his like again. The Jaffa boatmen are the noisiest lot of fellows in the world. The man who can shout louder or gesticulate more violently must have more lungs and life than one of them. From my knowledge of the world I do not believe the man exists. You would think that nothing less would satisfy them than the blood of their fellow-boatman who might be successful in getting a passenger or trunk. But, after all their noise and seemingly desperate intentions, they see their rivals row away with a boat-load, and their own boat empty, with the best evidences of good nature. You gradually discover that they are a lot of good-natured, good-looking, courageous fellows, whom you would soon get to admire if it were not for the noise and confusion they make.

We were about to visit Palestine at a season of the year when there are few visitors. A priest on the American mission cannot choose the season most pleasant for his travels. From the middle of March to the first of May is undoubtedly the best time for Palestine travel. In the first part of June the harvest is nearly over, and every week the weather is becoming more uncomfortably warm. But that this Biblical land may be better understood, it is well that its valleys and hills and towns should be described as seen by different eyes at different seasons of the year. We were about to enter the Holy Land when it was clothed neither with the beautiful verdure of spring nor with the barren desolation of autumn. Although there had been no rains for five weeks previous, neither all the green nor all the flowers of spring had yet faded. Heavy dews fell at night, and an occasional cloud was seen.

We soon landed, and the place whereon we stood was holy ground. Our baggage had to submit to a slight examination, and our passports were presented. We now learned the great convenience of a moderate use of "backsheesh."

Among the crowd that met us was one man whom you would readily recognize as a native of the Eastern States of our own country. We learned from him that he was a resident of Jaffa, who had come out with the now defunct American colony once planted here. It was a pleasure, so far away from home, to meet one of our own countrymen; and yet it seemed strange to see him choose to live in such surroundings. We can understand the reason of the choice in the case of monks and other pious persons, who live there because it is the Holy Land. He told us he was the guide of our great American general and of our new minister to Turkey when they visited the country. Followed by about a dozen others, he conducted us to the Franciscan monastery and hospice, where we were cordially welcomed by the good monks. It was our first introduction to the monks and their hospitality in Palestine. We had determined during our stay to make our home with them wherever possible, for we knew that they could better direct us, open the way to greater spiritual advantages, and more quickly animate us with the right spirit of the holy places. We were not deceived, and soon learned to love these humble sons of St. Francis and devoted custodians of the Holy Land, and prayers rise from our hearts whenever we remember them.

It was now early in the morning, and we were not to start for Jerusalem until about five o'clock, so we had sufficient time to see Jaffa. The time was past when we could travel here and there to places of interest in carriages. Horses, donkeys, and pedestrianism must take their place. We visited the traditional house of Simon the tanner, and ascended to the roof, where St. Peter went to pray, and where he beheld the vision of the sheet let down from heaven. It was certainly a pleasant place to which to retire, and takes in one of the most beautiful scenes of Jaffa, but not more lovely than that from the windows and terraces of the Franciscan convent. On our return to Jaffa, about two weeks afterwards, I had better occasion to appreciate the latter during a quiet Saturday and Sunday, when I had little else to do but to enjoy the scene and meditate. The waves of the blue sea were rolling in over the rocks that surround the peaceful little harbor, where a few sailing vessels were lying. Farther out an American man-of-war was riding at anchor, and the stars and stripes were a pleasant sight, one which we did not elsewhere see for a long time, except when they floated over our tent in Jericho. In fact, from the time we left New York Bay until we returned, while we frequently saw the flags of other countries, we saw our own only a few times. Our commerce seems to be destroyed and our flag banished from the ocean. What other eyes before mine have looked out upon this ancient harbor! Here the cedars were brought for Solomon's temple; here Jonas embarked; here also, without doubt, many of the Apostles departed to the ends of the earth to spread the Gospel and suffer martyrdom; and, dearest of all, St. John, the beloved Apostle, and the Blessed Mother of our Lord came here to the seaside to set sail for Ephesus. Jaffa is probably the oldest port, and is on the site of one of the oldest cities, of the world. It has an antediluvian origin. It is said that here Noe entered into his ark, and that his sepulchre is here, where one of his sons, after the flood, built a city.\

After our visit to the house of Simon the tanner we wandered through the narrow streets and saw their strange sights. We constantly wondered why all the cities of the Orient are not stricken with cholera during the summer season. Palestine is the home of the cucumber, a great favorite with the people. Thousands of them are bought daily and eaten raw, without being pared or seasoned. Yet, notwithstanding the seeming violation of nearly all the laws of health, they escape, and the really clean and careful cities of Europe are afflicted.

On our tour we had to make use of guide-books, and they are certainly useful, but we began to discover some of their discrepancies. The population of Jaffa, as given by Baedeker, is 8,000; by Bradshaw, 20,000; by the *American Cyclopædia*, 10,000. Besides the schismatical Oriental, there are in Jaffa Catholic Maronite, Greek, and Latin churches. The Catholic population of Jaffa is about 2,000. There is near Jaffa a German Protestant colony of the temple. Of the American colony of forty families who settled here in 1866 about half died, and the others, with the exception of four, returned home. Their idea was a religious one, but our American friend told us that the religious notion had long since departed.

The Germans have been more successful. It is their belief that it is the duty of Christians to settle in the Holy Land. Notwithstanding the numerous deaths that have occurred among them, they have prosperous colonies near Jaffa, Jerusalem, and Haifa. They have good cut-stone houses, fertile fields, and fine cattle. We also found them a very honest and industrious class of people; but we were told, whether truthfully or not, that the younger generation, for the most part, is growing up without religion. There is a telegraph-line and wagon-road from Jaffa to Jerusalem. This road, and one from Jerusalem to Bethlehem, and another from Haifa to Nazareth, are the only wagon-roads in Palestine. The German colonies have the best wagons. Their charges to Jerusalem in June are five or six dollars. Cook & Son have a carriage which will cost nearly three times that amount.

Towards evening we started for Jerusalem, and were in Ramleh by dark. We were accompanied about two miles out by our American friend, who rode a very fine horse. Not of our party were wagons before and behind, and on horseback, riding near us, a member of the temple community who keeps an inn at Ramleh, and a very picturesquely dressed Bedouin. Our American friend and the Bedouin indulged in the excitement of a horse-race, in which the American was winner. We passed on our way some fine groves surrounding various kinds of buildings, among them a Jewish school of agriculture. We were now crossing the renowned plain of Sharon. We were attracted by the remarkable hedges of cactus, which afterwards became very familiar to us, many of which are ten or more feet high.

The place where Samson tied together the foxes' tails, that he might burn the cornfields and vineyards of the Philistines, was pointed out to us. We did not go to the convent in Ramleh, as it was cooler travelling during the night, but took supper with our new German acquaintance, and then proceeded on our way.

From Ramleh not much of the country was to be seen until morning, but the journey was not accompanied by the usual stillness of the night. Many others besides ourselves were going over the same way. At length we came to a place called the "Gate of the Mountain"; on one side of the road is a restaurant, and on the other a watch-house. Here we stopped, with a number of others, and nearly every one took a short sleep or some refreshments. Our driver, who was a very sleepy-headed fellow, after caring for his horses "went to bed" on the ground. He probably would have stayed there until morning if we had not found him and got him again started on the journey. We now began to ascend—sometimes went down again, but usually up—until we reached Jerusalem. In the morning Neby Samwîl rose before our eyes to the north. It was the birthplace, residence, and burial-place of the prophet Samuel. It was the site of the famous city of Benjamin, where the people rejected God as their king and chose to have a king "like other nations." It is claimed by some to have been the place where arose the watchtower of Mizpah, "a place of lookout," where Saul was chosen king in the midst of the assembly of Israel. There might be much reason for the opinion that Mizpah—or Maspha—was in that neighborhood if it could be reconciled with the ancient and undoubtedly correct tradition that Neby Samwîl is the site of the home and tomb of the prophet Samuel.

Soon after we came to a wayside inn situated in the beautiful valley of Terebinth, six miles from Jerusalem, which was the scene of the battle between David and Goliath: "And all the children of Israel were in the valley of Terebinth, fighting against the Philistines." To the south, at the end of the valley, is the village of Ain Kârim, which the Christians call St. John's. It is the place of the Visitation of the Blessed Virgin to St. Elizabeth, and where St. John the Baptist was born. We afterwards made a visit there, which will be described in proper order.

After a short "rest" we again started over the weary road. The morning grew more sultry, and the sun beat down upon us with its intenser rays. The "everlasting hills about Jerusalem," on this side at least, were barren and desolate. Lizards in large numbers were gliding quickly over the burning rocks, about the only living thing manifest. Now and then we would pass a woman carrying on her head a load of some kind of produce to the city. A miserable village, clinging to the side of a hill or lying in a valley, would occasionally be seen. The general effect produced in the minds of tired travellers was a strange one, and it was hard to realize that this was the once rich "land of promise flowing with milk and honey." But it is hard to realize the natural changes, to say nothing of those that are supernatural, that take place in any country during three thousand years. Yet we could, without much effort, imagine the ancient people of God "going up to Jerusalem," the holy city on Mount Sion, to worship Him in His holy temple: "For thither did the tribes go up, the tribes of the Lord to praise the name of the Lord."

CHAPTER IX.

THE HOLY CITY, JERUSALEM.

We ascended hill after hill, and from each high eminence before us expected the long-sought vision to burst upon our joyous sight. The Crusaders went around by way of the north, and from the heights of "Neby Samwîl" first caught sight of the Holy City. Many travellers have also taken that route, and have enjoyed the sublime pleasure of first seeing the city from afar, and crying out: "Behold Jerusalem!" It is probable, however, that at the present time the vast number of pilgrims like ourselves take the smoother main road and find themselves suddenly in the suburbs of the city.

After having seen the desolate country through which we had just passed, we were hardly prepared for the city that now met our eyes. To me, at least, there was no disappointment in my first view of the walls and city of Sion. The modern city has extended out beyond the walls, and there are fine buildings in the suburbs on all sides of Jerusalem. If one did not know that such a city existed, and should come on it

BEHOLD JERUSALEM!

suddenly after a rough journey through the bleak hills surrounding it, he would hardly be able to believe his senses.

It was indeed to us a joyful surprise. We passed down the street outside the walls to the Jaffa gate. Wheeled vehicles are not allowed on the streets within the walls. So we stopped outside the gate, and were quickly surrounded by a number of men and boys anxious to take our baggage to any part of the city. Having chosen several, we directed them to Casa Nova, the hospice of the Franciscan fathers. They welcomed us with their usual cordial welcome, and the father-superior assigned us the rooms which we were to occupy during our stay; and right glad we were to have a good chance once more to take a quiet rest. Before we got to our rooms native guides were on hand to offer their services.

Guides are a necessary evil. They are of great use to you at times, and just when you begin to get independent you find them to be a necessity; but they are also a great bother, hanging after you when you would much rather be alone. There were two native Arab Catholic guides, who spoke English and wished to be employed; we chose the younger. We stayed in Jerusalem and vicinity eleven days, but did not see half that we wanted to see, and could not delay over and meditate on what we saw as long as we would desire; but we saw all that was of most interest to us.\

The population of Jerusalem is on the increase. I believe it cannot now fall much short of 40,000. The Catholic population is not so large in proportion as in several other towns of Palestine. The city probably contains about 3,000 Catholics of all rites, mostly of the Latin rite. Probably there are twice that number of Greek, Armenian, and other schismatics, nearly 10,000 Jews, and the remainder Moslems. Jerusalem is a much larger and finer city than I had expected to find it. It is situated on an elevated plateau of limestone, about 2,500 feet above the level of the sea, and is nearly surrounded by valleys on three sides: on the east by the valley of Josaphat, or valley of the Blessed Virgin, through which flows the torrent Kedron; and on the south and a portion of the west side by the valley of Ennom. Beyond the valley of Josaphat lies the Mount of Olives, which rises about 200 feet higher than the city; south of the valley of Ennom is the Hill of Evil Counsel. The walls surrounding the principal part of the city are 15 feet thick at the base, and from 30 to 50 feet in height, or a mean height of $38\frac{1}{2}$ feet.

with 37 towers, forming an irregular quadrangle of about 2¼ miles in circumference. Beginning with the northeast corner, the wall extends nearly south; from the southeast to southwest corner it runs southwest; from the southwest to northwest corner the direction is northwest by north; and the north wall runs northeast. The north and south walls are the longest. Mount Calvary is towards the northwest, Mount Moria at the southeast, and Mount Sion at the south of the city, to the west of Mount Moria. The streets are narrow and irregular, and not at all times clean. There are seven gates to the city, six of which are open a portion of the time; but the Golden Gate, leading up to the temple from the east, through which Christ made his triumphal entry, is now closed. The principal gates are: on the north the Damascus gate, on the east St. Stephen's or the Blessed Virgin's gate, on the south Sion gate, and on the west the Jaffa gate. Before I entered Palestine, Jerusalem lay in a well-defined picture before me, and I knew its celebrated sanctuaries, as if familiar sights, as soon as I saw them. Yet I was able almost every day to lose my way, and only found it when I turned up at the Jaffa gate.

The highest temperature of Jerusalem is 92° Fahr., the lowest 28° above, and the mean 62½°

Fahr. Snow falls in Palestine in the winter, but usually does not lie except on the higher mountains. The two chief seasons are the rainy and dry. The spring is the most pleasant part of the year, lasting from the middle of March to the middle of May. About the middle of May harvest begins, and ends about the middle of June. Very rarely in May there are thunderstorms, but from that time until October there are but few clouds and no rains, although at night there are very copious dews. During a portion of this time the heat becomes excessive, especially in the valleys. In October the "*early rains*" of Holy Scripture take place, and seedtime extends from the middle of October to the middle of December. In the latter part of November the trees lose their foliage, which they resume towards the beginning of February. The "latter rains" fall in March and April, during which months the whole country is covered with the choicest flowers and verdure. The climate in the lower valley of the Jordan is tropical, owing to its wonderful depression.\

At last we were in Jerusalem, eight thousand miles away from our home on the shores of Lake Michigan. We were in Jerusalem, city of the "vision of peace." "Our feet were standing in thy courts, O Jerusalem! Jerusalem!

which is built as a city, which is compact together." "The foundations thereof are in the holy mountains; glorious things are said of thee, O city of God!" Thou hast been great in thy joy, O city of Sion! and thou hast been desolate in thy sorrow, O city of Calvary! But in joy or in sorrow, thou dost ever attract the soul of the Christian; for the Lord "hath loved Sion," and the Son of God "wept over it."

Jerusalem was a city in the days of Abraham, when Melchisedech was King of Salem, which now is Jerusalem. It was a city of the Jebusites for five hundred years after the children of Israel had entered the Promised Land. It was finally captured by David, and made the royal city of David and Solomon, and of a long line of the kings of Juda. Here God dwelt in His holy temple, and here Jesus Christ closed the scenes of his life on earth by His Passion and Crucifixion. We could hardly realize that we were really in Jerusalem.

After we had rested a few hours we started out to visit those places which are the first and only thought of the Christian pilgrim when he enters the city—Mount Calvary and the Holy Sepulchre. On the streets the same Oriental scenes and costumes met our eyes to which we had become accustomed.\

The great change that almost necessarily occurs in the surroundings of any historical place in the course of centuries makes it more difficult to realize that this is the exact spot where a particular event took place. Yet a man would lack reason who would doubt when the proofs are convincing. Practically he rarely does doubt, except where some kind of opposing prejudice deprives him of the right use of reason. The natural and necessary changes in surroundings do not make an intelligent man less thoroughly convinced in judgment, but he may fail to realize as vividly as he might expect the fulness of what was once actual. This is the case when one approaches the Holy Sepulchre and Mount Calvary. But, like all things of great importance, they grow on you with time and repeated visits. Yet even at the first visit no one can describe the strange sensations that thrill the heart and the elevated thoughts that fill the mind. Here, just before us, was the church of the Holy Sepulchre, which covers the hill of Calvary, where Jesus Christ died on the cross and rose from the dead. I will not enter into details about the church, it has been so often described, and printed plans are familiar to almost every reader.

As you enter the church, at the left are a

few Moslem custodians, squatted on a slightly elevated bench, to whom you pay no particular attention, except to be reminded by their presence that many of the most sacred places of the Holy Land are in the hands of infidels—a fact which heresy, schism, and the indifference of Catholic nations permit. Not far from the door, and directly before you as you enter, is the Stone of Unction, where our Lord's body was placed when it was anointed by Joseph of Arimathea and Nicodemus: "They took therefore the Body of Jesus and bound it in linen cloths with the spices, as the manner of the Jews is to bury." It is the custom of Christians to kneel and kiss the stone as they enter. Not only Catholics but all kinds of schismatics do the same. So far as nearly all the sacred places are concerned, they are treated alike with reverence by all who bear the Christian name, except by the unfortunate followers of the Western heresy of the sixteenth century. Even Moslems look on many of them as sacred, and treat them with becoming respect. The Mohammedans treat the sacred places of the Christians with far greater reverence than do Protestants, with a few praiseworthy exceptions. To the right leads to Mount Calvary; we turned to the left, to the Holy Sepulchre: "Now there was in the place where He was crucified a garden; and in the garden a new sepulchre, wherein no man yet had been laid. There, therefore, because it was the parasceve of the Jews, they laid Jesus, because the sepulchre was nigh at hand." This account shows that the sepulchre was near Calvary. The distance is about 110 feet. The Holy Sepulchre is in the centre of a rotunda. A chapel 26 by 17½ feet encloses it. In front of the sepulchre is the "Chapel of the Angel," which you enter by a low door. The chapel is 10 by 16 feet. From it, through a small door, stooping low, you enter the Holy Sepulchre. It is 6 feet wide by 6½ feet long. At the right is a hewn stone nearly six feet in length, on which the body of our Lord was laid. It rises nearly three feet from the floor, and is covered with a marble slab. On the sepulchre, as an altar, the Holy Sacrifice of the Mass is offered. It is in the hands of the Greeks, Copts, Armenians, and Catholics. Here, as everywhere else in Palestine, the Greeks, through the aid of Russian money, have the chief influence and control. Catholics are usually allowed to offer the Holy Sacrifice only twice each day on this altar. By permission of the Holy See,

Catholics say Mass on the same altar, with a few necessary additions, as the schismatics. A large number of precious lamps are constantly burning over our Saviour's tomb, and devout native Christians and pilgrims from every land, at all times, are found kneeling here in prayer: "In that day the root of Jesse, who standeth for an ensign of people, Him the Gentiles shall beseech, and His sepulchre shall be glorious." Coming out, not far beyond the sepulchre is the place where St. Mary Magdalen met Christ and mistook Him for the gardener, and near by is her altar, on which I afterwards said Mass. To the right is the sacristy of the Catholics, and directly ahead the Chapel of the Apparition, built over the site of the house to which the Blessed Virgin retired after the Crucifixion, and where our Lord appeared to her after His Resurrection. It belongs to the Catholics, and contains a portion of the Pillar of Scourging.

From here we went back to Calvary, from the floor of the church ascending nineteen steps to the place where Christ was crucified. The Greek and Catholic chapels, really in one room, are forty-seven feet long and about the same in width. The altar over the place where the cross stood is in the hands of the Greeks, and no Catholic priest is allowed to say Mass on it. Beneath it is seen the hole where the cross was fixed in the rock, and a few feet away the rent in the rock: "And the earth quaked, and the rocks were rent." Very close to this altar, a few feet distant, is a Catholic altar of the Seven Dolors, where the Blessed Virgin stood at the foot of the cross and received the body of her Divine Son into her arms. I have not seen this altar marked on any of the printed plans of the church of the Holy Sepulchre. A few feet beyond it is the altar of the Crucifixion, where Christ was nailed to the cross, which is also in the hands of the Catholics. A number of persons are continuously approaching, to kiss the sacred rock where the cross was raised on which Christ died, and a priest in passing the spot, to say Mass at the other altars, makes a genuflection. We then descended beneath the chapel of the raising of the cross to the traditional tomb of Adam. It is directly under the place of Crucifixion, and certainly has very authoritative tradition in its favor, upheld by Tertullian, Origen, St. Epiphanius, St. Chrysostom, and St. Augustine. While St. Jerome in his commentary disfavors it, in his 46th Epistle he says: "It is said that in this city (Jerusalem), yea, at this very spot, Adam had lived and died, whence the place where Christ was crucified was called Calvary—that is, because there was buried the skull of the old man (Adam)—in order that the second Adam—that is, the blood of Christ dropping from the cross—would wash away the sins of the first Adam lying there." Calmet says, in his commentaries on the Holy Scripture, that "it is the opinion received in a great measure by the ancient writers, and in a great measure approved by the authority of the Church, that the tombs of Adam and Eve are on Mount Calvary."\

From this it seems probable that this place was called Calvary, or the place of a skull or skulls, not from its possible shape like a skull, nor because, being a place of execution, skulls may have been strewed there, but because it was known to the Jews that Adam was buried there Near by is shown the tomb of Melchisedech, the priest-king of Jerusalem and type of Christ, who, when he came forth to bless Abraham, offered the sacrifice of bread and wine in the valley of Josaphat.\

We afterwards visited the prison of Our Lord, chapel of Our Lady of Sorrows, chapel of Longinus, chapel of Parting the Garments, chapel of Mocking, chapel of St. Helena, altar of the Penitent Thief, place where the true cross was found, tombs of Joseph of Arimathea and Nicodemus, and the "Greek Centre of the World." After visiting the church we went out to make a visit to the *Via Dolorosa* (Sorrowful Way), over which our Lord made His sorrowful journey on His way from the house of Pilate to the place of His Crucifixion. It begins near St. Stephen's gate and extends in a southwesterly direction. The house of Pilate is now separated by the street from the place of Scourging. At the present time the former is occupied by Turkish troops, and the latter is a chapel belonging to the Franciscan fathers. I had already had the sad pleasure of going up the holy stairs of Pilate's house, on my knees, in Rome, where they are preserved. A portion of the Pillar of Scourging is in the church of the Holy Sepulchre, and another portion is in Rome. A little farther on is the arch and balcony where Pilate presented Christ to the people, saying: "*Ecce Homo!*"—"Behold the Man!" All along the *Via Dolorosa* are numbers indicating the different Stations of the Cross: where our Lord fell under the weight of the cross, where He met Simon of Cyrene and the women of Jerusalem, the house of St. Veronica, and where He met

His most afflicted Mother. The Sisters of Sion have a fine convent near the arch "*Ecce Homo.*" We afterwards, at different times, passed over this Sorrowful Way, and in our memory and imagination could ever see that sad procession more than eighteen hundred years ago; and we seemed to see the half-closed, blood-stained eyes of the Sorrowful Son as they met the tearful, loving eyes of the Sorrowful Mother.

The next day was the festival of Corpus Christi, and I had the privilege of saying Mass in the Holy Sepulchre. The usual Mass said in the Holy Sepulchre is the Mass of the Resurrection. But on great feasts like Corpus Christi it is the Mass of the feast. The same is true of Masses said on many other altars in the Holy Land. At the altar of the Seven Dolors that Mass is said, and at the altar of the Crucifixion the Mass of the Passion; at the altar of the Manger, in Bethlehem, it is the Mass of the Nativity, and at the altar in Nazareth the Mass of the Annunciation. Before saying Mass I vested in a crowded corner of the Chapel of the Angel. The chapel was packed with devout worshippers, but no one except the celebrant and server entered the small chapel of the Sepulchre. My server was a native Arab named Bulos Meo—Bulos means Paul,

Nearly all of the Catholics in Palestine are called Arabians, probably descendants of the ancient Chanaanites, who inhabited the country before its occupation by the children of Israel, and who were never driven out, but remained as slaves to the Israelites. A number of devout native women received Holy Communion at my hand at the door leading to the Sepulchre. Before my Mass was finished the Latin Patriarch of Jerusalem began solemn Pontifical Mass at an altar erected outside the Holy Sepulchre. He was a pale, thin, venerable, although young prelate, who wore a full beard, like all the priests that I saw in the East.\

As two of our number wore beards, the remaining member of our party was the only shaven priest I saw in the Orient, although a number of French and Spanish travellers were among them. I must acknowledge that this ancient, apostolic, and Christian custom very much pleased me. Jerusalem in some respects is more Roman than Rome itself. How grand and solemn was the stately Gregorian chant accompanying the Mass sung by the patriarch! Everything was Roman to the most minute detail. They have in Palestine the same convenient little cruets for wine and water for the Mass that are used in St. Peter's, Rome, and in almost all Catholic countries, instead of the awkward things which we use for cruets in this country.

I had wondered, when I read it in theology, that there was opposition in some countries to the use of a little spoon to measure the water poured into the chalice. But when I saw the Roman cruets I ceased to wonder, as it would be of no use when water could be poured drop by drop from a cruet without danger of too much.

When the priest recites the prayers after Mass in the Holy Land, nearly all the people present answer in Latin, and accompany him in the same language in the recitation of the "Salve Regina." In Palestine, too, Saturday as well as Friday is a day of abstinence, the same as in Italy.

After the Pontifical Mass a procession with the Most Holy Sacrament took place three times around the Holy Sepulchre. The boys, who are instructed by the Franciscan fathers, were almost perfect in plain chant, which to me was a much more than delightful surprise. The singers, the Franciscan fathers and brothers, the French consul and a few other European laymen, a number of native Catholics, and boys with large baskets of most beautiful flowers strewing them before the Blessed Sacrament, preceded the patriarch carrying the Sacred Host under a baldachin. The church was thronged with native Christians.

In succeeding days I had the joy of saying Mass four times on Mount Calvary: twice at the altar of the Seven Dolors and twice at the altar of the Crucifixion.

Offering up the Unbloody Sacrifice so near where Christ died, methinks I see the cross again raised on high, and, looking down upon me, the bleeding, sorrowful face of the Crucified; and I seem to hear that dying cry of utter desolation: "My God, my God, why hast Thou forsaken Me?" echoing for ever among these hills, and resounding to the ends of the earth. But the sweet thought consoles me that the beautiful garden of the Resurrection is so near the dread Calvary of Death, and the bright morning of Easter so soon succeeded the dark hours of the Crucifixion.

I gradually became accustomed to the church of the Holy Sepulchre; and the more familiar it became the more real did the scenes once witnessed there seem. Not only did the Sepulchre of Christ and Calvary seem holy, but the very walls and pavements, built by the hands of men, seemed to have become participators of the divine holiness of those sacred places.

The succeeding days were happy ones, bright with the sunshine of God, that shines on the walls and sacred temples of both the old and new Jerusalem. As early as we might start from Casa Nova, we found, either at the door or on the way, a young Christian Arab ready to serve our Mass. The fee of one franc, which we usually gave, was a great encouragement. One morning my usual server, a small brother of our guide, had gone with one of my companions; a little ragged Arab was ready to take his place. He accompanied me with delight; between fear and expectation he held the missal while I vested; and his eyes sparkled and his face beamed with joy when the good Franciscan brother told him to serve me, and on the way to the altar, as we met another brother, he looked at him with a look of triumph, which the brother returned with a good-natured smile. Thus do the children of the poor rejoice at what seem trifles to others, and their hearts are made captive by a smile of friendship or an act of kindness.

As you enter the square space in front of the church, you are met with numerous smiles and requests from the proprietors of various stands and mats to buy some of the articles of devotion which they exhibit for sale. They have olive-wood and mother-of-pearl worked into a great variety of forms. The Greek rosaries are very similar to the Catholic ones, having a tassel at the end instead of a cross or medal. The Mohammedans likewise use a string of beads in their devotions. Beggars are always waiting, and stretch out their hands for alms. Having once made an offering to two or three, I was instantly surrounded by a small army of them from every adjacent nook and corner. On my return from the church each morning I was followed by two little boys and a beautiful little girl about eight years of age, with the brightest dark eyes and rich, wavy hair, who, every few rods, would seize my hand and kiss it, and give me a look of deep, earnest supplication, yet altogether childlike.

I have sometimes wondered if the Divine Child Jesus, when He walked these streets or prayed in the temple, did not leave as a heritage to the children of the despised Chanaanites this look of sweet simplicity and deep earnestness mirrored from their souls. During my few weeks' stay I became greatly attached to these poor Christian children of Palestine. Like the Divine Child, they are poor in the goods of this world, but rich in the love and blessings which they have inherited from Jesus and Mary. I usually waited until near Casa Nova before making their hearts glad with a piece of money, for fear of the importunate crowd that would otherwise follow me. But they knew by experience that they would get it just the same. /

What strange and interesting sights you see on the streets of Jerusalem! The odd buildings and streets hold no comparison in ancient form and variety with the more peculiar costumes and people. But you soon get to feel at home in the midst of your strange surroundings. No one seems to notice what any one else wears. To attempt to describe the different modes of dress, to a man would be an endless confusion and final impossibility. You meet Catholic, Greek, Armenian, Coptic, Syrian, and Abyssinian monks in their various habits; Turks, Greeks, Europeans, Jews, Egyptians, Nubians, and natives of different races. Only the practised eye of an expert can distinguish by their dress to what particular class they belong, and I seriously doubt if he can. The guide-books say that they can thus be distinguished, but our dragoman in Alexandria told us it is not true, but that every man dresses according to his particular fancy and ability. A person long accustomed to the people might distinguish them, but any one else would make a mistake at least every other time.

Many, both Christians and Mohammedans, wear long robes, and turbans on their heads, some black, some white or green, blue or yellow. Many wear the red fez with black tassel, a flowing jacket with a close one under, and baggy breeches, or else a large, full garment, fastened at the waist, reaching half-way from the knees to the ankles, having openings for the legs, and stockings and shoes beneath. Some wear a simple white, blue, or other colored tunic, both cool and cheap, and nothing else except a fez or turban. The Jews are always easily distinguishable, having mostly colored gowns, usually a cap, which is sometimes fur, on their heads, and, although their hair is otherwise short, they have two long locks, sometimes curled, hanging down in front of their ears. But, as already remarked, peculiar dress will not be noticed in the East, except, perhaps, for its richness and beauty. I have my doubts if even an Esquimau from near the North Pole, dressed in his eternal winter dress of Arctic furs, would attract any vulgar attention. Yet it has frequently happened in our best American cities that the "Young American" rabble has thrown stones at Oriental Christian men in their own costumes. There is great need that "Young America" should be made at least half-civilized and much less vulgar. A young Englishman, who had always lived in Palestine, told me that he believed many costumes of the people had not changed their fashion in the last eighteen hundred years.\

The Friday after Corpus Christi I had forgotten my breviary in the Church of the Holy Sepulchre. I had not yet become used to the streets, and soon missed my way. I met an Arabian boy, and, not being able to speak Arabic, addressed him in Latin, as I found I was more frequently, for some reason I cannot explain, partially understood in that language than any other. I asked him to show me the church. He seemed to understand perfectly, and immediately led the way. Following him for some time, I reached the conclusion that he had mistaken my meaning. It dawned on my mind that it was Friday and he was taking me to the Jews' Wailing Place. Being very anxious to visit that place, I was well satisfied with the mistake. My suspicions were correct, and we soon arrived on the scene that draws sympathy from the heart of every man with a heart. There were not to exceed fifty persons present, of every age and both sexes. They were all evidently of the Jewish race. A very few asked and received alms. Some were sitting in silence, and, in the same posture, others were praying. Some were looking around with curiosity, but a number of men were standing with their faces to the wall, with books in their hands, and praying with great earnestness in a sad and mournful tone. The wall is over against the site of the ancient temple, an inside wall that surrounds Mount Moria. They seemed to try to peer through the cracks in the wall as they mourned over the desolation of Sion and the desecration of the Holy of Holies: "Behold, your house shall be left to you desolate."\

The wall of the Wailing Place is fifty-two yards long and fifty-six feet high. Some consider the lower courses of stones in this wall, which are very large, as very ancient. Sometimes, towards evening, the following litany is chanted:

Leader.—For the palace that lies desolate;
Response.—We sit in solitude and mourn.
L.—For the palace that is destroyed;
R.—We sit, etc.

L.—For the walls that are overthrown;
R.—We sit, etc.
L.—For our majesty that is departed;
R.—We sit, etc.
L.—For our great men who lie dead;
R.—We sit, etc.
L.- For the precious stones that are burned;
R.—We sit, etc.
L.—For the priests who have stumbled;
R.—We sit, etc.
L.—For our kings who have despised Him;
R.—We sit, etc.

Here is also another litany:

Leader.—We pray Thee have mercy on Sion!
Response.—Gather the children of Jerusalem.
L.—Haste, haste, Redeemer of Sion!
R.—Speak to the heart of Jerusalem.
L.—May beauty and majesty surround Sion.
R.—Ah! turn Thyself mercifully to Jerusalem.
L.—May the kingdom soon return to Sion!
R.—Comfort those who mourn over Jerusalem.
L.—May peace and joy abide with Sion!
R.—And the branch (of Jesse) spring up at Jerusalem.

Near the Wailing Place of the Jews is the very poor quarter of the Moghrebins, who are Moslems from the northwest of Africa.

CHAPTER X.

SOME SACRED PLACES NEAR JERUSALEM.

\ OUR next excursion was a more general one of the whole party. Starting from Casa Nova, early in the afternoon, might have been seen my companions and myself with our guide, four of us in all, dressed for very warm weather and astride four Jerusalem donkeys. It was not, however, our first experience in donkey-riding, as the reader knows. The donkey is deservedly a great favorite in the East. He seems to be one of the family, and always at home to company. He seems never to lose confidence, impudence, or self-possession. If any one "buys him for a fool" he will find that he has made a grievous mistake and has a donkey on his hands. They are of all colors, white, gray, black, and mouse-colored, and of many sizes. The Oriental donkey is much more intelligent than his Occidental brother.\

We rode past the church of the Holy Sepulchre, down the Via Dolorosa, and out of St. Stephen's gate, near which St. Stephen was stoned. This gate, on the east of Jerusalem, is also called both the gate of the Blessed Virgin

Mary and gate of Benjamin. Our road led down a steep declivity into the valley of Josaphat, or Jehoshaphat. Of this valley the prophet Joel speaks: "Let them arise, and let the nations come up into the valley of Josaphat; for there I will sit to judge all nations round about." "Nations, nations in the valley of destruction; for the day of the Lord is near in the valley of destruction. The sun and the moon are darkened, and the stars have withdrawn their shining. And the Lord shall roar out of Sion and utter His voice from Jerusalem. . . . And you shall know that I am the Lord your God dwelling in Sion, My holy mountain." Jews, Christians, and Moslems believe that this valley will be the scene of the Last Judgment. It is filled with Jewish and Mohammedan tombs. We passed over the brook Kedron; on our left, up the valley, was the tomb of the Blessed Virgin; on our right, down the valley, were the tombs of Absalom, the ungrateful son of David; of Josaphat, the pious king of Juda; of Zacharias, who was "slain between the temple and the altar"; and the tomb of St. James the Less, who was first Bishop of Jerusalem and a cousin of our Lord.

When the terrible events of the Crucifixion were taking place, the Apostles, weak and trembling, fled and hid themselves in caves and tombs near the city—"scattered like sheep when the shepherd was struck." After the Crucifixion St. James the Less retired to a grotto here, and ate no food until after the Resurrection. He ended his life by being stoned, and was buried at or near the place where he had formerly concealed himself. We did not go nearer these tombs, that chiefly attract the attention among the many everywhere visible. This valley was first called the Vale of Save, or King's Vale, where Melchisedech offered bread and wine as he met Abraham on his return from battle.\

We hastened on to the Garden of Gethsemani and Grotto of Agony at the foot of the Mount of Olives. We first entered the grotto. It is the place where our Lord retired a "little further to pray," and where, in His agony, the drops of bloody sweat fell down upon the ground. These are the same rocks which saw that scene of "sorrow unto death," and received those drops of the Saviour's blood. Oh! if they had voices they would cry out in anguish, until the end of time, with cries that would fill the whole earth with weeping for the spectacle that they witnessed on that awful night. The grotto and garden are in the possession of the Franciscans. The Franciscan in charge treated us very kindly and gave us some pieces of the sacred rock. We then went to the garden: "Then Jesus came with them into a country place which is called Gethsemani." It is surrounded by a wall, and the interior again by a high but sightly fence. Among about fifty olive-trees in the garden are eight more aged and venerable than the rest. As olive-trees live to a great age, and as these are very old and large, some of them nineteen feet in circumference, the claim is considered by careful writers as quite probable that some of the oldest date from the time of the Passion. The monks cultivate a fine flower-garden among the trees. The good brother gave us pieces of branches from the trees, and a package of dried flower-seeds to be planted in our distant American soil. We now turned back to the sepulchre of the Blessed Virgin. It is principally in the hands of the schismatic Armenians and Greeks. Catholics have sometimes had the privilege of singing Mass here on the festival of the Assumption.

As an instance of how well those authors frequently agree who try to be critical without regard to Christian traditions, we have in this place an illustration. Baedeker says: "It is ascertained, however, that a church stood over the traditional tomb early in the fifth century." The *American Cyclopædia* says: "Is the traditional tomb of the Virgin Mary, first mentioned in the eighth century." So it appears that the *American Cyclopædia* is at least three hundred years behind the times in matters of critical history. You descend to the tomb by long flights of very broad marble stairs. On the right, going down, are the tombs of St. Ann and St. Joachim, parents of the Blessed Virgin, and on the left is the tomb of her spouse, St. Joseph. Still farther down is the vacant tomb of our Holy Mother, where her pure, precious body was laid until it was transplanted into heaven. Next to the Sepulchre of Christ, the sepulchre of the Blessed Virgin is the tomb dearest to the Christian world. We passed out of the church, and up the side of the Mount of Olives. Nearly three thousand years ago King David went over this way "towards the way that looketh to the desert," and up this mountain: "But David went up by the ascent of Mount Olivet, going up and weeping, walking barefoot," as he fled from Jerusalem and his unnatural son Absalom. How many times did our Lord with His Apostles and Holy Mother pass up and down this mountain-side as they departed from or approached Jerusalem! Over this mountain He came from Bethany, when vast numbers of people met Him and cut down palm branches and strewed them in the way, and raised the shout "Hosanna!" as on the feast of tabernacles; but Jesus, "seeing the city, wept over it." We soon reached the summit, the place whence Christ ascended into heaven. The authors of guide-books and works on travel, and others who make little of sacred places traditionally held as such by Christians, almost unanimously reject this as the spot of the Ascension. They base their rejection on the passage from St. Luke: "And He led them out as far as Bethany, . . . and while He blessed them He departed from them, and was carried up to heaven." Baedeker, Bradshaw, and the genial author of *Orient Sunbeams* hastily conclude that He must have ascended from Bethany. St. Luke, the same inspired author, says in the Acts of the Apostles: "Then they returned to Jerusalem from the mount that is called Olivet, which is nigh Jerusalem, within a Sabbath day's journey." This agrees with the summit of the mount, which is about one mile or less, or a Sabbath day's journey, from the city.

Bethany is about two miles, or two Sabbath-days' journey, distant: "Now Bethany was near Jerusalem, about fifteen furlongs off" (St. John xi. 18).

It must also be remembered that in Holy Scripture events frequently follow each other in narration which did not occur in the same place. The account given by St. Mark, too closely followed, would indicate that the Ascension took place from Jerusalem. Besides this explanation, Tischendorf, the great Protestant Biblical critic, considers the clause in St. Luke, "and He was carried up to heaven," a very ancient addition to the original text. "The Codex Sinaiticus, Manuscript D of Cambridge, five Latin documents, together with St. Augustine, are against the genuineness of said passage." (*Four Gospels*, by Archbishop Heiss.) It may be further added that the text of the Latin Vulgate does not necessarily uphold our English translation, "as far as Bethany." It reads: "*Eduxit autem eos foras in Bethaniam*," which can be correctly translated: "And He led them out towards Bethany." The Latin word "in," denoting direction, is translated either "to" or "towards." The Mount of Olives is towards Bethany from Jerusalem. Thus we see that there is no good reason for rejecting the traditional site of the Ascension, handed down by primitive Christians to the days of St. Jerome and St. Augustine, and indicated in the Acts of the Apostles. The readiness with which it is done, even by some of the more intelligent Protestant authors, shows how little dependence can be placed on the hypercritical and superficial speculations of more prejudiced writers. The church that stood over the place is now turned into a mosque, in which Christians have the privilege of celebrating Mass on certain days of the year. We had some trouble to find the custodian, but he was at length found, as there were plenty of boys ready, if necessary, to search every building on the mount in hopes of backsheesh. It is the same all over Palestine: assistance is always at hand. A half-dozen or more are nearly always ready, if you have only the appearance of wanting something. /

We were directly shown the footprint of our Lord. which He left on His ascension into heaven. We knelt and kissed that sacred impress in the rock, as we did everywhere in the Holy Land not only the footprints but the footsteps of Him whose divine feet upon the mountains brought good tidings, peace, and salvation to the world. We retired a little farther to get an unobstructed view of the surrounding country. To the west the whole city of Jerusalem seemed to lie under our feet, with its towers, domes, and minarets; and its great eastern wall rose grandly out of the valley of Josaphat. To the south the heights about Bethlehem were visible; while to the east a farther and wider range of vision was presented—first was the "wilderness of Judea," which is a wide expanse of sterile, rocky hills and mountains; farther on was the valley of the Jordan, and at its southern extremity, lying far below us, was the Dead Sea, shining like a bright blue mirror in the sun. Although less than twenty miles distant, it is almost four thousand feet below the Mount of Olives, and three thousand seven hundred feet below the level of Jerusalem. Beyond it and the valley of the Jordan were seen the blue mountains of Moab and Ammon, among which is Mount Nebo, from whose height Moses beheld the Promised Land. To the north of these appeared the mountains of Gilead.

Whenever afterwards I had the opportunity of seeing that range of mountains beyond the Jordan, my eyes seemed riveted to them, as if at every instant I expected to see emerge from among them the vast army of the Israelites, coming forth from their forty years' wandering in the wilderness to take possession of the land of their forefathers.

Not far from here, on the mount, is the place where Christ taught the Lord's Prayer to His disciples. A pious French princess has built a convent over the spot, and around an interior court that Divine Prayer is inscribed on tablets in thirty-one different languages. Near by is the place where the Apostles came together and composed the Apostles' Creed. Perhaps they came to this place in memory of the fact that here they had learned from their Master's lips "how to pray." We rode part way down the mountain, and then turned on the road to Bethany. On the way ruins were pointed out to us as on the site of the ancient village of Bethphage, where the ass was procured on which Christ rode into Jerusalem. They now belong to the Franciscans.

We soon reached Bethany, which is situated on a southeast spur of the Mount of Olives. The Arabs call it El 'Azarîyeh, from Lazarus, or Lazarium. It has a population of about two hundred, who live in about forty miserable houses, all of whom are Moslems, except the family who have charge of the tomb of Lazarus and the house of Mary and Martha. I cannot agree with those writers who speak so disparagingly of modern Bethany. The village itself has few attractions, and its inhabitants seem poor, but the valleys and hillsides immediately around are well cultivated, and the landscape is made pleasant by groves of olive, fig, almond, and carob trees. Before I had seen that lowly village on the borders of the wilderness, outside of the noise and care, bustle and business of Jerusalem, my mind often dwelt on it with feelings of special affection; for our Lord loved it and its retirement. Beautiful, peaceful Bethany, where Jesus found a home and rest, love and sympathy! And the human heart of Jesus was moved by human love and tenderness, and the Gospel tells us: "Now Jesus loved Martha, and her sister Mary, and Lazarus." Who would not wish to live and die in a place so dear to our Lord? Who would not love a habitation and solitude in a place where Jesus loved to retire from the busy world? O Bethany, how fair thou art to the eyes of the soul! How dear thou art to him who loves his earthly home and desires a heavenly one!

We visited or passed through Bethany three times. On this occasion we visited the tomb of Lazarus, and south of it the house of Mary and Martha. They are not in a very good condition, but they are now in the hands of the Catholics, and Mass is sometimes celebrated here. A crowd of children constantly surrounded us, trying to sell a Bedouin dagger, "antique," or trying to do us some favor for backsheesh. As it was growing late we soon returned to Jerusalem, where we arrived after dark. It is not pleasant to ride in the dark through the rough-paved but slippery streets of Jerusalem, as your beast more frequently slips and stumbles than he does on the steep, rocky roads of the country.

CHAPTER XI.

THE JEWISH TEMPLE ON MOUNT MORIA, AND THE FIRST CHRISTIAN CHURCH ON MOUNT SION.

Our next visit was to be made to the site of Solomon's Temple, now occupied by the "Dome of the Rock," or Mosque of Omar. The surrounding courts, enclosed by a high wall, comprise about one-seventh part of the modern city. This was the ancient Mount Moria, but it was so closely connected with Mount Sion that it is frequently included in that name when the praises and glory of Sion are sung by the psalmists and prophets. At one of the western gates, through which we entered, we were joined by a Turkish military official from the Tower of David, near the Jaffa gate, dressed in a very showy uniform, who was to accompany us and pay all fees and manage all affairs connected with our visit. We had visited the alabaster mosque of Mehemet Ali in Cairo, and did not want a similar experience. Very few mosques would be attractive to our eyes after that combined attack on our pockets and good-nature. Although the Mosque of Omar is considered by the Moslems, next after Mecca, the holiest and the second most beautiful in the world, in all probability we would not have visited it if some stronger attraction did not compel us. Who would not be drawn to that place which was once the mountain of the Lord, even though now desolate?

I will not attempt a description of the Mohammedan surroundings of the present time, for it sickens the heart to think that this place, the holy mountain of God in the old dispensation, and in Christian times reconsecrated to divine service—in the Old Testament the dwelling-place of the God of Hosts, and in the New Testament so frequently sanctified by the presence of the Son of God—is now desecrated by the occupation of the infidel Moslem.

At the door of the mosque, as usual, slippers were put on over our shoes.

Our party would have attracted great attention anywhere else than in the Orient: the romantic looking Turkish officer, our gay-looking Arab guide, the mosque officials and attendants, and ourselves in American and tourist styles mixed, very much out of style in Jerusalem, and with huge colored slippers on our feet.

In the midst of the mosque is the Holy Rock, 57 feet long and 43 feet wide and about 6 feet high. From the earliest history this rock must have been a place of worship and altar of sacrifice. It is probable that it was on this rock that Abraham was about to offer his son Isaac. It is believed to have been anointed by the patriarch Jacob. It was at this rock that the angel of the Lord stood who slew the people of Israel because of the pride of David in numbering his people: "And the angel of the Lord was by the threshing-floor of Areuna the Jebusite. And Gad came to David that day, and said: Go up, and build an altar to the Lord in the threshing-floor of Areuna the Jebusite" (2 Kings xxiv.) Here Solomon afterwards built his temple: "And Solomon began to build the house of the Lord in Jerusalem, in Mount Moria, which had been shown to David his father, in the place which David had prepared in the threshing-floor of Ornan the Jebusite" (2 Par. iii. 1). It is probable that this rock was the place of the Holy of Holies, where the Ark of the Covenant rested, although some claim that it was the great altar of sacrifice. Not only did the Ark of the Covenant rest here, but it is said that it was hidden under the rock by the prophet Jeremias, and still lies buried beneath; but the Ethiopians believe that it was borne to their country, where it is yet preserved. Although Christians take advantage of the privilege of visiting so sacred a place, the Jews will not enter, through fear, it is said, of the sin of treading on the Holy of Holies. Excavations are not allowed to be made, and therefore much knowledge of the place must continue to be hidden. Not a "stone upon a stone" remains of the magnificent temple that once stood here. The temple in which Christ taught and prayed was not the temple of Solomon. Solomon's Temple was destroyed by Nabuchodonosor four hundred years after its building, and six hundred before the coming of Christ. After the return of the Jews from their Babylonian captivity it was rebuilt by Zorobabel, the son of Salathiel, and Josue, the son of Josedec. This was inferior to the first temple, which was a source of great sorrow to the Jews. Herod therefore determined to build a third temple more worthy of taking the place of the first. He employed on the cloisters and temple ten thousand skilled workmen and one thousand priests, whom it took eight years to build the cloisters, and a year and six months to finish the temple. Yet it was more than sixty years before it was wholly completed. The temple proper was surrounded by great cloisters or courts, 600 feet square, made from the richest materials and by the most skilful artisans. The outer cloister was the court of the Gentiles; the second cloister, into which under pain of death none but Israelites might enter, was divided into an outer court for the women and an inner court for the men. Into the third cloister none but priests were permitted to enter. Within this was the temple itself, and before the temple was the great altar of sacrifice. Within the temple was the sanctuary or holy place, and farther in the background, in a deeper recess, was the Holy of Holies. From this we see that the courts of the Lord have become more glorious than His inner temple, for " He has glorified the place of His feet," "and all that slandered Thee shall worship the steps of Thy feet, and shall call the city of the Lord the Sion of the Holy One of Israel." With memories and reflections like these we wandered around the courts and within the sanctuary of God's ancient temple; and in that reverent spirit with which men walk on holy ground, our eyes were closed to the present, and we seemed to see the Holy Family, St. Joseph, the Mother Mary, and the Divine Child Jesus, accompanied by the holy priest Simeon, coming up the steps of the courts of the temple. On our way to the church of the Presentation of Mary, in the southwest corner of the grounds, now the mosque of El-Aksa, we had pointed out to us the judgment-seat of David, and where Solomon prayed at the dedication of the temple, and many other interesting places. The mosque of El-Aksa was originally built by the Emperor Justinian in honor of the Blessed Virgin. In this part of the temple grounds tradition states that the Holy Family remained some days in a dwelling occupied by the holy priest Simeon. On the east is the beautiful Golden Gate through which Christ came in His triumphal entry, which is celebrated by the Church on Palm Sunday. During the time of the Crusaders, on Palm Sunday the patriarch rode through it on an ass in grand procession from the Mount of Olives. It is now walled up, because the Moslems have a tradition that on some Friday a Christian conqueror will enter this gate and retake Jerusalem. May God hasten the day!

After visiting El-Aksa we went out and looked over the walls to the south. Across the deep valley, on the other side, is the village of Siloam, on the declivity of the Mountain of Offence, said to be the site of Solomon's idolatrous sacrifices. The inhabitants are all Moslems and noted for their thievish propensities. The caves which serve as dwellings for many of them were formerly inhabited by hermits. But we had other places to visit and could not delay. We soon found ourselves outside the temple walls, where our gallant Turk left us. /

Mounted on donkeys, with a donkey-boy running behind with a rod to make them more lively, we followed the leadership of our Arab guide. We first went to the Jews' Wailing Place, which my companions had not yet seen. Soon after we dismounted and entered one of the chief synagogues of the Jews. It was Saturday, but there was a great difference in the devotion manifested here and at the place we had just left. We did not long delay, for our way was over to Mount Sion. We passed out of the gate of Sion, for the objects and sanctuaries of greatest interest are now outside the walls. When one tries to compare the sacred places as to relative importance and sacredness, he finds himself at a loss to decide between them, and is happy in the thought that it is not necessary. What place can be more holy than the one we were about to visit? The Cœnaculum of our Lord is now a Mohammedan mosque. It lies in the midst of a cluster of buildings called by the natives "Prophet David." We were readily admitted by the Moslem custodian, and ascended into the "large upper room" where our Lord ate the Last Supper with His Apostles. This is the place spoken of in the Holy Scriptures: "But David took the castle of Sion, the same is the city of David." Here was his royal palace, and here he prepared his tomb where he was buried. The tombs of David and Solomon are in the east part of the building, at the end of the Cœnaculum. It is quite certain, according to ancient authors, that this building escaped destruction when Titus took and destroyed Jerusalem. The Mohammedans have a superstitious dread of entering the tomb of David. Our guide told us it was believed that one who entered it would immediately die It is related by Benjamin of Tudela, a Jewish rabbi who travelled extensively in the East in the twelfth century, that when two workmen once raised a stone that revealed the mouth of a cavern, they entered and found two grand, palace-like tombs, ornamented with marble, gold, and silver, and crowns and sceptres were lying on tables. They saw also other tombs of the royal house and family of David. On trying to enter they were repulsed by a whirlwind, and a voice was heard saying: "Arise, and go from this place." This wonder was related before a learned Jew, who said it "was the burial-place of the house of David, prepared for the kings of Juda." Josephus writes that it is stated that when Herod attempted to enter David's tomb "two of the guards were slain by a flame that burst out on those that went in." As we stood there in that plain, uncared-for, unornamented room, we said within ourselves: Is it possible that this is the actual room in which the Holy Eucharist was instituted by the Son of God, and which witnessed the wonders of Pentecost? What mysteries of divine love and power have been accomplished in this place! Read the first and second chapters of the Acts of the Apostles, and it will appear plainly that there was one "large upper room," called in the Latin Vulgate

"Cœnaculum," a word having different meanings, but in this case evidently applied to the same place, which was the common sanctuary of holy life, prayer, and mystery; which Christ sanctified by His great mystery of love, and the Holy Ghost made glorious by the manifestation of His divine power and the communication of His divine gifts; where earth and heaven seemed to meet and commingle; where those who were yet among mortals raised their hands and touched the heavens, and where the glorified yet loved to linger; so that men could then and even now exclaim: "How terrible is this place! This is no other but the house of God and the gate of heaven."

To summarize the events of this place: Here David and Solomon lived; here do their bodies rest. Here our Lord instituted the Holy Eucharist, and here, after His resurrection, He appeared to His Apostles and instituted the Sacrament of Penance as He breathed on them and said: "Receive ye the Holy Ghost"; here also the doubting Thomas was led to exclaim: "My Lord and my God!" Here the Holy Ghost descended. Here Matthias was chosen by lot to take the bishopric of Judas; here St. James the Less was made bishop of Jerusalem. Here the Apostles dispersed to go forth to fulfil the divine commission to teach the nations of the earth; here they assembled in the Council of Jerusalem. Here the seven deacons were chosen, and among them St. Stephen, the first Christian martyr; and here his body was brought after his death. And this was the home of St. John and the Blessed Virgin after our Lord's Ascension, where St. John celebrated Mass in her presence. Here the Blessed Virgin died, and was borne from here for burial. *This was the first Christian church.* It is now a Moslem mosque, but Mass is yet offered in this holy place on Holy Thursday. The Franciscan superior is yet styled "Guardian of Mount Sion." "Arise, arise, put on thy strength, O Sion! put on the garments of thy glory, O Jerusalem, the city of the Holy One! Shake thyself from the dust, arise, sit up, O Jerusalem! loose the bonds from off thy neck, O captive daughter of Sion!"/

From the Cœnaculum we went to the Armenian monastery of Mount Sion. It is situated on the site of the house of Caiphas, the high-priest, where Christ was led and where Peter denied his Lord. The prison of Christ is shown, and the stone which was placed against the door of the sepulchre. We then rode out through a cemetery, and to the very brow of Mount Sion toward the south. We looked away to the south while the dearest memories filled our minds, because in that direction, only six miles distant, lies Bethlehem. How often King David, from his palace on Mount Sion, must have looked in the same direction; for Bethlehem was his native place, and there he was anointed king. Mount Sion was the home of his manhood and greatness, of his wives, sons, and daughters; Bethlehem was the home of his childhood and simplicity, of his father and mother. Which do you think was dearer to him? I cannot decide, but I must cry out: O happy man whose eyes in his mature and declining years can rest, as his could, upon the home of his birth and the scenes of his youth! Our Lord likewise looked out from this hill towards Bethlehem; and the eyes of the Blessed Mother also wandered over those southern hills as she remembered that dark and dismal stable and that cruel night. Wandering among the tombstones scattered over the hill were several black ecclesiastics from Abyssinia, like ourselves quietly enjoying the scene. How frequently does it occur that on these holy hills Europe, Asia, Africa, and America are represented, drawn from the corners of the earth by a fact which seems so simple and is so powerful, that One who was spoken of as the "carpenter's Son" here lived a brief life in poverty, and here died an ignominious death nearly two thousand years ago! After we had sufficiently dwelt on the scene with mind and eye we turned homeward, around the southern and western wall, through the valley of Hinnom, or "valley of the son of Ennom," *i.e.*, "valley of the children of groaning," called also Topheth and Gehenna—used in Scripture to designate the hell of the damned—because in this valley children were sacrificed to the idol Moloch. Across, on the southern side of the valley, are the Field of Blood and Hill of Evil Counsel, where the death of our Lord was plotted in the country-house of Caiphas. On the hill is the "tree on which Judas hanged himself." It is a solitary tree, with none others near it, and can be seen from every direction. It seems to me quite probable that this one is a growth from the actual tree. I have said above, "homeward," for Casa Nova seemed like home. We were always welcomed back with a friendly, cordial welcome by those whose faces had become familiar. I can never say enough in praise of the Franciscans of Palestine, nor admire sufficiently their humility, labors, self-sacrifice, and genuine Christian hospitality. Their beds and rooms were clean and neat, their food good enough and served with care and politeness. They were ever ready to yield their own convenience to the desires of the pilgrim-priest, especially in the matter of saying Mass at the first opportunity on those altars where only two Masses can be celebrated each day. Next to the glory of God and the salvation of their souls, the welfare and pleasure of Christian pilgrims seem to be the chief aim of their lives.

There are not a great number of visitors in Palestine in the month of June, so we soon got acquainted with the pleasant faces daily around the pilgrims' table. Some remained a part of the time and others all the time of our stay. Among them were two Jesuit fathers from their college in Beirout, a priest from France, another from Spain, and about a dozen sisters from France, going to Nazareth to establish a house. With them was their chaplain, a fine old Capuchin father, who had been a missionary in the East Indies. The pleasant, friendly superior of Casa Nova usually spent a part of the time with us at both dinner and supper, and seemed especially to enjoy the conversation with his American friends. Perhaps we are naturally inclined to be interested in what is or comes from very far away in distance.

The Patriarch of Jerusalem has a new and

beautiful church, where we went on the afternoon of Corpus Christi. There was to be a grand procession in honor of the Most Holy Sacrament. A large number of priests, some of them of Oriental rites, were in the sanctuary. There must have been fully two thousand persons present, which convinced me that it is quite probable that the Catholic population of Jerusalem is even greater than claimed. When a very large procession was outside, the church was nearly filled with women. The procession was like all similar ones, but those who appeared in it were quite different from those who take part in more western lands. The patriarch and numerous clergy presented a very venerable and Oriental appearance; while it would be impossible to describe the picturesque effect of the long line and surrounding throng of dark-complexioned Syrian Christians of all classes in their strange and graceful varieties of dress. I was pleased to see pews in the patriarchal church; for, whatever may be said of them, they conduce to good order and respectful devotion, and are usually accompanied with the Christian instruction of the people, as we saw by a comparison of the different countries of Europe. Where chairs are stationary with kneeling stools they answer the same purpose as pews. Of course there are churches—like the Holy Sepulchre, and St. Peter's, Rome—where they would be out of place.

CHAPTER XII.

BETHLEHEM.

We had now seen the chief places of interest in Jerusalem; it was time to visit those farther away. I will proceed in the order of visitation.

Bethlehem naturally comes first. It is only six miles away to the south. There is a so-called carriage-road reaching there, but we preferred our favorites. We took our guide with us. Although not necessary, his company was useful. It is always understood that a donkey-boy runs behind to urge on the donkeys and take care of them. The ride to Bethlehem was a very pleasant one. The afternoon was fine, and a large number of people, walking and riding, were constantly passing in both directions over the road: natives on foot, and riding on donkeys or horses; others driving or leading long lines of heavily laden camels, such as you meet on almost every road in Palestine; Greek and Armenian priests and monks, and once in a while the brown-robed sons of St. Francis, two by two, on foot, like the Apostles of old. Having passed out of the Jaffa gate, and down and across the valley of Ennom, we left the hill of Evil Counsel and the tree of Judas on our left, and the new German temple colony on our right, frequently looking back to get new glimpses and views of the city, walls, and surroundings of Jerusalem. From the east and southwest the "Daughter of Sion" appears to advantage, "sitting in silence" in the midst of the "everlasting hills." We were now in the valley of Raphaim, the plain where David overcame the Philistines in battle. This plain descends towards the southwest to the Valley of Roses. To the right is shown the house of holy Simeon, and still farther on is the "Well of the Wise Men from the East," where the star again appeared to them as they "went their way" from Jerusalem to Bethlehem. We then ascended a hill, near the summit of which is a schismatic Greek monastery, where they show the impress of a man in the rock, where they say the prophet Elias slept when he was fleeing from the impious Jezabel. I do not pretend even to mention one-fourth of the places pointed out as scenes of historic events of the Old and New Testaments; it would be impossible, for Palestine is a land of small extent, and the time from Abraham to Christ covers a period of nearly two thousand years. Too many things confuse. I try, therefore, to bring out only those landmarks of sacred history which are especially prominent to the physical, intellectual, or spiritual eye. Here is a view that I could spend a lifetime beholding with the eyes of the senses and the eyes of the soul. To the south lies Bethlehem, to the northeast Jerusalem, both in full view—the birthplace and the burial ground of kings, where kings have been anointed, and where they have been crowned, and where they have laid aside their crowns and sceptres: the royal David and the royal Son of Mary, of the house and family of David. The sceptre of the one was powerful and his crown glorious, but they rust in the tomb; the sceptre of the other was the reed of scorn, His crown the crown of thorns, but they are for ever enthroned on high. It was a beautiful sight which I shall never forget, the first sight of Bethlehem, still beholding that other city which, as in olden times, is now the city of the "vision of peace."

A monk told me that Jerusalem seemed a city of sorrow and Bethlehem a village of joy. It does not seem to me, however, that the city is altogether sorrowful that possesses the Cœnaculum, and where the Resurrection and Ascension took place. To the north, beyond Jerusalem, rose Neby Samwil, and to the east the mountains beyond the Jordan.

The country, from Jerusalem to Bethlehem, is tolerably well cultivated, and around Bethlehem seems quite fertile. To the right is the residence of the schismatic Greek patriarch, and, farther on to the right, Beit Jala, the beautiful residence and seminary of the Catholic patriarch, surrounded by vineyards and olive groves. Nearly a mile before we reached Bethlehem we came to the tomb of Rachel. The love of Jacob for Rachel furnishes one of the most beautiful stories of the Old Testament. Jacob himself thus relates her death: "Rachel died from me in the land of Chanaan in the very journey, and it was spring-time; and I was going to Ephrata, which by another name is called Bethlehem." Her tomb is reverenced by Christians, Jews, and Mohammedans. It is now about 3,600 years old. Near here a road branches off to the Pools of Solomon, from which, by means of aqueducts, water was formerly supplied to Jerusalem. To the left we saw the hills where the shepherds were "keeping the night-watches over their flocks," and heard the angelic song of great joy: "Glory to God in the highest, and on earth peace to men of good will."

It is just such a picturesque spot as where they might be expected to guard their flocks during the night, neither high up on the hills nor yet in the valley.

At the present time there is a church, belonging to the Greeks, over the place where the angels appeared. Not far distant, on the side of the mountain, is the village where the shepherds lived, and which is now occupied by about fifty families of Greek and Catholic Arabs. Even to this day the dwellers in this rural abode partake much of that simplicity which characterized the humble shepherds who adored the Infant Jesus in Bethlehem. And as in olden times, so now they go over to Bethlehem, and, going down into the Grotto of the Nativity, they kneel and adore Him who was once an infant there.

We soon arrived in Bethlehem, which is situated on the brow of a hill overlooking a deep valley, and in the distance presents a pleasing appearance. It is surrounded by a verdant, well-cultivated, and fruitful country. The name signifies "house of bread."

At the present time it is an enterprising

village, manifesting a better growth and more healthy life than any other town that I saw in Palestine. Along the street through which we entered the village a goodly number of fine hewn stone buildings were being erected. Bethlehem has a population of about 5,000. Of these 3,000 are Catholics, 1,500 schismatic Greeks, and 500 others. They are for the most part a prosperous people, possessing some of the best characteristics of a Christian community. It is a very ancient town, and possessed of great historical importance. We know that it was already in existence more than seventeen centuries before the coming of Christ. Bethlehem was the scene of the charming story of the book of Ruth, who gleaned wheat after the reapers in the field of Booz, whom she afterwards married, and from whom the family of David was descended. It is distinguished as the birth-place of David, but far more as the birth-place of our Saviour, where, nearly nineteen hundred years ago, shepherds and kings knelt on a common level and adored the King of kings. "And thou, Bethlehem Ephrata, art a little one among the thousands of Juda: out of thee shall He come forth unto me that is to be the Ruler in Israel; and His going forth is from the beginning, from the days of eternity." Wherever in the whole world the joys of Christmas day are known, the hills and plains, the houses and people of Bethlehem, and the scenes and events of the Divine Nativity and of the succeeding days, have been a hundred and a thousand times pictured. It is enough; in Bethlehem the Son of God and the Son of Mary was born. And the thought keeps running in my mind: Is Bethlehem or Nazareth dearer to me? If, after our Lord's birth, He had lived in Bethlehem until His ninth or tenth year, all doubt would disappear. Bethlehem was the place of His birth, which witnessed the mutual love of Mother and Son the first time that they looked into the depths of each other's eyes; but Nazareth was His home, and home, to the human heart, is next to heaven. And the Sacred Heart of Jesus loved His home, for it was the sanctuary of the Immaculate Heart of Mary. That home was the Holy House of the Holy Family, which they yet love on earth, even though they dwell in the heavenly mansion of the Eternal Father. And I believe, if it were possible to be home-sick in heaven, that the Holy Family would be home-sick for the Holy House of Nazareth. Home and family are the foundations of society, planted by the fiat of God in nature, and cemented and consecrated by Jesus, Mary, and Joseph in the love and miraculous care and preservation of the Holy House of Loreto.

Such thoughts must enter the mind of any Christian who passes through the streets of the sacred towns of Palestine. We soon arrived at the portals of the great monastery and church built over the Grotto of the Nativity. As ever, we were kindly welcomed by the monks. The monastery at Bethlehem, in parts at least, is a little more richly furnished than others in the Holy Land; the wine also is better. But the kindness and hospitality shown the pilgrim are the same in all.\

Soon after our arrival we went to visit the grotto. It may be entered from different directions, and one not used to the entrance or exit is liable to lose his way. The crypt which served as a stable is about forty feet long, twelve feet wide, and ten feet high. At the east end is the Altar of the Nativity, and under it is a silver star with an inscription round about: "*Hic de Virgine Maria Jesus Christus natus est*"—"Here Jesus Christ was born of the Virgin Mary." As in all similar holy places, a large number of lamps, belonging usually to the Catholics, Greeks, and Armenians, are always burning before the different altars. A few paces distant from the spot of the Nativity are the Chapel of the Manger and Altar of the Wise Men, which are the places where the Infant Jesus was laid in the manger and where the wise men adored Him.

The manger itself is preserved in the church of Santa Maria Maggiore in Rome. The Altar of the Nativity belongs to the Greeks, and the altar of the manger to the Catholics, although the Catholics can say only two Masses daily at their altar, as it is in the same room with the Altar of the Nativity. We also visited the chapels of St. Joseph, of the Holy Innocents, and of St. Jerome and St. Paula. The next morning I had the privilege of celebrating Mass in this holy grotto at the altar of the manger. At the time appointed I found that a Pontifical Greek Mass, sung by a schismatic Greek bishop, was in progress. I put on my cassock and waited in the grotto, without vesting, until it was finished. I had to wait more than an hour, but in the meantime was very much interested. The bishop was vested in a vestment similar in appearance to our cope, and had on his head during a portion of the service a very high crown with a cross at the summit. An attempt at a description of their ceremonies would serve to confuse and mislead rather than inform the reader. Assisting, were four or five clergymen in vestments similar to that worn by the bishop. All wore beards, and very long hair parted in the middle. During the Mass the *Kyrie eleison* was frequently sung by the bishop, accompanied by the clergy and choir. The use of incense was much more frequent and common than with us. There were also several processions through the chapel. At one time he gave what I suppose was blessed bread to many of those present. He turned towards me to see if I would receive it, but I indicated that I would not, and he passed on. When they had finished I went to the Catholic sacristy and vested, and then had the great privilege, which until lately I had never expected to enjoy, of offering up and adoring the Sacred Host in the exact spot where the Divine Infant lay and was adored on Christmas night, and afterwards by the Magi, nearly nineteen hundred years ago. Whenever we said Mass in any of the sacred places a goodly number of native Christians were present and assisted.

We returned to Jerusalem that day. The pilgrim will always find that the journey from Jerusalem to Bethlehem and return is one of the most pleasant in all Palestine.

CHAPTER XIII.

JERICHO AND THE DEAD SEA.

Our next excursion was to be a longer one, and more tiresome and subject to danger. It was to Jericho and the Dead Sea. Greater preparations were necessary; but these were all under the supervision of young Auwad, our guide and dragoman. Much to our disinclination, we had to take horses instead of donkeys. We were accompanied by two parties: first the cook and men with tents, whom we only saw a portion of the time, and then our own party: ourselves, the dragoman, the muleteer—who owned all the horses and donkeys, and who was a Turk—and our Bedouin guards. Our guards were the sheik of Abu Dis and his two sons. Sometimes one was with us, sometimes another. As there were only a few travellers at that season of the year, the three made the journey with us. I may as well say it right here, I like the Bedouins and almost everybody else in the Holy Land. The Bedouins seem like children in disposition and friendship, but they are brave men when courage is required. They were careful—and almost childlike—to point out their native village or their homes, and I have to acknowledge that I took at least as much interest in them as in the country seats or palaces of the noblemen and princes of Europe. And that little village had a new interest for me as the birthplace of our Bedouin guard. They are a showy, warlike-looking lot of fellows, with their dark faces and large, black moustaches, in their strangely fashioned dress, double-barrelled gun slung over their shoulders, daggers and pistols in their sashes, and mounted on their Arab steeds. But they are nevertheless as good-natured, kind, affectionate, and honest fellows, towards those to whom they think these qualities are due, as you would wish to meet.

Very early in the morning we passed out of the Jaffa gate, around the northern wall of the city, to the eastern side. The city was silent, and as we looked upon the grotto of Jeremias to the north, where he wrote his

Lamentations, we were better able to appreciate his mournful words: "How doth the city sit solitary that was full of people." We rode over the Kedron, and around the southern side of the Mount of Olives towards Bethany. The place of the barren fig-tree which Christ cursed was pointed out to us. We rode on through Bethany, ever beautiful and ever dear to us, and soon after were joined by our Bedouin guard, whose village was visible on a hillside towards the south. From here, until we "drew near to Jericho," we were in the region called the "desert of Jericho," which is an expanse of barren and partly barren hills.

We soon descended into the "Valley of the Watering-Place," and reached the "Spring of the Apostles," which is so called because Christ and His Apostles must have many times rested here and drank water from this spring on their way from Jericho to Bethany and Jerusalem. It must have been to the weary Apostles of our Lord one of the pleasantest fountains in the whole land. So it seemed to me as we returned from Jericho after a tedious ride; and for several miles I eagerly looked forward to see it come in view. How cool and refreshing did its waters seem, how delightful was the place! This was the ancient "fountain of the sun" spoken of in the book of Josue.

The morning sun sends its sparkling rays down through the valley, and its first beams shine on the fountain. This "Valley of the Fountain," with its every-day beauty and its thirty-three hundred years of tranquil history, has all the elements of idyllic poetry. It must have been near here that Semei, of the house of Saul, cursed David in his flight, but afterwards asked forgiveness, and his life was spared.

From here to Jericho and back again we met several hundred Bedouins, sometimes only two together, sometimes in bands of twenty, with horses, camels, donkeys, and flocks of sheep and goats. Flocks of sheep and goats were usually together, the former of the large-tailed variety. Of the several hundred men whom we met, only two were unarmed. All the rest had guns of various patterns, most of them old-fashioned fire-arms with flint-locks, and long barrels bound with brass and inlaid with mother of pearl. Our guard was the best-dressed and best-armed of any.

About half-way to Jericho is the traditional place where the man fell among robbers, as related in the parable of the Good Samaritan. He could not have found a more fitting spot for such an occurrence. It would seem perfectly natural to the locality to have a band of robbers appear before you, rob you, and leave you half-dead. It is a dreary and dangerous-looking place. There is a large, unoccupied building standing there, one of only two or three that we saw in a distance of fifteen miles. Along the route enough grass is frequently found for grazing purposes, and now and then a tree spreads its sheltering branches. The road, while fairly good, was often very precipitous. In many places it was cut through the rocks, and the white limestone, reflecting the hot sun, dazzled the eyes and formed a heated oven, in which we sweltered. Sometimes we came into the cool shade of a rock, and thought of the refreshing simile of Holy Scripture: "As the shadow of a rock that standeth out in a desert land." We were approaching a tropical climate in June.

For a long distance we had seen the mountains beyond the Jordan, but at last the plain of Jericho, the valley of the Jordan, and the Dead Sea burst upon our sight. Far below us, running by the side of the road, was a deep ravine through which runs the ancient torrent of Carith, or Cherith, out into the plain and past the modern Jericho, into the Jordan.

We soon descended the last hill and found ourselves in a beautiful, fertile, and very green plain. The plants and fruits of the valley are semi-tropical, on account of its great depression. Jericho is called in the Scriptures the "city of palm-trees." When Moses looked down from Mount Nebo he saw a wide plain, luxuriant in vegetation, and rich in fields of grain and groves of palm-trees, and in its midst a large city, surrounded by walls, and rich in gold and silver.\

It was on this plain that Josue saw the "prince of the host of the Lord" "standing over against him, holding a drawn sword." At the command of the Lord the valiant men and priests went around the city seven times; the seventh time the priests sounded the trumpets and the people raised a great shout, and the walls fell down and the entire city was destroyed. In this vicinity took place many of the events described in the lives of the prophets Elias and Eliseus. Here David fled and passed over the Jordan from the pursuit of Absalom. Near here St. John the Baptist preached penance, and our Lord was baptized by him in the Jordan. About two miles to the north rises the barren, desolate Mountain of Temptation, where Christ fasted forty days, and was afterwards tempted by the devil. Near here He cured the "blind man Bartimeus, who sat by the wayside begging." Here also He was a guest at the house of Zacheus, "chief of the publicans." And from here He began His last, sad journey towards Jerusalem. We passed down the almost level valley of the Carith, through pleasant groves and gardens, to an inn, built of wood and looking very much like an American farm-house, kept by a Russian family. How tired we were! As for myself, I was so stiff and lame from horseback riding over such a long, hot, rugged road, that I was hardly able to dismount, and, once on my feet, scarcely able to walk; but a certain degree of elasticity quickly returned. We were shown a well-ventilated, comfortable upper room, where we soon settled ourselves for a few hours' midday rest. The old sheik, father of our guards, who had arrived before us, made us a call. He was a venerable, dignified old Bedouin, with whom we spoke through an interpreter.\

About four o'clock in the afternoon we remounted our horses and started for the Dead Sea, about six miles distant. We tried to make ourselves believe that a cool breeze had modified the temperature, but it was of no use. There was a breeze, but imagination would not help us; the atmosphere was too glowing. For warm weather commend me to the Dead Sea region in summer-time; yet I prefer it to the furnace-like blasts that come from the desert at Cairo. Modern Jericho contains about sixty families, most of whom are Moslems and live in miserable huts. There is a Greek monastery, and a few other buildings are connected with their colony. After riding some distance we again came to the valley of the torrent of Carith, at the place where the prophet Elias was fed by the ravens. As we approached the Dead Sea vegetation gradually disappeared, although not entirely. Like the soil, it was coated with salt and gypsum.

The Dead Sea is forty-six miles in length, and at its broadest place ten miles in width. It contains in its waters no animal life, although birds fly over and even swim on its surface. At near six o'clock in the afternoon the thermometer stood 105° above, Fahr., in the shade of the most corpulent member of our party. It is said that the water has an oily appearance. There was a breeze coming from the sea, which produced small waves breaking upon the shore, which caused much foam; otherwise it did not seem to me different than other sea-water. But it is, in fact, as chemical analysis shows that it contains twenty-five per cent. of solids, one-half of which is salt. The mean depth of the sea is about eleven hundred feet. It is calculated that six million tons of water flow into the Dead Sea daily, and it has no visible outlet. It is called in the Scriptures the Salt Sea, the Eastern Sea, and the Sea of the Plain; by the Greeks the Sea of Asphalt, and by the Arabs the Sea of Lot. Where this sea and barren plain now lie in dreary, desolate grandeur, surrounded by the high mountains on either side, was once a luxuriant plain, adorned with prosperous and populous cities. This was the plain chosen by Lot nearly four thousand years ago, and described in these words: "And Lot, lifting up his eyes, saw all the country about the Jordan, which was watered throughout, before the Lord destroyed Sodom and Gomorrah, as the paradise of the Lord." Mountains from fifteen hundred to twenty-five hundred feet in height nearly surround it, those on the east side being the higher, and their blue slopes form a rugged and grand framework to the blue mirror which they enclose. Notwithstanding the dread desolation of the place, it is, after all, a very beautiful picture on which the eyes rest. The scenery is a wonderful commingling of the beautiful and sublime.

We did not attempt a full bath in the heavy waters, but contented ourselves with bathing our hands.

Taking in the entire surroundings, we meditated on what they once were by God's blessing, on what they now are by God's curse. Our reveries, as we looked upon those scenes, were not so prolonged as they would have been had the heat been less intense. We were easily convinced that we had gone far enough, and were satisfied to look upon the green course of the Jordan from the distance, rather than farther overheat ourselves in the great natural oven which we had entered.

Therefore, returning directly through Jericho, we passed to our camping-ground near the fountain of Eliseus (or Elisha). It was dark after leaving Jericho, and we rode two miles through groves, near Bedouin encampments, and across streams exceedingly difficult of passage, until we reached our tents. In the dim light of the evening we could see over the larger tent prepared for us the Stars and Stripes floating in the warm breeze of the plain of Jericho, and, like ourselves, a long way from home; but the flag of our country cheered our weary spirits. We were quickly off our horses and in our tent. Although during the day we frequently drank the cool water from an earthen jug carried by our muleteer, and replenished by him at every good fountain, we were as thirsty as if we had been drinking from the Dead Sea. Lemonade is easily procured in Palestine, and we drank more of it that evening than was really good for us. A most excellent meal was soon placed before us in different courses—soup, three kinds of meat, and various delicacies. It was really a marvel of good food and good cookery. But, alas! we had lost our appetites; we were too tired to feel like eating. Hunger was gone, thirst had taken possession of us. My two companions fell out by the way at the first course of soup. The one of our number whom God had blessed with the most magnificent appetite had completely lost it, and was the first to relinquish the contest, which he scarcely began. I alone determined, notwithstanding my feelings, not to disappoint the cook, and partook something of every course. We had very nice beds, but the night was excessively warm. Our Bedouin guards did constant sentry duty during the entire night. We had noticed on our way to the Dead Sea and return that the guard in charge frequently took close observations of the mountains of Moab, as if to note any indications of the presence of hostile tribes, and at night they showed more particular anxiety and vigilance. We were not inclined to apprehend danger in any part of Palestine, as many travellers do, but we concluded that night that there was at least some show of danger. Without doubt there are many dangers lurking in the mountains east of the Jordan, liable at any moment to make their presence felt, especially at a time of the year when there are but few travellers, where less hindrance might be expected on account of less numbers to oppose. The Bedouins beyond the river are less tractable, and often make incursions to the western side for purposes of robbery, although when once they have become your escort you are perfectly safe in their hands. It was so sultry in our tent during the night that a good sleep was out of the question, and the fleshiest member of our party might have been seen in the middle of the night, in his shirt-sleeves, sitting at the door of his tent like Abraham of old, and now and then negotiating with one of the guards to go to the spring of the prophet Eliseus to bring him a drink of cool water.

CHAPTER XIV.

A MORNING AND DAY IN PALESTINE.

WE were out of our beds and dressed at dawn of day. Having partaken of a slight meal, and while the tents were being taken down, packed, and loaded on the mules, we visited the fountain of Eliseus. This is the spring spoken of in the Holy Scriptures: "And the men of the city said to Eliseus: Behold the situation of this city is very good, as thou, my lord, seest; but the waters are very bad and the ground barren. And he said: Bring me a new vessel and put salt in it. And when they had brought it, he went out to the spring of the waters, and cast the salt into it, and said: Thus saith the Lord: I have healed these waters, and there shall be no more in them death or barrenness. And the waters were healed unto this day." The spring is a large one, copious and beautiful, and sends forth pure water and fertility to a large tract of country./

It was a splendid morning; a cooling breeze fanned our cheeks and invigorated our bodies, while all nature gladdened our hearts; the rising sun darted its golden beams over the purple mountains and through the green valleys of the east, gilding the tops of the gray mountains of the west, and sending a thousand beautiful reflections upon the shining surface of the Dead Sea, until we could no longer draw the dividing line between the gray, blue, green, and purple of the earth and the azure of the heavens. The joyous vision of these things which are seen, united with hallowed and historic associations of four thousand years, raised our souls to the contemplation of the unseen and spiritual things of God, to praise and thanksgiving for His everlasting love and bounty. I looked back four thousand years to that terrible morning when "the sun was risen upon the earth and Lot entered into Segor," and I seemed to see towards the south the fires of divine anger hurled forth from heaven like awful thunderbolts upon the fair cities of that luxuriant plain, crushing and consuming them from the face of the earth, that an hour before had been bathed in the warmth, richness, and glory of God's sunlight. I looked back more than three thousand years, and I seemed to see shining among those eastern mountains the "pillar of the cloud by day and the pillar of fire by night," covering the tabernacle of the Lord in the midst of the camp of Israel, coming to the banks of the Jordan and in its waters for ever vanishing, but a figure to be fulfilled in that same place and in those same waters fourteen centuries afterwards in the baptism of Christ; for the holy Fathers teach that the "pillar of fire" was a figure of Christ, and the "pillar of the cloud" a figure of the Holy Spirit.

I looked back nearly two thousand years, and I seemed to see in the plain below a small company of men of venerable appearance, in long, flowing, graceful robes such as are seen everywhere in Oriental lands, who are departing from Jericho, slowly ascending the first hill and disappearing among the mountains. One among them seems more noble than the rest, more perfect in form and bearing, and I seemed to see even in the distance that He had a more godlike brow, and eye, and face than the others; and—I could not tell, it was so far distant—it may have been the morning sun that formed that bright halo around His head, but it seemed to me milder and yet more radiant. It is the last sad, solemn procession of Jesus and His Apostles on their way to Jerusalem, where He goes to be crucified.

And in those three pictures I saw the terrible anger, the holy fear, and the sweet love of our God.

We rode around the base of the desolate Mountain of Temptation, and in a few miles got back to our old road by which we had come from Jerusalem. The usual return of travellers is by the way of Mar Saba and Bethlehem, but on account of the great heat that road appeared longer than we wished to undertake. As we gradually ascended the mountains, on every higher eminence we looked back to see if we could still distinguish Mount Nebo, and to give ourselves up to speculations perhaps somewhat romantic. I have heard it stated, but without reference or citation of proof, that there is an old prophecy that the East will be reconverted to Christianity by priests from America. If the longings of some hearts could be realized, it surely would be fulfilled. As the sun rose higher it became warmer, but luckily we were now ascending towards Jerusalem, to cooler heights. After a few hours we anxiously looked forward down the valley to catch a glimpse of the Fountain of the Apostles, which once reached, we quickly threw ourselves from our horses. An old Moslem, with his family, was lying in the shade ready to assist travellers in any way possible. The water is most excellent, but a cloth must be placed over the mouth of the vessel to strain it, on account of leeches. As we came near Bethany our guard bid us "farewell," and turned to the left to his own village; he afterwards came to see us at Jerusalem.

We soon after reached Bethany, and decided to stop there and lunch in a beautiful olive orchard near the house of Mary and Martha. We were immediately surrounded by a large number of the women and children of the village. Every one wanted to do us a service. The woman, with her family, who has charge of the tomb of Lazarus, was there with a jug of water. The boy who sold "antique" Bedouin daggers was also on hand; and many others, with jugs of water or pleading looks, made up the company, all expecting backsheesh. Water for drinking purposes seemed to be the chief staple product of the place; but the water of Bethany is very good. We, however, seated on the ground under the protecting shade of a large olive-tree, confined ourselves to lemonade, wine, cold chicken, and other solids. On our way to Jericho we had met the funeral procession of a man who died in that village, but whose native place was Bethany, where he was borne by his friends for burial. As soon as we met them they started a mournful cry or song of sorrow. They were now down below us in a green, shady valley, singing their mournful dirge during one hour at midday, which, I was told, is repeated for eight days. As for myself, I kept constantly falling asleep, and slept a good portion of the time that I sat in the midst of that motley crowd. But, half-dreaming, with the happy voices of children and the sad voices of mourning sounding in my ears, Bethany seemed to me more lovely than ever. When wilt Thou, O Lord, call out: Come forth from your spiritual graves, ye men of the village of Lazarus; and ye daughters of Bethany, dry the tears of your mourning that is without hope?

After about an hour we started for Jerusalem, and rode around the southern brow of Mount Olivet, and in a short time familiar scenes were once more before our eyes. We passed through St. Stephen's gate, up the Via Dolorosa, and soon stopped before the ever-hospitable portals of Casa Nova, where we were received like old acquaintances. Our rooms, where we left our large leather travelling-bags, in which were so many things to remind us of our home in America, and which we missed so much in a few days' absence, seemed like a second home to us. As I now write, that travelling-bag is in an adjoining room, but it does not seem so intimate as it did then; it even seems to have put on more foreign airs than its master, and to be pervaded with a certain Oriental atmosphere; but it is nevertheless the old companion of my travels, which I can never forget. /

CHAPTER XV.

THE "HILL-COUNTRY OF JUDEA" AND HOUSE OF THE VISITATION.

Our next excursion was to Ain Kârim, or St. John's in Montana, where St. John the Baptist was born, and where the Blessed Virgin visited her cousin St. Elizabeth: "And Mary, rising up in those days, went into the hill-country with haste into a city of Juda." It is about seven miles distant from Jerusalem, nearly west, through valleys and over hills. We were again mounted on our favorite donkeys, and from practice were enabled to get considerable speed out of them, even over rocky roads and down steep hills. The country around Jerusalem is rocky beyond ordinary imagination ; but wherever there is an attempt to cultivate it, not only in valleys but even on hillsides, trees, gardens, and vineyards are successful, for the soil is so rich that but little of it is necessary. Almost everywhere flowering shrubs of various kinds were seen ; they were still green, and many of them contained a sprinkling of flowers, although no rain had moistened them for more than seven weeks. Small flowers also were seen peeping up among the rocks and stones, as bright-looking as if they had just caught in their beautiful cups the refreshing drops of a spring shower.

In spring Palestine must be the land of flowers. From north to south it is the same everywhere ; every blade, plant, and shrub seems to produce flowers of rich or delicate hue. It would be difficult to describe the richness of some and delicacy of others, and the never-ending varieties.

Descending a high, steep, rocky hill, we were in Ain Kârim. Our first visitation was to the place where the Blessed Virgin hastened to meet St. Elizabeth. We left the village, and passed by the Fountain of the Madonna, which the Blessed Virgin must many times have visited. It is the most beautiful and picturesque fountain that I saw in the Holy Land. A number of girls and women were around it, washing clothes in its waters as they flowed down and away. In their strange, various colored dresses, and with their dark eyes and hair, they presented a most pleasing Oriental picture not quickly forgotten. We passed around and up the side of a hill, perhaps a quarter of a mile from the village. To our right was a convent, the country house of the Sisters of Sion, and to our left a church, where once stood the house of the Visitation, probably the summer-dwelling of Zacharias. Between the two is a tasty flower-garden. The church stands in the midst of the grand, solid ruins of a church built by the Crusaders. We entered, and standing directly before us was an altar with an inscription beneath it stating that it is of constant and perpetual tradition that this is the place of the "Magnificat," the place where the Blessed Virgin and St. Elizabeth met, and where St. Elizabeth called her "blessed among women," and where the Blessed Virgin with divine rapture answered: "My soul doth magnify the Lord," etc. We knelt and repeated the joyous and grateful words of that inspired Canticle.

Oh! how beautiful are those places that have been made holy by our Blessed Mother's feet. No wonder that a pious legend says that the roses of Jericho sprung up in the desert wherever the Blessed Virgin placed her foot. We were shown a small cave near by, where St. John the Baptist was concealed during the slaughter of the Holy Innocents.

We were at the end of the valley of Terebinth, which we had crossed on our road from Jaffa to Jerusalem. From the ruins of this ancient church we could see far up the valley, beyond the Jaffa road, to Neby Samwîl rising in the distance. It is a fertile valley of green groves and orchards, and near Ain Kârim it is wholly covered with well-cultivated gardens, delightful to the eye. St. John's has a population of about seven hundred, of whom about six hundred are Moslems and one hundred or more are Catholics. We passed down the hill and by the fountain to the castellated monastery and church of St. John the Baptist, where he was born. This is where the holy priest Zacharias uttered that other inspired canticle, "Benedictus"—"Blessed be the Lord God of Israel." Having knelt at the various altars, and having commended ourselves to the Blessed Mother, to St. John the Baptist, to St. Zacharias and St. Elizabeth, who once dwelt here, we started back to Jerusalem.

The time was drawing near when we must leave Jerusalem. We had intended to visit Hebron, the home and final resting-place of the patriarchs. We had also intended to go north overland, and have the privilege of drinking at Jacob's Well, which is four thousand years old, and where our Lord sat, weary, conversing with the Samaritan woman. But our weeks were quickly passing, and we had a limited time for our absence from home; and we would remain in Rome some weeks, and then extend our travels up through the countries of central Europe. So we concluded to omit Hebron and other places of interest, and go to Nazareth over the easiest route, by way of Jaffa and Mount Carmel.

The good and kind superior of Casa Nova, and the sisters who were about to found a house in Nazareth, and their simple-hearted, pious old Capuchin chaplain, were about to make the same journey by the same route. We went in different parties.

Having received sacred mementoes from almost every one in the house—mementoes on the border-land of relics, which we shall ever sacredly treasure—we were ready to start. A number of natives had come to the convent to see us off and to assist us. After all, even though those who assist you expect a little reward, does the little given in any way repay the kindliness of spirit with which you are served? And that which is expected is frequently sadly needed. In most instances it is given to the poor; and how often it is the case that the poor wonderfully control themselves when it is a real pain to do so, because of their necessities! Under that half-concealed look of anxiety hunger and want are frequently hidden. I have no patience with those who do not wish to give a reasonable fee to those who serve them; for to fee is often to feed the hungry, whether that fee is called backsheesh or goes by some other name. On our way to the Jaffa gate a considerable number came to bid us "good-by." They were those whom we knew, and we were somewhat surprised to think that we had made so many acquaintances in Jerusalem. We were soon in our wagon, bade "adieu" to our friends, and once more were on our journey. We looked back from time to time, but in a little while the walls of the Holy City disappeared from our vision, probably for ever. But may our eyes at length catch sight of the glorious walls of the heavenly Jerusalem, the Holy City of the Living God!

The road to the valley of Terebinth did not

seem half so long as it did the morning of our arrival. The *café* in the valley, like many similar places in Palestine, has, besides various kinds of liquors, imported beer from Vienna and Marburg, in Austria. Our driver on this trip was an Arab, and was not so sleepy as the Russian driver of the former journey. About two o'clock in the morning we arrived at Ramleh, but made only a short stop. As usual, a number of other travellers were taking a brief rest, and among them were several Turkish soldiers in charge of a Bedouin who had stabbed four or five men. We again saw them the next morning in the plain of Sharon, riding on their horses, marching him before them, until they finally turned into a guard-house. The poor fellow looked dusty, tired, and dejected, and I could not help pitying him, although he may have been getting his just deserts. We were in Jaffa at an early hour and at the doors of the convent, where we were welcomed by familiar faces. The sisters were there before us, and one of them was appointed to deliver us an address. It was about as follows: "We meet so often in the Holy Land, we hope that we will also meet in heaven." We expressed a reciprocation of the good desire, and shall pray that it may be fulfilled. As soon as possible we took a much-needed sleep, and, thus refreshed, were prepared to enjoy during the remainder of the day and evening that singularly peaceful and beautiful scene./

CHAPTER XVI.

"NOBIS DONET IN PATRIA."

Towards evening, while the rays of the sun, already set, lingered on the distant waters of the Mediterranean at the western horizon, and as the evening breezes were springing up from the great sea, cooling the parched day, and silence began to take the place of busy noise, the sisters, who had assembled together on one of the higher, court-like terraces of the monastery, commenced to sing, and sung a few plaintive, pious melodies, which sounded to me like the sad songs of exiles who never again expected to see their native land./

But we are all exiles in this world, longing for our heavenly home and country. I cannot imagine a sadder land to the Christian exile than Palestine, nor one nearer or surer of heaven. O home! thou art dear to the homesick heart, but our real home is heaven. Therefore the pious exiles of the Holy Land, who are exiles by their own will for the sweet love of Jesus and Mary, are the favored ones of God.

The next day was Sunday, and we had the privilege of offering up the Holy Sacrifice in the church of Jaffa. We enjoyed the remainder of the forenoon looking out upon the sea, and gave ourselves up to our imagination; for this is the great sea of whose majesty and wonders the inspired psalmists and prophets so frequently sing.

In the afternoon we took the steamer for Haifa (or Caifa). A number of Franciscan fathers, and the sisters already spoken of, were also aboard. The steamer belonged to the Austrian Lloyd line. While on the Mediterranean we sailed on steamers of four different lines: from Brindisi to Alexandria on the P. and O. steamers, an English line; from Alexandria to Jaffa on a Russian steamer; from Jaffa to Haifa and back to Alexandria on the Austrian Lloyd; and from Alexandria to Naples on a French steamer. The passenger rates were by far the dearest on the P. and O. line, and next dearest on the Austrian Lloyd. The food was best on the French line, about equally good on the Russian and Austrian, and poorest on the P. and O. line;

but the steamers of the last-named were fine and large. On the French and Russian steamers wines were free, and on the other two lines to be paid for extra. In the first cabin of all the lines everything was very clean and neat, the English steamer having East Indian table waiters and the others Europeans, whom I very much preferred.

It was ten or eleven o'clock at night before we arrived at Haifa. The wind was blowing, the waves were rolling, and it was very dark. The small boats put out from the shore as soon as we had anchored, each with a solitary lantern, but with an abundance of suppressed noise and confusion, ready to burst all bonds and bounds as soon as the steamer was reached. I must acknowledge that I do not like the mode of landing. We had to go down a dark gangway, and then step off into—we knew not what—a boat, if we could, that was rising and sinking, and tipping about among twenty other boats, each one trying to push the others away from the foot of the gangway. We all managed to step into a boat instead of the sea, although it was so dark below that we could not discover which until we found ourselves in the bottom of the boat. A gentleman, accompanied by his wife and two small children, was in the boat with us, and attended to the custom-house officer in the usual way. He proved to be a German in the employ of the English Missionary Society for the conversion of the Jews. He had been operating in Jerusalem, but had lately been transferred to Safed, the "city seated on a hill" at the north end of the Sea of Galilee, where there is a large Jewish population. We decided to stay at the Hotel Carmel, of the German colony, which is some distance out of town; but it proved to be an excellent inn, and on the direct way to the convent of Mount Carmel. We awakened early the next morning, and after breakfast went out to take a look around us.

CHAPTER XVII.

MOUNT CARMEL—THE MOUNTAIN OF THE PROPHETS AND OF THE BLESSED VIRGIN MARY.

HIGH above us rose Mount Carmel, which branches off from the mountains of Samaria, and extends towards the northwest to the sea. It is about fifteen miles long, and rises in places to a height of more than seventeen hundred feet. Along its northern base is the great plain of Es-

MOUNT CARMEL.

tended to the custom house officer in the usual way. He proved to be a German in the employ of the English Missionary Society for the conversion of the Jews. He had been operating in Jerusalem and had lately been transferred to Safed, the "city seated on a hill" at the north end of the sea of Galilee, where there is a large Jewish population. We decided to stay at the Hotel Carmel, of the German colony, which is some distance out of town; but it proved to be an excellent inn, and on the direct way to the convent of Mount Carmel. We awakened early the next morning, and after breakfast went out to take a look around us.

CHAPTER XVII.

MOUNT CARMEL, THE MOUNTAIN OF THE PROPHETS AND OF THE BLESSED VIRGIN MARY.

High above us rose Mount Carmel, which branches off from the mountains of Samaria, and extends towards the northwest to the sea. It is about fifteen miles long, and rises in places to a height of more than seventeen hundred feet. Along its northern base is the great plain of Es-

Mount Carmel.

draelon. This mountain was the residence of the prophets Elias and Eliseus, and the seat of the "school of the prophets." It slopes towards the great sea, into which it juts, a high and bold promontory, on which the convent of Mount Carmel is situated, four hundred and eighty feet above the water. The convent, seen from land or sea, is a very conspicuous object. Carmel is covered with trees and vegetation, and even now is beautiful and majestic; therefore does Solomon sing in the Canticle of Canticles, in reciting the praises of the Spouse of Christ: "Thy head is like Carmel." Christ, the invisible Head of the Church, is here signified. But, like all other places in Palestine, Carmel is not what it once was, but rather the mournful prophecy of Isaias is fulfilled: "And gladness and joy shall be taken away from Carmel, and there shall be no rejoicing nor shouting in the vineyards. He shall not tread out wine in the press that was wont to tread it out: the voice of the treaders I have taken away."

On this mountain the prophet Elias called down fire from heaven, which consumed the holocaust upon his altar, to the confusion of the prophets of Baal, so that the people cried out: "The Lord He is God." And the false prophets were brought down from the mountain to the ancient torrent of Kishon, or Cison, and were slain on account of their impiety and imposture.

On this mountain Elias prayed when there had been no rain for three years and six months, and while he prayed "a little cloud arose out of the sea"; "and while he turned himself this way and that way, behold the heavens grew dark with clouds and winds, and there fell a great rain." The place of the sacrifice of Elias is yet pointed out, and the convent of Carmel is built over the cave where he dwelt. From time immemorial this mountain has been occupied not only by the prophets, but by saintly anchorites before the time of Christ, and after His coming by Christian hermits until the present time. The Carmelites have the prophet Elias as their founder.

The fourth and fifth lessons of the Divine Office of the Roman Breviary for the Commemoration of the Blessed Virgin Mary of Mount Carmel relate the following: "When, on the sacred day of Pentecost, the Apostles by heavenly inspiration spoke in divers tongues, and, having invoked the most august name of Jesus, performed many wonders, it is related that very many men who followed in the footsteps of the holy prophets Elias and Eliseus, and had been prepared by the preaching of John the Baptist for the coming of Christ, . . . forthwith embraced the evangelical faith, and by a certain especial love began so to venerate the Most Blessed Virgin—whose converse and familiarity they had happily been able to enjoy—that first of all on that place on Mount Carmel where Elias formerly saw the cloud rising, marked as a type of the Virgin, they built a chapel to the same most pure Virgin. Therefore, gathering frequently every day at that new chapel, with pious rites, prayers, and praises, they worshipped the Most Blessed Virgin as the particular patroness of their order. For which reason they came to be called everywhere the Brothers of the Blessed Mary of Mount Carmel."

The German colony has reclaimed considerable land between the base of the mountain and the sea. It is a wide, level plain of fields and orchards. Their houses are good and substantial, constructed of fine hewn stone. Their yards and gardens are well kept and ornamented, and among the trees here and there are a few graceful palms. Across the bay we could see the town of Acre, or Ptolemais, and far beyond the waters of the bay, to the east, the hills of Galilee.

During the forenoon I determined to make a

visit to the convent. My companions thought the day was too warm and would not accompany me, so I set out alone on foot. The path, which was quite good, was pleasantly lined the whole distance by shrubs and trees, so that when I felt the heat was too intense I always found the welcome shade of a tree near at hand. These occasions of rest also gave an opportunity to enjoy quietly the beauty and grandeur of the scenery. From this holy mountain of Carmel, the mountain of God and the mountain of the Blessed Virgin, many a pure and holy eye has lingered for the last time on the blue, beautiful sea, and over the green plains and hills of Galilee, quickly to catch a glimpse of the home of eternal rest and the divine delights of the celestial country. It is, surely, a holy place in which to pass a lifetime, and a divine place from which to pass from earth to heaven.

I soon reached the monastery, and received a most cordial welcome from the Carmelite monks. The convent of Carmel looks out from its heights over the Mediterranean Sea, and from its influence over the world. I became acquainted with an aged Carmelite father, wearing a long, white, flowing beard. He was a Belgian, and had been on the missions in the East Indies and knew English well. He delighted in making eloquent quotations which he had formerly committed to memory from *Paradise Lost*. In about half an hour after my arrival my two friends, having reconsidered their morning resolutions, arrived on donkeys at the monastery-gate. Our venerable Carmelite guide showed us over the building. The most interesting part was the cave of the prophet Elias. In how many ways these monks of Mount Carmel, who have gone forth to the ends of the earth "with the spirit and power of Elias," have proven themselves to be the true sons of Elias, quickened by a new fire consuming and working wonders to the confusion of the false prophets of the world, and making men cry out: "O Jesus of Nazareth, Thou art the Son of the Living God! and O Mary, thou art indeed the Mother of God!" We also knelt before the altar of St. Simon Stock, who lived six years in this holy retreat. We were cordially invited to stay over-night and as long as we pleased, but, having to start for Nazareth that afternoon, we could not accept the kind invitation. In returning to Haifa I was glad to have the privilege of walking down the side of the mountain alone and in silence, meditating on the history and mysteries of Carmel.\

Nazareth is about eighteen miles distant from

Haifa, between which places is a fair wagon-road, over a level country, except the last few miles of the approach to Nazareth. We employed a member of the German colony to convey us, and were pleased to see on what good terms many of these simple and industrious men apparently live with their Catholic neighbors, especially the Catholic monks.* Fraternity seems to be one of the prominent characteristics of a large portion of the inhabitants of the Holy Land. In saying this I am not unmindful of the robberies and contentions that sometimes take place, but which only appear to serve to unite more closely the larger number of the people.

CHAPTER XVIII.

THE LIGHT OF NAZARETH.

Leaving Haifa, for some distance we passed between hedges of cactus and groves of various kinds of trees, crossing once or twice the an-

* Since writing the above I have seen it stated, on seemingly good authority, that members of the colony at Haifa have interfered with the rights and property of the monks on Carmel. If this be so, it would very much detract from the estimate that I formed of them; but I should hope that not all the colony joined in any such injustice.

NAZARETH

Haifa, between which places is a fair wagon-road, over a level country, except the last few miles of the approach to Nazareth. We employed a member of the German colony to convey us, and were pleased to see on what good terms many of these simple and industrious men apparently live with their Catholic neighbors, especially the Catholic monks.* Fraternity seems to be one of the prominent characteristics of a large portion of the inhabitants of the Holy Land. In saying this I am not unmindful of the robberies and contentions that sometimes take place, but which only appear to serve to unite more closely the larger number of the people.

CHAPTER XVIII.

THE LIGHT OF NAZARETH.

Leaving Haifa, for some distance we passed between hedges of cactus and groves of various kinds of trees, crossing once or twice the an-

---

* Since writing the above I have seen it stated, on seemingly good authority, that members of the colony at Haifa have interfered with the rights and property of the monks on Carmel. If this be so, it would very much detract from the estimate that I formed of them; but I should hope that not all the colony joined in any such injustice.

NAZARETH.

cient river Kishon, and continued through its wide, fertile valley for some miles along the base of Mount Carmel. At the present time Galilee seems much more verdant, fertile, and well timbered than Judea. In the valley of the Kishon we saw many flocks, herds, and cultivated fields. The villages along the way, however, made but very humble pretensions, worthy of humble Galilee. A portion of the country is not unlike what we call the "oak openings" of our Western States. Other parts of it are very dissimilar. I believe that it would be a good country for the settlement, farms, cities, and homes, of fifty thousand industrious and courageous European and American Catholic Christians, who could thus live in the midst of the constant sacred associations of the Holy Family. But why indulge in such dreams? Nevertheless they may have been the dreams, in another form, that led the Crusaders to offer up their lives by sickness and in battle for the restoration of the Holy Land to Christ. The Cross of Christ before our eyes leads us to imaginations and desires which never on this earth will be fulfilled, but which shall be realized in perfect form and being in heaven. Having passed out of the valley of the Kishon, we entered a woody tract which extended some distance without any sign of habitation. After a while the plain of Esdraelon appeared on our right. It is called also the Great Plain, the Plain of Jezreel, and Plain of Megeddo, and was one of the great battle-plains of Jewish history. We passed through various estates and villages, near most of which extensive piles and stacks of grain were waiting for the threshers. Darkness came on some time before we reached Nazareth, and towns were pointed out to us by lights seen shining in the distance. One light shone out, far away beyond the plain of Esdraelon, towards the south; we were told that it was in the "city of Naim," where our Lord restored to life the widow's son. O mild and bright light of the mercy and love of Jesus Christ! Soon afterward, to the left, near the highway, appeared the town of Yâfa, the Japhie of the book of Josue, which was the native place of the holy Apostles "James and John, the sons of Zebedee"; our driver called it St. James. We were now entering the region where the Apostles lived and toiled before they were called to be the disciples of the Lord; in which our Lord also lived, and chose the sons of His own simple, humble neighbors to be His Apostles, the teachers of the wise, and the spiritual conquerors and rulers of nations. Not long after the lights of Nazareth appeared. How can I express my feelings as we approached Nazareth? There is hardly a square rod of ground in it or about it that has not been sanctified by the footsteps of Jesus, our Saviour, in His childhood and manhood.. And where He walked, Mary His Mother walked, and Joseph the carpenter. In connection with Nazareth 'I love to use these names, so simple and yet so powerful—Jesus, Mary, and Joseph. How many times did the lights of Nazareth bring joy to our Lord and His weary disciples as they drew near home! We rode into the city and through the streets until we came before the portal of the Franciscan hospice, which is situated not far from the church of the Annunciation. Our coming was in some way known, so we were not unexpected guests, and, although we were somewhat late, supper was almost immediately ready. Here we found the same kind welcome as elsewhere, the last, perhaps, which we ever should receive from our kind entertainers and friends, the Franciscans of the Holy Land. Their reward awaits them in heaven.\

We retired to our rooms, to awaken in the

morning to see Nazareth for the first time by daylight. For a long time I could do nothing but look out of the window and watch the men going to their work, and the women going to the fountain of the Blessed Virgin, and the children at play or accompanying their mothers, and think of the same scenes more than eighteen hundred years ago. Many also were going to the church to assist at one of the early Masses. Nazareth contains a population variously estimated at from six to ten thousand. Of these from fifteen hundred to twenty-five hundred are Catholics of the Latin, Greek, and Maronite rites, all of whom have churches. The remaining population is about equally divided between Greek schismatics and Moslems. The greater part of the town lies on the steep slope of a hill, and the remainder on a level at the base, with a beautiful, green, shady valley immediately at the east. It is surrounded by mountains, from some of which an extensive view is obtained. As soon as we were ready we were conducted to the church of the Annunciation, where we were to have the happy privilege of saying Mass at the altar of the Annunciation, on the very spot where the Incarnation of the Son of God took place, when the Angel Gabriel declared unto Mary: "Behold, thou shalt conceive in thy womb, and shalt bring forth a son; and thou shalt call His name Jesus." We entered the church, and very soon saw that, in architectural design, and artistic finish, it is one of the most attractive churches in Palestine. Above, at the farther end, was a high altar, but below it, by steps leading down from the body of the church, we descended to the chapel of the Annunciation. Beneath the altar of the chapel are these words: "*Hic Verbum caro factum est.*"—"Here the Word was made flesh." Above the portals of the grand Christian basilica which the Empress Helena had erected here, she had these words inscribed: "This is the ground whereon the foundation of human Redemption was laid." This chapel and altar stand on the rock where once stood the Holy House, in which dwelt the Blessed Virgin, and afterward the Holy Family. We had the privilege, after our return to Italy, of saying Mass in Loreto in the Holy House, which was translated from Nazareth by miracle.

The Blessed Virgin belonged to a family of Judea that seemed to have partially settled in Galilee. It is generally believed that she was born in Jerusalem, where her parents lived for a time, just within the walls at St. Stephen's gate, and where the church of St. Ann now stands. As already mentioned, the tombs of the parents of the Blessed Virgin are down in the valley below the same gate. It is also commonly believed that both St. Joachim and St. Ann were born in Galilee, in Sepphoris, a little more than three miles north of Nazareth; although some ancient writers claim with good reason that St. Ann was a native of Bethlehem.

It is piously related that St. Ann, born in Bethlehem and retaining her virginity until her twentieth year, was informed by the Angel Gabriel that she should go to the temple in Jerusalem, where she would meet St. Joachim, whom she should marry. St. Joachim was also informed by a messenger of heaven that he should likewise go to the temple, where he would meet St. Ann, who should become his wife. They were both obedient to the will of God, although they kept the communications made to them secret from each other; but for twenty years their marriage was without fruit. At the end of that time St. Joachim, having brought his offerings to the temple, while praying in the court of the Israelites was cast out by the priest Issacher as a dead branch of Juda. He went forth meekly, but prayed that he might return the following year, bearing offerings and a hope for the family of David. At this time St. Ann received a second vision from the Angel Gabriel, in which it was revealed to her that she would be the mother of the Virgin Immaculate, who would be the Mother of God. How beautiful and marked by divine goodness and love are the revelations of Christ to His saints!

The following immediate genealogy of the Blessed Virgin, as given by St. Hippolytus, who received the martyr's crown A.D. 252, is interesting :

"Before Herod's coming to the throne of Judea, under the reign of Cleopatra in Egypt, and Carsoparia in Persia, there dwelt in Bethlehem a priest named Mathan, of the race of David by Solomon. By his wife, Mary, he had three daughters. The eldest, called Mary, after her mother, married at Bethlehem, and had a daughter named Salome. The second, called Sabe, also married in Bethlehem, and was the mother of St. Elizabeth, the mother of St. John the Baptist. The third, Ann, the mother of Mary, of whom Jesus Christ was born, dwelt in Nazareth with an Israelite named Joachim."

We said the votive Mass of the Annunciation, and had the joy of repeating the angelical salutation in the Holy Sacrifice in that very place where Mary first listened to it, as it was borne, not from earth to heaven, but from the royal court of heaven to the abode of humility on earth, by the resplendent messenger of God. Adjoining this chapel, but separated from it, is the chapel and altar of St. Joseph, with the inscription: "*Hic erat subditus illis*"—"Here he was subject to them." Near by is the kitchen of the Blessed Virgin, where, as well as in the workshop of her holy spouse, labor was sanctified.

As in the church of the Holy Sepulchre and the church of the Nativity, so here, numerous lamps and candles are always burning, lighting up dim and dark places with a strange and holy beauty; and silence reigns everywhere, except broken by the musical, solemn chant of the Divine Office or the Holy Sacrifice of the Mass. And, filled with a mysterious awe and love, the soul bows down before its God in praise and rapture, and cries out: "This is the House of God and the Gate of Heaven." How many holy feet have pressed these pavements and this ground since the time when the Holy Ghost overshadowed this place with His power, and the Son of God "bowed down the heavens and descended," and the Eternal Father looked down with a complacent eye, and loved the place which had witnessed the great mystery of the Incarnation! The Blessed Mother of God, her holy spouse St. Joseph, Gabriel, the arch-angelic messenger of Heaven, St. Ann, St. Joachim, and all the holy Apostles of our Lord, knelt here and adored. An ancient tradition says that "immediately on the Ascension of our Lord into heaven, the Apostles and the primitive faithful turned the house into an oratory, wherein they repaired to pray, and that they kept it in great veneration." Here St. Helena came and built a magnificent basilica. Besides the many great saints who came here in the following centuries after St. Helena, in later times came two most eminent servants of God, and wept and prayed on this sacred spot: St. Louis of France, the great crusader, and St. Francis of Assisi, who chose the Holy Places for his earthly inheritance and the heritage of his Order. And since the time that this holy spot was last visited by the Blessed Virgin and St. John, probably no saint has ever here prostrated himself with a more profound spirit of adoration, deeper sentiments of love for the Divine Child Jesus and His holy poverty, and more ardent transports of spiritual joy than St. Francis.

After Mass one other member of our party and myself determined to visit Mount Thabor. The other member preferred to stay in Nazareth. We had only a short time left before taking the steamer for the return voyage. It was our first intention to go to the Sea of Galilee; but our experience of the valley of the Jordan in summer time had already been sufficient. We also had intended to visit Beirout and Damascus, and return to Italy by way of Smyrna and Athens. But on account of the date of the sailing of the steamers, and their tardy connections, reluctantly we had to conclude to retrace our old route Two of us, therefore, determined to get as good a view as possible of the Sea of Galilee and all the surrounding country, from such a commanding position as the summit of the "high mountain" of the Transfiguration.

CHAPTER XIX.

"HIS OWN COUNTRY."

It was yet early in the morning when, mounted on our horses, and with a dragoman to accompany us, we started on our way. Mount Thabor lies about six miles to the south of east of Nazareth. The country intervening is very hilly, and the road, or rather path, very uneven. Just as we left the town we passed by the fountain of the Madonna, where many women were filling their earthen jugs with water. It is the only spring of good water in Nazareth, and every hour of the day, on all the streets, women are seen going to and returning from the fountain with the water-jars upon their heads.

We know but little of Nazareth before the coming of Christ, but we know that in His time the same daily scene was witnessed. And the Blessed Virgin Mary, during her long residence here, must have gone daily to this fountain, often accompanied by the Divine Child Jesus.

From the base to the summit of Mount Thabor the path is very steep and rocky, and to a certain extent dangerous, especially in the descent. Sometimes for a rod or more there would be only a smooth, precipitous rock, with hardly a place on which the horse's foot could catch, so that its feet would slide some distance, and by a slight mishap one would be hurled down the precipice. It takes one hour to ascend or descend the mountain, which is in the form of a truncated cone and rises more than two thousand feet high. It stands almost entirely alone at the east side of the plain of Esdraelon, from which it abruptly rises. It is covered with shrubs and trees, and abounds in game. The entire summit is surrounded by an ancient wall; and the level plateau at the top contains schismatic Greek and Catholic convents, and some massive ruins, evidently of a primitive church and of the time of the Crusaders. It is claimed by some that a town existed here more than a thousand years before the coming of Christ, which met with the various successes and reverses of human fortune. Whether this be true or not, there is nothing in history to indicate that, in the time of our Lord, there was any such settlement here as to preclude this being the place mentioned in the evangelical narrative of the Transfiguration.

The Franciscans have a hospice here in which there were only two members of their order. Several persons besides ourselves were likewise on a visit, and among them a very gaily costumed and gentle-mannered Asiatic young gentleman from Haifa. He was very agreeable towards us, and tried to make our brief stay pleasant and interesting.

Out among the ruins we wandered to the place that beheld the Transfiguration. The scene that was presented to the eyes was magnificent. Towards the east lay the beautiful Sea of Galilee glistening in the sun, and nearer to us the hill of the Beatitudes, where Christ preached the "Sermon on the Mount"; at the base of which was the field where His disciples plucked the ears of corn as they walked on the Sabbath day. As I looked down on the shores of that sea and over that Eastern scene, the quiet and repose of that Sabbath day still seemed to linger. Beyond the lake were the fortress-like mountains of Hauran, in the ancient land of Bashan, and south of them the mountains of Gilead. To the north of the lake appeared the city of Safed, situated high on the mountains, and so prominent to the eye that its visibility seems its chief characteristic. It is the "city seated on a mountain that cannot be hid." Farther north were the ranges of Lebanon and the Great Hermon: "Thabor and Hermon shall rejoice in thy name." To the south and west was the plain of Esdraelon. In every direction numerous villages dotted the hill-sides and plains. Among them to the south, across the plain at the foot of the hills, was Endor, where the witch called up the spirit of Samuel that Saul might consult him and learn of the disasters about to overwhelm him in the battle of Gelboe; and to the southwest was Naim, whose lights we had seen on our way to Nazareth. Beyond them was Little Hermon, and still farther beyond were the mountains of Gelboe (or Gilboa). The range of Carmel stood boldly and grandly against the western sky. The wide-extended plain of Esdraelon, even in summer, appeared very fertile, green, and beautiful. At the foot of Thabor, to the northwest, nestled the little village of Debbora the prophetess; for it was here that Barac the son of Albinoem, and Debbora the prophetess, leading down the mountain-side the army of the Israelites, met and destroyed the hosts of Sisara. This view takes in a large portion of northern and central Palestine; and this vicinity has been the scene of battles between the Jews and Romans, the Moslems and Crusaders, and Napoleon and the Turks. With the eyes of the memory and imagination I seemed to see all these events passing before me, one after the other, in grand historical procession, until the mountain seemed left alone in its solitude.

The sun shone as brightly, but it flashed not upon the bright arms and armor of contending hosts; the shouts of battle and of victory had died away, and the last notes of the victorious canticle of Debbora and Barac, "So let Thy enemies perish, O Lord: but let them that love Thee shine, as the sun shineth in his rising," had melted away into eternal silence, or to burst forth again in the eternal harmonies of heaven. And while the top of the mountain yet seemed to belong to earth, the bright atmosphere a few feet higher seemed bathed in the sunlight of God's glory; and in its midst three forms appeared, "with garments white and glittering as snow, and faces shining as the sun"; and on the top of the mount three humble forms bowed down, men clothed in the poor, coarse garb of Galilean peasants, whose poor, thin faces were pale with fear. The poverty of earth caught a glimpse of the glory of heaven, and was prostrated to the earth in terror, and the peaceful words from the throne of God only transfixed their hearts with a new and greater fear. But how quickly it passed away when Jesus, their Lord, touched them, saying: "Arise, fear not." O happy moment, when the humble heart that has suffered long years from doubts and fears shall hear the reassuring words of its Saviour! Great will be the change in that instant!/

In whatever direction we turned our eyes we saw some road where Christ walked, some place where He taught by parable, revealed a new truth, or performed a miracle. This was indeed "His own country."

Having partaken of the dinner prepared for us at the hospice, we returned to Nazareth. We met numerous parties of Bedouins on horseback wending their way towards the east over the uneven paths between the rocks, and now and then a camel-train bearing burdens of various kinds and going in the same direction.

On our return, although weary, we started out to visit the holy places of Nazareth. Next in interest to the house of the Blessed Virgin, where the church of the Annunciation stands, is the workshop of St. Joseph, which was his home before his espousal to Mary, and which was then and afterwards his workshop, where our Lord as a child and as a young man daily assisted him. It was on the way from the Holy House to the fountain. How frequently then did the Blessed Mother pass this way and stop here and rest, and converse with them as they toiled for their daily bread!

The carpenter-shop of St. Joseph is very attractive to me. In it, as in the home of Mary, human labor was sanctified. When our first parents were driven out of Eden they had been cursed to toil; it was now changed into a blessing, and those most favored of Heaven were appointed to the—humanly speaking—hard lot of daily toil and poverty. St. Joseph is the great model and patron of workingmen, and under his patronage Jesus and Mary will change home into heaven, and the blessings of toil into the treasures of eternity. St. Joseph's workshop was the model workshop of the world. The tools he used were perhaps very primitive and clumsy, and his income was probably very scanty. But his arm was willing and his heart simple and sincere ; his life was honest, and his home purest of the pure. He was a true friend to his neighbor, and Jesus and Mary loved him as he loved them. Oh ! who, in our day, can preach rightly to the workingmen of the world, except he preach from the workshop of St. Joseph? For "him God sanctified in his faith and meekness, and chose him out of all flesh. He glorified him in the sight of kings, and gave him commandments in the sight of his people, and showed him His glory." The labor question can be solved only by aid of the light that still burns on the altar of the workshop of St. Joseph in Nazareth. The site and chapel now belong to the Franciscans. The chapel is an humble one, but it has a beautiful marble altar, beneath which are the words : "*Hic erat subditus illis*"—"Here He was subject to them."

We next went to the schismatic Greek church of the Archangel Gabriel. It is situated over the spring which supplies water to the fountain of the Madonna, to which it is conveyed by means of a conduit. According to the Greek tradition, here the archangel appeared to the Blessed Virgin, who afterwards retired to her house, where she received the heavenly messenger and gave her consent to be the Mother of God. We drank some water from the spring, and then started for the western part of the city. In passing through the streets I noticed that Nazareth is not an over-clean place—in fact, in parts it is rather dirty. But I did not notice any of that extraordinary filth that is spoken of by some writers, a number of whom are Catholics. If a man is looking for filth I suppose he could find it in almost any city or village of the world. The Oriental cities and towns are certainly not any too clean. But where some writers hunted up their piles of filth I cannot imagine. It is natural for some persons to find fault with everything, but they are not usually very honest writers. Their own bile makes everything look bilious to them, and they paint all their pictures for others in the same unnatural colors.

In the western and upper part of the town

is the chapel of Mensa Christi, or Table of Christ. It contains a large, thick, flat stone, ten by twelve feet, in the shape of a table, on which, it is said, Christ ate with His Apostles both before and after the Resurrection. Near it is the Maronite church. On our way back to the hospice, but nearer the centre of the town, is the synagogue, a house like building, which is now the church of the Greek Catholics: "And He came to Nazareth, where He was brought up: and He went into the synagogue, according to His custom, on the Sabbath day; and He rose up to read." The book of Isaias the prophet was delivered to Him, from which He read a prophecy relating to Himself, and, having given up the book, sat down: "And the eyes of all the synagogue were fixed on Him. And He began to say to them: This day is fulfilled this Scripture in your ears." "And they wondered at the words of grace that proceeded from His mouth, and they said: Is not this the son of Joseph?" or, according to another Evangelist: "Is not this the carpenter, the son of Mary?" We had not time to visit the Precipice, nor the chapel of Tremor, where the Nazarenes brought Christ, "that they might cast Him down headlong," and seeing which, in the distance, His holy Mother was seized with a great fear.

Having returned to the hospice, and having made a farewell visit to the church of the Annunciation, we started back to Haifa. Some of the children followed us out of the city for backsheesh. We passed through the country by daylight, which we had not seen before on account of the darkness. We met many loads of grain and straw on donkeys and camels going to the city; and at a fountain about a mile out of Nazareth a Bedouin wanted us to give him tobacco, with which request the smoker of the party readily complied.

The afternoon was pleasant, and towards sunset we halted for a brief rest under the shade of some fine trees on the borders of the valley of the Kisson, or Kishon, and not far distant from the side of Carmel. Some native men, in groups along the road, were returning from the work of the day. A few villages with trees near them appeared as if asleep at the base of the mountains. All nature was in a state of repose, or so quiet in its movements and manifestations of life that its tranquillity was undisturbed. We should soon bid adieu to Palestine, and this peaceful hour at the close of a day sacred in our lives would soon pass into a holy twilight, and the sable curtains of night would quickly descend to shut from our sight the fading scenes of the last day of our pilgrimage in the Holy Land.

For the benefit of those who are interested in ancient biblical narrative I will state that during our journey through Palestine, Jaffa and the road towards Jerusalem for some distance lay in the portion of country allotted to the tribe of Dan, while to the south along the sea-shore our eyes rested on the land of the Philistines, to the east of which appeared the land of Juda, and on the north we beheld the hills and mountains of Ephraim. Jerusalem and the road to Jericho are in Benjamin, while Bethlehem is in Juda. Across the river from the plain of Jericho we saw the portions of Ruben and Gad. In the north, Nazareth and nearly the whole of Galilee through which we passed were in Zabulon, although Mount Thabor is on the borders of Issachar, and the principal part of the great plain of Esdraelon belonged to the same tribe. Across the Sea of Galilee, as well as beyond the mountains of Carmel, lay the land of Manasses. Towards the north our eyes wandered over the lands of Nephtali and Aser, which latter we entered as we approached the sea-coast, for "it reacheth to Carmel by the sea."

CHAPTER XX.

DEPARTURE FROM THE HOLY LAND.

It was rather late at night when we arrived at the Hotel Carmel, of the German colony, and we rose early the next morning to take the boat, which, however, did not start until noon.

Nearly all the afternoon we sailed down the coast of Palestine, looking away over the sea and intervening space at its blue mountain ranges, dreaming dreams of commingled joy, sadness, and solemnity. The mountain of Carmel, ever grand, seen from sea or land, gradually sunk beneath the wave. But the mountains of Ephraim, and lastly the mountains of Judea, had appeared, and I said to myself: "This is the last time that I shall look upon the sacred mountains of the Holy Land." What a strange old land it seemed to me! And I could do nothing but look and dream until night settled down upon the sea and land, and we could see nothing but the lights of Jaffa. The next morning we were still in the port of Jaffa, but set sail during the day. We watched the mountains until they disappeared, and then said, in our hearts, "Farewell!" We were leaving Palestine, but we were returning home.

When we were well under way we noticed a Franciscan father on deck reading a newspaper, and, taking closer observations, we saw that he was reading the New York *Freeman's Journal*. Seeing one of our favorite American Catholic papers, we drew nearer, and recognized a good Franciscan that we had met in Jerusalem, to whom I had twice made my confession. Our first greeting over, we learned that he had been transferred to Alexandria. He had been in the Holy Land about a year, having been previously many years in America. He related many things of interest to us about Palestine, its cities, people, and religious condition; the relations of the various religious bodies—Latins, Greeks, Armenians, and others, Catholic and schismatics of various rites; and the difficulties, hardships, trials, and consolations of the guardians of the sacred places. He said that the authorities at Rome seemed to favor the Oriental rites in the East for a reason readily perceived. He said, if there was any difference, that the Greek Catholics seemed more tenacious of their ancient rites and discipline than the schismatics. He informed us that a Greek, Armenian, or other schismatic, who wishes to become a convert, is not allowed to become a Latin, but is obliged to become a Catholic of his own rite, where a congregation of his own rite exists. How truly Catholic is the Church of God, that takes into consideration all the prejudices, national traditions, and, above all, religious customs held in just reverence by the nations of the earth! We were introduced, on board the steamer, to the postmaster at Jaffa, who is an Arab Catholic of the Greek rite.

To a Catholic from Europe or America it seems strange to find in the Orient Catholics and Catholic churches of so many different rites in the same city, and each rite under a different local ecclesiastical jurisdiction. The ancient city of Damascus might be taken as only a fair example of this frequent occurrence. In 1840 its population was probably under-estimated at 110,000, and the number of Christians was stated to be about 12,000. Of these the schismatic Greeks numbered more than 5,000, Greek Catholics more than 5,000, Maronites about 300, Armenian Catholics about 300, Syrian Catholics about 600, and the Latins a few hundred. Whatever the Christian population in reality may have been in 1840, it is probably double the foregoing figures at the present time, the Catholic Greeks being about equal in numbers to the Greek schismatics, and the other Catholic Oriental rites considerably surpassing in numbers, wealth, and position the corresponding schismatical bodies, which is the reverse, however, in a number of the other cities of Syria.

North of Palestine, in the region of the Lebanon, the Maronites are a very important body of Oriental Catholic Christians. One day, as we were waiting in the hall of the Casa Nova in Jerusalem, four tall, venerable, and dignified strangers, wearing the usual flowing robes of the East, entered the door and passed through to a room in the building. As they passed they saluted us by bowing and placing the right hand to their foreheads and then on their breasts in the Oriental manner, as token of their respect in mind and heart. We were glad of the opportunity of meeting these manly and heroic Christians of northern Syria. Probably we had already seen some of their number, but were unable to distinguish them from others of the finer specimens of Palestine manhood. They number about two hundred thousand and chiefly inhabit the mountains of Lebanon. They claim never to have departed from the orthodox faith or from obedience to the chair of St. Peter. Like all the other Oriental Catholic bodies, they have their own rites and liturgy, and the Church discipline peculiar to the East. They use the Syriac language in their liturgy, the very language which Christ our Lord used when He instituted the holy mysteries. The secular and regular clergy number about twenty-six hundred, and the monks possess many fine monasteries in the Lebanon.

We arrived in Alexandria at noon on Saturday. All the guns of the British war-fleet were about to fire a royal salute. It gave us a good idea of the bombardment of Alexandria without its terrible results. It seemed the more real, as we recognized the names of several war-ships that took part in that battle. We went on shore and drove to Abbat's Hotel. There we saw late papers for the first time in a month, in which we learned the name of the nominee of one of the great political parties for the Presidency of the United States, and found a confirmation of the rumors which we had heard in Jaffa that cholera had broken out in southern France. Towards evening we took a walk through the streets to get a last good look at Oriental scenes, which now we might enjoy, although they were no longer possessed of novelty.

The next day was Sunday and the Feast of the holy Apostles Peter and Paul. We celebrated Mass in the cathedral of St. Catharine, and for my Mass I was directed to the altar of St. Peter. Some of those who assisted at the Mass which I celebrated were afterwards with us on the steamer. /

EUROPE.

CHAPTER XXI.

FROM ALEXANDRIA TO NAPLES.

On our arrival in Alexandria we were undecided as to the route by which we should return to Europe; but, as we were desirous of making haste on account of the summer weather, we decided to take the French steamer which sailed on Sunday forenoon for Naples. It is a more lonesome route than some others, but we were rewarded with the sight, within the space of the last twenty-four hours, of the three great volcanic mountains—Etna, Stromboli, and Vesuvius. We drove to the harbor in a carriage with an Egyptian guide, who told us that our former guide was taking a vacation, as he was able to do so, being quite wealthy. He appeared to feel at home with us and to enjoy himself, and laughed quite heartily as he narrated the efforts of some English ladies to convert him to "Christianity."

An hour afterwards our vessel steamed out of the harbor, and by noon the Egyptian coast disappeared from our sight beneath the distant horizon of waters, and to us the East, the dream-land and wonder-land, lived only in the past and in our imagination. Until some time beyond the middle of the afternoon of the fourth day we saw only the blue billows of the deep. But the sea was not so dreary as the ocean, for nearly always some white-winged messenger of peace and plenty—which under the bright rays of the sun appeared like fleecy clouds of snow and then again like transparent golden banners —skirted the horizon or moved majestically onward at a more neighborly distance. The cabin passengers were all French except ourselves and a solitary German who seemed to possess both a gentlemanly and sensitive nature, but who did not appear to feel at home among so many Frenchmen. As for us, we thoroughly enjoyed our French company, and we had a good opportunity of observing their polite bearing, light hearts, and genial dispositions, ever unchangeable during the voyage. We had music, songs, and lively conversations; and sometimes the ladies and gentlemen, including the captain and first mate, skipped the rope like children, to see who could make the best record, which was always greeted with rounds of applause. Sometimes the sea itself seemed to catch the infectious spirit of jollity, and would take on playful moods and start into quick motions that would set all the passengers dancing until they were sick of it.

About two or three hours before sunset we came in sight of Sicily, and rising high among its mountain peaks was volcanic Etna, whose summit, ten thousand feet above the level of the sea, marked a short line against the blue sky. Nearer and nearer we approached the land, and the great mountain gradually revealed more clearly its grand proportions. We sat on deck and looked out over the smooth sea towards the land and mountains until night settled down over all. What a sublime and terrific sight that mountain would have presented to us two years later, as it cast forth its liquid streams of fire into the black heavens of night, lighting up mountains, land, and sea with its lurid light!/

The next morning at dawn there was something about the movement of the vessel that made me think we were not far from land, and I hastily arose and looked out of our state-room window. The land was near by, and we were passing between the Scylla and Charybdis of the ancients, where, according to Grecian mythology, two horrid monsters dwelt on opposite sides, ever ready to swallow up unlucky navigators. In former ages it was certainly considered a dangerous place in navigation, but in modern times it has lost most of its terrors. I dressed as hastily as possible and went on deck, but by that time we were gradually moving out into wider waters, and the narrower channel was left behind. Huge banks of jagged clouds rested over the land, and they stood so calmly, with their white-capped and gray-mantled peaks, that at first I mistook them for high mountains, and it took close observation to dispel the romantic illusion. /

About the middle of the forenoon we came in sight of Stromboli, which is a volcanic mountain island, rising three thousand feet out of the sea. Although we could discern at the base of the mountain a space containing a town of many houses, it otherwise looked like an island formed of a single mountain, rising directly out of the waves into a solitary peak. It is said to have been an active volcano for two thousand years, and is called the "light-house of the Mediterranean," but we did not discover any signs to indicate, at the present time, the fitness of the name. From about half-way up its sides it was covered with a cloud, which at times would break in pieces, revealing the summit, which would again quickly be hidden.

The remainder of the day we sailed up the uneven Italian coast, with nothing more to interest us than the sight of land, and sailing-vessels scudding over the water in every direction, and dignified steamships, under clouds of smoke, starting on their journey to southern and eastern countries.

Towards evening we came in sight of the Bay of Naples. It was one of the rarest and most beautiful scenes ever painted on my memory. The entrance to the bay, from Cape Miseno on the north to Cape Campanella on the south, is twenty miles in width. To our right, at the south of the bay, were mountain heights adorned with numerous villages and cities, many of which were founded by Grecian colonists five hundred years before Christ. Immediately at our left was the high, rocky island of Capri, looming up like a grand, impregnable fortress. This island was the favorite resort of the Roman emperors Augustus and Tiberius, and of many of the old Roman nobility. Towards the north entrance rose the island of Ischia, noted for its earthquakes and volcanoes. Before us was the fair bay, beyond which was the beautiful city. And towering over all was mighty Vesuvius, belching forth its black and threatening volume of smoke, which, as evening came on, became at frequent intervals a lurid red, for an instant appearing like an angry demon lighting the darkness with his infernal torch. But when we first entered the bay and rounded the southern coast all was calm, bright, and beautiful; a clear blue sky overhead, the blue waters of the sea beneath, and on the land commingled green and white, and changing colors everywhere; and all—sky, water, vessels with their white sails, cities, and land—were bathed in the limpid light of the setting sun. An American man-of-war in the harbor was covered with flags and bunting, for the next day was the Fourth of July.

As we came to anchor and the shades of evening began to deepen, we heard the loud, distinct voice of military orders on a neighboring Italian man-of-war, followed by the beat of drum and the clear, musical notes of the trumpet; and the dark pall of night rested on the bright scenes of day, as the pall of death rests upon the fair face of beauty. And the lights that quickly rose in the city, like those of the death-watch, added an appearance of reality to the comparison.

The next morning, as we stepped on shore, we realized that we were in a new world. The sacred places and associations of the Holy Land were no longer ours, but our feet rested on a land that, with all its faults, is still Catholic. And everywhere over the land were sanctuaries and sacred temples, hallowed by the divine presence of Jesus Christ in their holy tabernacles.

But our first impressions on landing were not pleasant. The chief officer of the custom-house happened to be present, and the under-officials showed great zeal in unpacking our baggage and hunting in every nook and corner for tobacco—which two of us never use—and for articles of devotion, such as rosaries and crucifixes, some of which we had bought in Rome but most of which in Palestine, and which we were carrying through Italy as presents to our friends and parishioners in America. Perhaps we did not sufficiently "possess our souls in patience," or pay the duties, which we had to pay, with sufficient meekness, nor did we speak complimentary words of the decency of a government that is Catholic even in name and does such things. We blamed the officials, in which we were probably wrong, as they were only the dutiful servants of a needy and greedy government, whose own people everywhere feel the slavery of a grinding taxation. It was the Fourth of July, and we were perchance a little inflated with the spirit of American independence, and expected too much. We were foolish enough to expect decency in a matter where we knew that the legislators had a right in law to disregard it. We expected too much when we looked for decency from a government that steals convents and churches and robs the Vicar of Christ. Yet in justice I must add that all over Italy we found many officials, both civil and military, who were kind and obliging in their manners, and gentlemen in every respect. And, so far as I am personally concerned, I have no complaints to make of my treatment by the Italian people, and I got to like the greater number of those with whom I formed any acquaintance. In few countries would I sooner live than in Italy, only I would not wish to become a citizen of the Italian kingdom. I consider the Italian population as a too patient people, Catholic at heart, toiling under the burdens and oppression of ambitious rulers and the unprincipled classes who uphold them. We afterwards noticed over the customhouse a beautiful statue of the Immaculate Conception, which quieted our disturbed feelings. No one has a more sincere loyalty to the flag of his country than I have for the Stars and

Stripes, but I was never in love with the brazen goddess of liberty. May the day quickly come when the Immaculate Queen of Heaven will be invoked by our nation to bless the starry banner of freedom!

CHAPTER XXII.

"SEE NAPLES AND THEN DIE."

WE took a carriage and drove to the Hôtel de Rome. During the forenoon we made arrangements with a guide for a carriage and driver and his own service for a visit to the ruined city of Pompeii. It is situated twelve miles southeast of Naples, yet the houses along the streets were so continuous that we hardly perceived that we had left the city. Naples possesses more than three hundred churches, and we passed many of them on our way. From the inscriptions on those which we saw we learned that a large number of them are dedicated to the Blessed Virgin under some one of her titles; and at almost every corner there was a picture of the Blessed Virgin, or the Blessed Mother and Divine Child. Some special festival of the Blessed Virgin had lately been celebrated, and hanging across the street, through which we drove for about a mile, as nearly as I could judge the distance, were cords and wires—only a brief space apart—each one upholding many lights of various kinds. It must have been a grand display and illumination in honor of the Queen of Heaven, and Naples appeared to me in a better and more beautiful light than it ever had before, for I have great confidence in a people that has such tender love and devotion for the Mother of God. After we had gone a certain distance we noticed that a cross was marked on all the houses, and on many of them was a painting representing a bishop making the sign of the cross towards Vesuvius. This is in honor of the miracle that occurred on that terrible day in December, 1831, when the city was experiencing repeated shocks of earthquakes, and the dread fires of Vesuvius were rolling down towards the city, threatening it with destruction, when the archbishop went forth bearing the blood of St. Januarius, and with it made the sign of the cross over the burning mountain, and its devouring torrents of fire were stayed in their course and the city was saved. When I saw these pictures on the houses I took them to represent St. Januarius making the sign of the cross over Vesuvius, but it is probable that they are representations of the archbishop with the reliquary.

The road to Pompeii led near the bay, along whose shores were charming villas surrounded by pleasure-grounds and flower-gardens, such as can be found only in a climate as delicious as that of Naples. With frequent glimpses of the bay and its surrounding peopled heights, and a constant view of great Vesuvius before us, and frequent changes of nearer passing scenes, we journeyed over the road. On our arrival at the entrance to Pompeii we heard a party of about twenty singing familiar words to a familiar air; they were evidently citizens of the great republic of the West, over which the sun shines at his zenith during about one-eighth part of the time of an entire revolution of the globe. They were singing the "Star-Spangled Banner." They were about to make the ascent of Vesuvius, and, as we were to visit Pompeii, after a short and friendly acquaintance we separated, perhaps to meet but once in our lives, and then at the gates of a dead city in a far-off foreign land. As they left us it occurred to me that it was not the first Fourth of July that our countrymen had approached "the crater" beneath which slumber volcanoes. We were soon afterwards inside the walls of Pompeii. This was a city five centuries before the coming of Christ, and how much older it is history does not inform us with sufficient certainty. In the year 79 A.D. it was destroyed by an eruption of Vesuvius, and lay buried under volcanic deposits for seventeen centuries, to be brought to the light in our age, revealing to our eyes the homes, customs, and domestic life of the Roman people two thousand years ago.

We walked through silent streets and entered tenantless houses whose last masters had left them in haste, so that they were found eighteen hundred years afterwards just as they were when last occupied, the furniture in its place, and sometimes the table with its dishes and food ready for a repast. The owner's name is often inscribed over the door, and the various rooms are pointed out which the family occupied for different purposes; even the profession or trade of the householder and his manner of life can be determined. Frescoes are painted on the walls adorning the different rooms, revealing the tastes and enjoyments of their former occupants. Their wine-shops where drink was sold are well preserved, and cavities in stone where different kinds of drink were kept, and slabs of marble on which wines and liquors were dealt to customers, look as if they might have been used yesterday. The places of amusement and the military barracks are not different than those which are well preserved in other cities. The temples of the pagan gods and goddesses, with their statues, and altars on which sacrifices were offered, are well kept, and in many respects appear very much as they must have looked had we entered them the day before their terrible visitation. The streets are narrow, and it is not far from the curbstone of one sidewalk to that of the other; but they are well paved with stone, in which are well-worn ruts made by the chariot-wheels of those early times.

In the museum near the entrance were several petrified bodies of human beings and animals, in the exact position they were, and with the expression of agonized terror that was on their faces, when they were overtaken by the element that destroyed life but preserved all else. About one third of the city has been excavated, and laborers are constantly employed by the government at the same work. When we were there it was the time of their siesta, and they were lying in the shade of ancient walls, some of them fast asleep. This unfortunate city occupied one of the fairest sites that the earth could afford. As I looked around me on that early afternoon I did not wonder that the ancients built a city in such dangerous proximity to Vesuvius. On the one side were the calm, blue waters of the bay with its picturesque frame; on the other side was the grand mountain raising its giant head into the azure heavens. Between the mountain and sea was a plateau, sufficiently large for a city, and gradually sloping downwards to the surrounding country with its groves and farms, gardens and villas, over which the eye could wander at pleasure; and this fair scene reposed under the clear, dreamy sky of southern Italy. Having bought some mementoes of the place from soldiers and others, we returned to Naples.

Among the prominent objects in Naples which frequently attract attention are its castles. Three are especially noticeable: Castel del' Ovo—the Egg, so called on account of its oval form—occupying an island near the shore and built in the eleventh century; Castel Nuovo, on the mainland near the Port, and built in the thirteenth century; and Castel St. Elmo, on the heights overlooking the city. We rose rather early the next morning, as we wished to make a few remaining visits before leaving on the train for Rome early in the afternoon. Having dressed, I was looking out of the window at the morning street scenes when I saw coming up the street a priest in surplice and stole, walking under a baldachin, and bearing a ciborium with the Blessed Sacrament. Several persons with colored lanterns preceded him. He was a priest from the neighboring parish church of St. Lucy returning from a sick-call. The people on the street, for the most part, showed proper reverence for the Most Holy Sacrament by kneeling as it was borne by, and just in front of the hotel a street-car was passing down the street. The driver immediately stopped the car and knelt in his place; more than one-third of the passengers got out of the car and knelt in the street, and more than half the rest knelt in the car, while a few remaining persons kept their seats with more or less indifference. I suppose they belonged to the class of infidels and free-thinkers who disgrace modern Italy, or some of them may have come from those unfortunate countries where faith is looked on as superstition. But, taken all in all, the scene was edifying, and one which is frequently witnessed in Catholic lands.

After breakfast we took a carriage and rode first to the church of St. Dominic, in order to see as much as possible of the locality made sacred by the presence and labors of St. Thomas of Aquin. We saw several places of his more public ministry, but were unfortunate in not being able, for some reason or another, to enter the room where, raised from the floor in fervent prayer, a voice was heard directed to him from the crucifix: "Thou hast written well of Me, Thomas: what recompense dost thou desire?" To which he answered: "No other than Thyself, O Lord." We were shown, however, the tombs and skeletons of the Anjou princes, which we did not care to see; although St. Alphonsus Liguori, who was born in Naples, would probably have made them the subject of a meditation on death.

We next drove to the National, formerly Bourbonic, Museum, one of the finest and most extensive in the world. It contains hundreds of frescoes brought from the ruins of Pompeii; and although the best of them have been transferred to the museum, I better appreciated those that I saw on the walls where they were painted, and overlooking the rooms which they ornamented for their owners in the long-departed past. I do not intend to publish a catalogue of any museum, but I may state that among the thousands of curiosities and works of art contained in this one, those of world-wide fame are the Farnese Hercules and Farnese bull.

When in Palestine we had expressed to a Franciscan father our intention of visiting Bologna to see the body of St. Catharine of Bologna. He advised us to go to the Franciscan church in Naples to see the incorrupt body of St. John Joseph. We therefore next drove to the Franciscan church for that purpose. On stating the object of our visit to one of the fathers, we were taken through the sacristy to an interior chapel, where he lighted the candles over the altar, and, drawing two curtains aside, revealed the body and face of the saint. We could see only the face clearly, but it was perfectly incorrupt and natural, and, while evidently the face of a corpse, it looked like the face of one who had died yesterday. Having knelt and prayed to this pure saint, whose pure body lay before us, and having received some pious mementoes of the church, we returned to the hotel.\

We would leave Naples in a few hours, and during that time we could not be idle; so we sauntered through the streets until near train-time, enjoying the gay life and lively manners of the people. It is not to be expected that the traveller will relate the story of his rambles through the streets of different cities; but after all it may be to himself one of the most pleasant, interesting, and instructive parts of his travels. I may not often speak of it, but we never failed to make such walks necessary incidents of our visits. Since the cholera broke out in Italy I have frequently heard the expression, "dirty Naples." These words may be true of some sections of the city which I did not see; one of my companions says he met with such districts, and on our first visit I noticed that the neighborhood of Virgil's tomb possessed an unsavory atmosphere. But on our last visit I rode and walked many miles through its streets, and I hardly found a cleaner city in Europe; and I remember several in northern Europe and in America that were much dirtier, although their climate may be more favorable to their sanitary condition.

The afternoon found us moving out through the suburbs of the city, past gardens and vineyards, towards the north on our way to Rome. The luxuriant foliage of the frequent clumps and groves of trees was much more pleasing to our eyes than it was on our downward journey, for since that time we had become accustomed to the more barren scenery of Palestine. A little past the middle of the afternoon we again came in sight of Monte Cassino. For a full half-hour we had the privilege of beholding its grand, fortress-like walls, while we were stopping at the station and as we continued our way up the beautiful valley. It is, indeed, a grand old fortress against "the world, the flesh, and the devil." The first rain-storm that we had seen since we left for the East now threatened us. The dark clouds rested over the tops of the mountains and deepened the shadows in the valleys, but it proved to be a mild, refreshing shower, without thunder and lightning.

The monastery stands on the brow of a mountain, looking down upon a fertile plain, which is nearly surrounded by mountains and extends into the narrower valleys north and south through which the railroad runs. The mountain scenery is stern and grand, but the valleys below are fair and smiling. St. Benedict certainly chose a grand solitude for the mother house of his Order; but to what extent since that time the wilderness has blossomed into roses and the surrounding country grown rich in fields of golden grain, by means of the self-denying toil of his monks, I will not stop to narrate, as we must hasten on towards Rome, from which this sacred and impregnable mountain has received its divine strength, and of which Monte Cassino has been, during fourteen centuries, a mighty fortress, sending forth from its gates legions of Christian soldiers to the four corners of the earth. As I beheld that long line of conquerors marching out of those venerable monastic walls, as the pale, ascetic faces of many of them were revealed in the first rays of the morning sun, I saw that they already glowed with the light of victory; and even now around the heads of some shone the aureola of sanctity, growing brighter and more beautiful as they advanced, changing at times into the radiant and glorious crown of prophetic martyrdom.

CHAPTER XXIII.

THE ETERNAL CITY.

Towards evening we were again passing through the charming remote environs of Rome. It was dark when we arrived in the city, and we took the omnibus of the Hôtel Minerva. We secured pleasanter rooms than we had occupied at the time of our first visit, and we engaged them for ten or eleven days, with breakfast and *table-d'hôte*, the latter at four o'clock.

The next day was Sunday, and, as we had not yet presented our papers to the cardinal-vicar to get our "Celebret," we decided to attend Mass at St. Peter's. We crossed the bridge of St. Angelo, built by Hadrian more than seventeen hundred years ago to connect his tomb with the city, and passed near the Castle of St. Angelo, built by the same emperor to be his tomb, where the Roman emperors and their families were buried until the time of Septimius Severus, and perhaps later. We were now approaching the ancient Vatican mount, which in the time of the Roman Republic was occupied by suburban gardens, where dwelt those in humble life, which under the Empire were turned into public pleasure-gardens and parks; and on that eminence just before us, where rises the grandest structure of the world, was the circus of the infamous Nero. In this vicinity St. Peter was crucified, and the cross of the Vatican, like that of Calvary, became symbolical of suffering and victory. And beneath the centre of that wondrous dome his body was laid at rest.

We soon reached the Piazza of St. Peter, which is 1,100 feet in length by about 800 feet in its extreme breadth, partially encircled by colonnades, each having four rows of columns,

284 of which and 88 buttresses forming three covered passages, whose roofs are surmounted by 162 statues of saints. In the centre of this piazza is an Egyptian obelisk, brought from the city of Heliopolis in the first years of the first century of the Christian era, and placed in the Vatican circus by Caligula, third emperor of Rome. It was placed in its present site in the sixteenth century. On either side is a large fountain, whose waters, rising in jets and spray, shone with prismatic colors in the bright light of a summer morning sun.

Before us to the right was the immense palace of the Vatican, which is the largest palace in the world. It is said to contain 11,000 halls, chapels, salons, and private apartments. It is many stories high, and covers an area about 770 feet in width by 1,150 feet in length. Only a relatively small portion is set apart for the direct use of the papal household. Even under the present civil rule the palaces of the Vatican and Lateran, and Castle Gandolfo, are declared by the Italian "guarantees" to be exterritorial.\

As we entered through the great doors of St. Peter's we seemed to witness the vast procession of pilgrims who in past centuries had passed over this same ground, even if in earlier ages their feet had not trod the same pavement, to pray before the tomb of the Prince of the Apostles; for the poor, illiterate Galilean Fisherman has become the Prince of Christendom. This church was founded by Constantine the Great; and Charlemagne and Alfred the Great, and a long line of emperors and kings, have here received their crowns from the Successors of the Fisherman. Near the entrance is a round block of porphyry on which the emperors were formerly crowned. The length of St. Peter's, including the portico, is about 700 feet, and its width—that is, the interior length of the transept—is 450 feet; its height to the summit of the cross is 435 feet. When we entered, Solemn High Mass was in progress at an altar erected before the crypt. The singing, which was without organ accompaniment, was a delight not merely to the ears but to the soul. I noticed that the celebrant did not sit during the singing of the Credo, but continued the Mass. Having assisted at a good portion of this Mass, we began to watch the sacristy door in order to discover a priest about to celebrate a Low Mass which we might attend. We had not long to wait. A half-dozen men of the working-class attended the same Mass, who knelt during the whole time, and seemed to assist with true devotion. At first it may strike the stranger, passing his first Sunday in Rome, that but few people attend the different Masses. At some Masses there might be not more than half a dozen, and at others from one to two hundred persons were in attendance. But when we consider that there are 365 churches for a population of about 300,000, that many of these are children and persons not bound to attend Mass, and the large number of Masses in nearly all the churches, and the number of priests, students, and religious, male and female, who attend Mass in their own chapels, the number of those who assist at the Holy Sacrifice must be relatively large. Having fulfilled our obligation, we were attracted to a crowd of persons collected at the end of the church under the chair of St. Peter. On approaching we found that a bishop was confirming a number of children, and the parents and friends were gathered around.

During the remainder of the day we visited a number of other churches, even the names of which I cannot now remember; but I believe that the Pantheon was among them, as it was only a short distance from our hotel. It was built by Agrippa about twenty-seven years before the Christian era, and it was probably called the Pantheon because, being lighted by a single opening in the centre above, it bears resemblance to the vault of heaven, the supposed residence of the gods. In the year 609 it was converted into a Christian temple and dedicated to the Blessed Virgin and all the martyrs; and it was at this time that the Festival of All Saints was instituted by Pope Boniface IV. It is the best preserved and noblest former temple of paganism in Rome. It has a portico in front, 110 feet wide and 44 feet deep, which is supported by 16 Corinthian columns of Oriental granite, with bases and capitals of white marble. They are 41½ feet in height and 15 feet in circumference. The main building is round, 143 feet in diameter and the same in height, with walls 20 feet in thickness. It contains the tomb of Raphael and the tombs of many other celebrated artists. Victor Emmanuel is buried here, and over his tomb were hung the symbols of mourning. The Pantheon is still used as a church.

That afternoon we paid a visit to the American College, where we were kindly received by the pro-rector, Rev. Dr. Schulte, who offered to send our papers to the Vicariatus, that they might be endorsed with the permission to celebrate Mass while we remained in the city. During our stay in Rome I celebrated Mass six times: three times in St. Peter's; once in the crypt at the altar beneath which rest the body of St. Peter and a good portion of the body of St. Paul; once at the altar over the bodies of the holy Apostles St. Simon and St. Jude; and once at the altar over the body of St. Gregory the Great. I celebrated Mass twice in the Gesù; once at the altar over the body of St. Ignatius, founder of the Society of Jesus; and once at the altar of St. Francis Xavier, my patron saint. Often had I desired to visit the cathedral of Goa, in the far East, where the body of St. Francis Xavier is preserved incorrupt; but, not having that joyful privilege, I took advantage of the opportunity to say Mass at his altar in Rome beneath his incorrupt hand and arm, which are preserved over the altar in an oval golden plate—that glorious hand that was so often raised towards heaven in God's ministry, that baptized so many pagans, that was raised so often in the sacrament of reconciliation, and that touched with such reverence and bore aloft with such a profound spirit of adoration the body and blood of Jesus Christ. I also celebrated Mass once at the principal altar in the church of Santa Maria sopra Minerva. Beneath this altar is the body of the wonderful "dear St. Catharine of Sienna." This altar has been remodelled and renewed, and consecrated by Pius IX, and the body of St. Catharine has been brought from a side-altar and placed under it; but after all it is the same altar before which the great doctor of the Church, St. Alphonsus Liguori, was consecrated bishop. Since we had but a short time before said Mass on Calvary and in the Holy Sepulchre, and in other sacred places of the Holy Land, it might be doubted if we properly appreciated the full value of the privileges that we now enjoyed. In a certain sense we valued them much more than we would have otherwise; for to the heart which Jesus Christ has lately touched the whole world seems on fire with love. /

On Monday forenoon we drove to the convent of St. Calixtus in Trastevere, which is occupied by the Benedictines of St. Paul. I had a letter of introduction — which had kindly been given me by an American bishop — to Right Rev. Dr. Smith, O.S.B., Consultor of the Holy Office, and who since that time has become an abbot. As Dr. Smith is a member of several of the Roman congregations, he was absent from the convent in attendance at one of their meetings. We left the letter, and Dr.

Smith called on us early the next forenoon at the Minerva with offers to show us any kindness in his power. As we knew that he must be very busy, and perhaps often bothered by travellers, we requested of him as little as possible, but hold in grateful remembrance his ready willingness to be of service to us. On leaving the convent we visited the church of Santa Maria in Trastevere, which is in close proximity to St. Calixtus.

This church was founded by Pope St. Calixtus in the year 224, and was the first church in Rome dedicated to the Blessed Virgin. It was built over a fountain of oil which miraculously sprung up at the time of the birth of Christ, as attested by ancient writers, both pagan and Christian. The present edifice was rebuilt in the twelfth century by Pope Innocent II. We were now in the region of the city where the inhabitants boast of being descendants of the ancient Romans. It is narrated that once when one of them wished to see the Holy Father, and was repulsed by a Swiss guard, he proudly replied: "Barbarian, I am of ancient Roman blood, and moreover of Trojan." Whether the Swiss understood what he said is not related; nor do authors inform us whether the Trasteverian had been reading light literature.

During the remainder of this day and on following days we made various excursions through Rome, but I will not attempt to date the particular days on which they were made, describing them only in the order, or nearly the order, of their occurrence. Before making any more journeys it may be well to preface them with the following introduction: Rome was founded by Romulus—descended from Æneas, Prince of Troy—753 years before the birth of Christ, and reached the summit of its greatness under the Empire in the time of Augustus. Including its thickly-populated suburbs, it must have extended over an area thirty miles in diameter, possessing from 3,000,000 to 5,000,000 inhabitants, and was adorned with many thousand magnificent palaces and temples. Seated on her seven hills, she was queen of the whole civilized world. Though her citizens travelled to the most distant lands and entered the gates of strangely foreign cities, a Roman soldier stood on guard at every gate. On the shining waters of every sea then known to the civilized nations of the earth, the oars of the Roman galleys flashed in the bright sunlight. In order that the reader may revive a few facts in his memory, I would remind him that ancient Rome was built on both banks of the Tiber, but was chiefly situated on its eastern side. It occupied seven hills, and in fact extended upon several others. Commencing at the northeast, and continuing down the eastern part of the city towards the south, the Quirinal, Viminal, Esquiline, and Cælian lie in irregular order. Southwest of the Cælian and near the Tiber is the picturesque Aventine, north of which is the Palatine, adorned with the palaces of the Cæsars; and northwest of the Palatine is the Capitoline, the site of the citadel and of the great temple of Jupiter, and the smallest but most important hill of ancient Rome. Northwest of the Capitoline is the famous Campus Martius, enclosed in a bend of the Tiber. Across the river are the Janiculum and Vatican hills, the latter northeast of the former. At the present time the northernmost hill on the east side of the Tiber is the Pincian. I have not pretended to be exact in my description of the relative position of these hills, but have rather attempted to give a rough sketch, which the mind will be apt to retain. For example, while I have stated that the Quirinal is north of the Viminal, I have left out the fact that it also bounds its whole western extent; for to draw every boundary line in an entire city which is not familiar to most readers, would only serve to confuse them. To give a too full description is often hardly to describe at all.

One of our first excursions was over a portion of the way with which we became partly acquainted at the time of our first visit. We entered the ruins of the mighty Coliseum—called also the Flavian amphitheatre—one of the greatest works of men. It is situated between the Palatine, Esquiline, and Cælian hills, and was commenced and finished in the first century of the Christian era. It is four stories high, built in the form of an ellipse, attaining a height of 157 feet, and 630 feet long by 513 feet wide, covering six acres of ground, and capable of accommodating more than 100,000 spectators. In the celebration of some of its great feasts 5,000 wild beasts and 10,000 gladiators were engaged. St. Ignatius, a convert of St. John the Evangelist, and Bishop of Antioch, and thousands of early Christian martyrs, moistened the soil of its arena with their life-blood. I saw with sadness that Christianity has taken away the emblems of religion and abandoned it again to paganism, but the blood of its martyrs is the seed that shall give birth to the new army of heroes and saints who at no distant time shall destroy modern heathenism with the fiery, avenging sword of Christian charity. We next visited the ancient church of St. Clement. It is partly in the hands of the Irish Dominicans. St. Clement—who is spoken of by St. Paul in his Epistle to the Philippians—was third pope after St. Peter, and this church was erected over the site of the house of his family. From excavations that have been made in modern times the ruins of an older, grander, and much more extensive church have been found beneath the present edifice; and still lower has been discovered masonry belonging to imperial and republican Rome. Under the high altar are the bones of St. Ignatius, St. Clement, and Flavius Clemens, a martyred cousin of the Emperor Domitian.

In this church is a marble slab which contains an inscription that tells such a touching story of piety that I will transcribe it from a celebrated work on Rome: "In the sixth century there lived at Rome a holy beggar named Servulus. He was paralyzed from his childhood, and could neither stand straight, nor raise his hand to his mouth, or turn himself on his bed. His brother and his mother watched over him, and carried him each day to the church of St. Clement, and placed him in the vestibule. He gave to the other poor all that he received in charity, beyond what was necessary for his own wants. He used to stop the faithful, and ask them to do some charity for his soul. They willingly read for him some chapters from the holy books. He listened so attentively that he soon knew the entire of Holy Scripture. He then daily passed his time in singing the praises of God. His sufferings only rendered his fervor greater and his voice sweeter. One day, as he lay on his bed in the vestibule of the church, he asked the poor and pilgrims who were around him to pray and sing for him, as he knew his end was approaching. He joined with them in their songs of praise. Suddenly he desired them to stop and listen to the sweet melody of the heavenly choir. At these words he expired, and his soul went to join the angels in their eternal song."

The Irish Dominican father who accompanied us through the edifice would not go with us, at that season of the year, into the excavations under the church, for he said that he had once got the Roman fever in that way; so we lighted our tapers and went alone. It was not so interesting as it would have been if we had studied the subject better beforehand, and had been perfectly sure that we might not at any moment fall into the bowels of the earth. It contains a number of figures and frescoes extending through seven centuries, but which could not be seen to such good advantage as those in the Christian museum of the Lateran, or those in the long staircase leading into the church of St. Agnes outside the walls. /

During the afternoon we again visited the basilica of St. John Lateran. This church is situated on the Cælian Hill, near the walls, in the southeast part of the city. In front of the church is the largest Egyptian obelisk in the world, and the oldest object in Rome. With the pedestal it is 153 feet in height and weighs 600 tons. It is of red granite, and was erected before the temple of the sun in Thebes nearly thirty-five hundred years ago. The church of the Lateran is the cathedral church of the Pope, and takes precedence of all other churches in the world. Hence it bears upon its noble front the inscription: "The most holy Lateran Church, the mother and head of all the churches of the city and world." It was founded by Constantine, and was so magnificent in gold and silver that it was called the Golden Basilica. But I must conform to my original intention, and not write a guide-book or one filled with dry and uninteresting details. For what are even artistic statues and paintings in comparison with the spiritual beauty and historical greatness of the edifice? Yet I did not pass by its colossal statues and ancient mosaics—even though I omit to describe them—without a profound admiration for the vast and skilful labors that genius has bestowed on the construction and adornment of this venerable cathedral. At the time of our visit a very expensive restoration was being made, which has since been brought to a completion worthy of the ancient fame of the "mother and mistress of churches."

The papal altar of St. John Lateran contains a large portion of the one on which St. Peter offered the Holy Sacrifice; and over it are the heads of St. Peter and St. Paul. In this church are preserved the table on which our Lord instituted the Holy Eucharist, a part of the purple robe put over His shoulders in the court of the palace of Pilate, a piece of the sponge filled with vinegar and gall which they offered Him to drink, a part of the tunic which St. John the Evangelist wore, and a part of a chain with which he was bound, as well as other relics of many saints and martyrs. Five general councils have assembled within the venerable walls of this basilica, and a long line of popes have here been enthroned. As on our first visit we had ascended the Holy Stairway near the Lateran, we did not on this occasion perform that sorrowful devotion. We paid a brief visit to the Lateran palace, which was the residence of the popes for a thousand years. It is now turned into a museum, where we saw a fine collection of sarcophagi, engravings, and inscriptions, taken from the catacombs and ancient churches and basilicas. /

We next went to the church of Santa Croce in Gerusalemme. The church of the Holy Cross in Jerusalem is situated east of the church of St. John Lateran, and on the southeastern extremity of the Esquiline. After Constantine had seen the sign of the cross in the sky, and had been converted to Christianity, his mother, St. Helena, found the true cross in Jerusalem. She brought it to Rome, together with a large quantity of soil from Mount Calvary. For their reception Constantine then built this church, which has since been several times restored. The church and relics are now in the hands of the Cistercians. We were conducted by a monk to a chapel in connection with the church, where we were shown some of the most sacred relics anywhere preserved—a large portion of the true cross, thorns from the crown of our Saviour, one of the nails that was driven through His sacred flesh into the cross, one of the fingers which St. Thomas put into the wound of His side, and a large part of the cross of the penitent thief. This church also contains the inscription placed over the head of the Crucified: "Jesus of Nazareth, the King of the Jews." In the pavement of the church are a number of stones brought from the hill of Calvary. At the present time the situation of Santa Croce seems like a country place in the suburbs of the city.

Our next visit was made to St. Maria Maggiore, called also St. Mary's of the Snow and St. Mary's of the Crib. It is the largest and chief church in Rome dedicated to the Blessed Virgin, and is one of the oldest churches in the world. About the middle of the fourth century a noble Roman husband and wife, desiring to devote their patrimony to the Blessed Virgin for the honor and service of God, saw in the night a vision of the Blessed Mother, who directed them to build a church in her honor on the place which on the following morning should be covered with snow. When the next day dawned upon the world it revealed the Esquiline hill covered with a beautiful mantle of snow, although it was in the month of August, a season of extreme heat in Rome. Pope Liberius and the noble patrician John came to explain to the people the meaning of the miracle, for a great number had gathered together to witness so strange a sight. A grand church was soon erected and dedicated to the Mother of God, which, although several times restored or enlarged, was the same one we now entered. In its construction as well as in its more recent restorations rich and rare materials were used that have been obtained from different sources, the ceilings being gilded with the first gold brought by Columbus from America.

The most important relic preserved in this church is that which gives it one of its titles—the crib or manger in which the Divine Child was laid in the stable of Bethlehem, and which is placed on the high altar during Pontifical Mass on Christmas. Beneath the high altar and in other parts of the church are many notable relics of the Saints of God—members of their bodies, and sometimes the entire body—among which are very important relics of the Apostles and of the companions of their apostolic labors. Here are also some very ancient mosaics which were referred to by the Council of Nice. Over the altar of the Borghese Chapel is an ancient picture of the Blessed Virgin, said to have been painted by St. Luke, which Pope St. Gregory the Great carried in solemn procession through Rome in the sixth century. It was not exposed to view on the day of our visit, so I returned on the following Sunday, when I saw it. A man who pointed out to us some of the objects of interest, having keys which admitted to various chapels, at length brought us into a sacristy, and desired to take our order for an altar, a tabernacle, or some other article of church furniture, to be made of variegated Italian marble. Judging from the specimens which he showed us and the prices he gave, one in need of artistic articles of this kind could make from him a satisfactory purchase. During the remainder of the day we visited other churches and places of interest, but I have now forgotten which ones they were.

CHAPTER XXIV.

THE HOLY FATHER—EDUCATION, RELIGION, AND ART.

WHEN we arrived in Rome on our second visit the time for public audiences given by the Holy Father was ended for the summer. As we had no reason for a private audience, we should have felt guilty of robbing the Pope of some of his precious time if we had obtained one; although we were told that we should probably be received by His Holiness if we made application through those with whom our friends had influence. But as we only wished to see our Holy Father and receive his blessing, we accepted the kind offer of Dr. Schulte to obtain for us tickets of invitation to a discussion in theology and canon and civil law, to take place in the Vatican, at which His Holiness was to preside. The next day, at the appointed hour, we passed the Swiss Guard, and were directed to the large hall where the intellectual contest was to take place. It was soon filled with several hundred students and priests, and a large number of monsignori and bishops. We had the pleasure of seeing some of the most distinguished professors and men of learning in Rome or the world. Among those present was occasionally seen a priest without the tonsure, indicating that he came from some land less Catholic in its customs. I also noticed one priest of the Greek rite, distinguishable not so much by his beard—as others present wore one—as by his long hair, parted in the middle, to which we had become accustomed in the East.

In a short time side-doors were thrown open, and several of the Noble Guard led a procession the most distinguished that I had ever seen. About fifteen cardinals entered, wearing over their dark cassocks beautiful scarlet silk ferraiolos, and on their heads skull-caps of the same color and material. Following them,

<blockquote>
In robes of purest white,
Christ's Vicar came, reflecting heaven's light.
</blockquote>

Leo XIII. was before me. His great piety, his highly cultivated classical and literary abilities, his profound learning, his broad grasp of intellect, his high rank among men of science, his intimate knowledge of men and public affairs, his enlightened Christian statesmanship, were almost forgotten in the one thought that filled my mind: He is the Vicar of Jesus Christ whom mine eyes behold! The exercises lasted about three hours, and during almost the entire time the countenance of the Holy Father, who sat in a chair in the middle of the platform, was lighted up with a pleasant and benignant smile. The opening address was delivered in Latin, the language of all the exercises, by Cardinal Parocchi. After the discussions the Holy Father delivered a short address. He seemed very animated, but I noticed that he was, notwithstanding, very deliberate in his utterances.

When all was over we retired to the church of St. Peter, which we commenced to visit with more reference to details, beginning on the right of the door of entrance, with guide-book in hand, and making the circuit of the entire church. This visit could not be finished in a few hours, but had to be continued on the following days. While it took so much time and care, it was continuously interesting, and, once completed, our after-visits possessed an attraction and pleasure which they could not before enjoy. In writing about St. Peter's it is useless to enter into particulars; a good sized volume might be written on this great church, and the subject not be half-exhausted. I prefer to leave such description to guide-books and to those who make a specialty of it. I delighted to wander in its every chapel, to kneel at its wondrous shrines, and to breathe in the broad and grand catholicity which seems to have a living existence within its majestic walls.

Having had my name registered, I received the privilege of celebrating Mass in its Sacred Crypt at six o'clock on Sunday morning. As I nearly always wore the cassock, ferraiolo, and clerical hat when I visited the Roman churches, and having a full beard, I do not think that any of those around, except those to whom my papers were presented, suspected my nationality or race. When I said Mass at other altars in this church I was accompanied from the sacristy by the server, who carried with him two wax candles, which he placed on the altar and lighted. I do not remember that the bell was rung at any Mass that I said in Rome. If it was ever rung it was an exception. I noticed that we always had in the Mass an "oratio imperata," which was changed several times during two weeks. On the morning that I said Mass in the Crypt I was accompanied from the sacristy by two young men, one of whom unlocked the gates and doors and prepared the altar, and the other served my Mass. They were older than my former servers, being, I should judge, more than twenty years of age, and wearing Roman collars and purple cassocks. They were very obliging, and did all that they could do to serve me, and we parted without any mar of politeness and without disappointment on the part of either of us. The Romans everywhere pleased me, and no people that I saw abroad made a better impression on my mind. I do not remember to have seen a brazen-looking girl—except in statuary—during our stay in Rome. When I had finished my Mass I observed that they were preparing for the celebration of the next Mass by a bishop. I made my thanksgiving and retired, accompanied by my server. As we came out through the last gate the episcopal procession came in sight. It was probably a not unusual, but after all it was a strange procession for St. Peter's. The bishop was accompanied by two priests, dressed like himself in the awkward-looking clerical coat of heretical lands, regulation pantaloons, and carrying the usual high silk hats in their hands. The clergy were accompanied by several ladies, stylishly dressed, who were doomed to disappointment. When they came to the first gate, which was unlocked for the clergy, the ladies were turned back, as females are not allowed to enter the Crypt except by papal permission, and thus the beautiful symmetry of the procession was broken.

Although we remained in Rome only a short time, St. Peter's became very familiar to me, and even now I seem once more to walk over its pavements on my way to its holy shrines and altars; and I seem once more to hear in the morning requiems, when but few worshippers were in the church, the solemn, musical voices floating majestically but sweetly through the aisles and chapels, and among the arches of the world's cathedral.

A few evenings after our arrival in Rome we had a pleasant audience with His Eminence Cardinal Simeoni, Cardinal Prefect of the Propaganda. He probably does more hard work than any other cardinal in Rome. Nevertheless he is as pleasant and affable as if he had nothing else to do but entertain visitors from America. I felt a twinge of conscience that we should take up so much of his valuable time, but, as it is Roman etiquette that the cardinal should make the sign for departure, we could not transgress the proprieties; so we talked about America, the newspapers, and ecclesiastical affairs, while he asked us numerous questions. But he seemed really more interested about affairs in the Orient than in the Occident, rather confirming a preconceived opinion that Rome at the present time is taking special interest in the return of the Oriental schismatics to the Church. We retired from his presence with a great confidence in his splendid ability to perform the vast labors of his high office with the best results to the missionary portion of the Church of God\

Our next visits were made to the Sistine Chapel and the various galleries and museums of the Vatican. The Vatican Palace was founded by Pope St. Symmachus, who reigned during the last years of the fifth and opening years of the sixth century. We passed the Swiss Guard in their picturesque and artistic uniforms, and went up the Scala Regia and were admitted into the Sistine Chapel. This is the papal chapel, and possesses as an altar-piece the celebrated fresco by Michael Angelo, "The Last Judgment." It covers the entire end-wall, and is sixty-four feet in width. Many years before this fresco was produced the ceiling was painted in twenty months by the same artist. Both these paintings are considered by different authorities as the greatest masterpieces in fresco, and the culmination of modern art. The "Last Judgment" is very much dimmed by age and incense, and it would require an artist fully to appreciate its merits. Photographers were taking photographs of some of the figures on the ceiling, throwing light on them artificially to get a clearer picture. We next went to the Stanze of Raphael, which consists of allegorical, biblical, and historical paintings. These works are considered by many to be his greatest efforts, and rivalled only by Michael Angelo's frescoes in the Sistine Chapel. We then studied the beautiful biblical scenes in Raphael's Loggie, called "Raphael's Bible." The time for closing came and we should return another day. Leaving the Vatican, we spent several hours in St. Peter's.

The following day we went directly to the "Picture Gallery," which contains some of the most important masterpieces in existence. Among them are the "Transfiguration" and the "Madonna of Foligno," by Raphael, and the "Last Communion of St. Jerome," by Domenichino, a number of others by Raphael, Murillo, Leonardo da Vinci, Titian, Perugino, Guercino, and other world-renowned artists. We spent about two hours contemplating these great works of genius. We then visited the

Vatican Museum, or collection of antiquities. Collected in its vast halls and galleries are hundreds of the most remarkable works of ancient art. It was but reasonable that we should select for special inspection the statuary most highly prized by artists of cultivated taste, whose own works have proven their capability of just appreciation. Before two masterpieces I remained much longer than before any others, however worthy of attention. The genius of the minds that conceived them and the hands that chiselled them is evident even to the eye less skilled than that of an artist. The first of these is the famous group of the Laocoön, who with his two sons is being strangled by serpents. It was executed by artists of the Rhodian school. The second is the beautiful statue of Apollo Belvedere, probably of the same age as the other in the history of art.\

These masterpieces of genius are in a state of almost perfect preservation. It is different with some other specimens of remarkable excellence. Among those that are most noted are a bust of Zeus, or Jupiter, formerly regarded as a faithful copy of the Zeus of Phidias, the greatest of the Grecian sculptors; a "Daughter of Niobe," probably a work of Praxiteles or Scopus, both of whom were among the most distinguished of Grecian artists; a torso of Hercules, by Apollonius the Athenian; "Apoxyomenos," an athlete cleaning his arm with a scraping-iron, probably a true copy from Lysippus, and several other fine copies of the great Grecian artists. It is altogether probable that some of the fragments of ancient art contained in this Clementine museum are the actual productions of some of the greatest sculptors that Greece or the world ever saw. For want of time we did not visit many other museums, but afterwards I was sorry that we did not enter them and see one or other piece of statuary which most interested us. In this way we might have seen the "Dying Gladiator" of the Capitoline, and the "Sophocles" of the Lateran, one of the finest specimens of ancient art to be found in Rome. We returned by the way we came, making the circuit of St. Peter's, which enabled us to realize better the vast extent of that magnificent structure. We were invited to enter the Vatican stables and inspect the grand papal carriage of state, ornamented with scarlet and gold. My companion wanted to enter it, but was not permitted; he also wanted to sit on the throne of Naples, but was unsuccessful; and he ascribed all his ill-luck to us who were less ambitious.

CHAPTER XXV.

SACRED AND HISTORIC PLACES OF PAGAN AND CHRISTIAN ROME.

/ ONE of our excursions while in Rome was past the palace of the Cæsars and the baths of Caracalla, and out on the ancient Appian Way—built 312 B.C.—to the church of St. Sebastian, one of the "Seven Churches of Rome." We passed out of the gate of St. Sebastian, and rode over the Appian Way, which in the days of Rome's glory was the highway on which were witnessed the diversified scenes and triumphal processions of her historic centuries. I seemed to see marching out of the great gate and over the regal road, which led to the thousand highways on land and sea that reached the extremities of the earth, the military legions of imperial Rome, their arms and armor flashing in the golden sunlight of a land of sunshine, and their imperial banners floating in breezes that seemed like the divine breath of the gods of war. Proud Roman forms march beneath those ever-victorious battle-flags, and brave, intellectual Roman faces are lighted with the smile of the lover in remembrance, and of the hero whose eyes are directed towards the aurora which will usher in a day of martial deeds, and victory, and undying glory to proud and adored Rome.

Better far that those brave Roman soldiers shall die on the field where Roman eagles triumph than return to the welcome and debaucheries of the imperial mistress of the world. We seemed to see the decimated legions returning from foreign lands and conquest. Their step is more wearied, but none the less that of Roman soldiers; their smile is changed; from the faces of some it has departed, for they return to desolate homes; on the faces of others its brightness has been toned into fairer lines and sweeter expression by hardships in strange lands, and wounds upon the battle-field, and perhaps gentle and kind-hearted deeds towards friend and foe; on the faces of others it has developed more fully into cynical pride, or even downright cruelty of expression. How many times this regal road has echoed to the steps and chariot-wheels of returning victorious armies, when the lofty Roman gateways have opened to receive them, and the Roman people, proud of their conquests, have met them with shouts of welcome and applause! Captives from distant and strange lands have seen those

Roman gates close upon them, the seal upon their living tomb of liberty, and the symbol of a life-long slavery. The songs of victory by the victors are often the death-notes of liberty to the vanquished. /

In a short time we came to the wayside chapel, "Domine quo Vadis." It is related that St. Peter, having been rescued from the Mamertine prison, was prevailed on to make his escape from martyrdom, and fled over the same road on which wearily he had entered the city twenty years before. At this spot he was met by his Lord bearing His cross and going towards the city. St. Peter asked Him: "Lord, whither goest Thou?" Our Lord answered: "I go to be crucified again." St. Peter returned to Rome and received the crown of martyrdom. This tradition is considered by candid historians to be well verified. About one and one-fourth mile from the gate appeared the entrance to the catacombs of St. Calixtus, shaded with cypresses. These are the most interesting and important catacombs in or about Rome. As it is deemed unhealthy to enter them during July, we had to be satisfied with alighting and making an inspection of the surroundings, and plucking a few flowers as mementoes of the ancient tombs of saints and martyrs. Such a visit is seemingly superficial, but oftentimes since, in the recitation of the Roman Breviary, when I have read that the body of some early martyr was buried and reposes in the cemetery of St. Calixtus on the Appian Way, it has added a new spirit to my devotion. It is well known that the catacombs are chiefly composed of underground streets not more than three feet wide, and from seven to fifteen feet in height, where the dead were buried in tiers of graves on either side. There were in all 160 different catacombs bordering on public ways, and containing about 900 miles of streets. It is estimated that each seven feet in length contains five graves on each side, which would show the whole number of graves to be more than six millions. /

In another quarter of a mile we had arrived at the church of St. Sebastian. The original church was founded by Constantine the Great, and was dedicated by St. Sylvester. It was built over the entrance to the catacombs of St. Sebastian, in which the body of that brave Roman soldier was buried. An inscription near the door by which they are entered states that 46 popes and 174,000 martyrs are buried here. In these catacombs a number of saints spent many hours in prayer; among them St. Charles Borromeo here passed entire nights; here divine love so moved and inflamed the heart of St. Philip Neri that his ribs were broken by its power; and here St. Bridget was rapt in ecstatic vision; here also for some time were concealed the bodies of St. Peter and St. Paul. When we entered the church one of its priests was conducting through it a party of Italian soldiers, who appeared to belong to some other district of Italy, for the time being quartered in Rome. They were listening with respectful attention, and were looking at the relics and sacred places with respectful demeanor. Italy is without doubt Catholic at heart. Whenever the entire voting population takes part in the municipal elections in Rome, Naples, and many other cities, the Clerical party carries them by immense majorities. /

Among the relics in this church are the heads of Popes St. Calixtus and St. Stephen, an ancient leaden chalice containing the ashes of St. Fabian, the head of St. Fabian, an iron point of one of the arrows which pierced St. Sebastian, and the footprint of our Lord in stone, taken from the place where He appeared to St. Peter. Beyond the church, and rising on a slightly higher eminence, we could see the round, high tomb of Cecilia Metella, who was the wife of the younger Crassus, son of the triumvir. It is 65 feet in diameter and of corresponding height. We did not proceed farther, but returned over the same way to the city; when we arrived at our hotel it was near dark.

Another day we visited the church of St. Paul outside the walls, passing out of the city through the gate of St. Paul, near which is the pyramidal tomb—one hundred and twenty-two feet in height—of Caius Cestus, who lived in the time of Augustus, and who prepared the solemn banquets of the gods in the temples on certain important occasions. The present structure of St. Paul's is modern, and is probably the finest church edifice built during the nineteenth century. The interior is 75 feet in height, 195 feet in width, and 390 feet in length, and is rich in its varieties of fine marble and rare stone. It contains several lofty pillars of yellow alabaster, presented by the viceroy of Egypt, four of which, fifty feet in height, support the baldacchino over the high altar. Used in the construction of this and the side-altars are many expensive and beautiful gifts of malachite from the Emperor of Russia. The two side-altars presented by him are valued at $100,000. Malachite, possessing a beautiful green color, under almost any form is very pleasing to the eye. The mosaics are numerous, and among them are some that are ancient, rescued from the fire which destroyed the old basilica. Among the modern mosaics are portraits of all the popes from St. Peter to our time. Each is about five feet in diameter, and taken as a whole they are an interesting study. My clerical companion, who, as well as myself, wore a beard, took special notice of that particular aspect of these historical pictures. He afterwards told me that fully three-fourths of the entire number of popes had worn a beard in one form or another. I had noticed the same general fact, but had not reduced my observations to such mathematical precision. The ancient basilica of St. Paul was built by order of Constantine, under Pope St. Sylvester, over the place where the body of St. Paul was buried. By order of St. Sylvester his body was afterward divided, and half placed here and half in the basilica of St. Peter.

Usually these visits to churches within the city or outside the walls were only a part of our daily routine. Frequently we would dismiss our carriage at the Trajan or the Roman Forum, or at some other place of interest in ancient or modern Rome, and, choosing a favorable position where the crumbling monuments of old, pagan Rome mingle with the venerable temples of early Christian times, we would dream day-dreams of the departed centuries.

And these memorable places of antiquity seemed peopled once more with the living men who in quick succession occupied them, and lived their part in history, and left their monuments behind them to tell to future generations what they had thought and done. To the imaginative mind the historical procession of centuries is an interesting one, with its ever-changing faces and scenes, now peaceful, now warlike, pagan and Christian, as it moves through the streets, always the same, but sometimes changed in name, stopping finally to arrange itself picturesquely around the self same arches and broken columns that raised themselves in the midst of the actual, living events of the past.

The forum of Trajan contains the celebrated column of Trajan, built in the year 112 A.D., 147 feet in height, and having around it from top to bottom a spiral band three feet wide and 600 feet in length, having in bas-relief 2,500 human figures, besides animals, engines of war, etc. It was erected by the "Senate and Roman people, to the Emperor Cæsar Trajan, son of the divine Nerva Augustus, German Dacian, high-priest, 12 times tribune, 11 times consul, father of his country." The Roman Forum is far more interesting than that of Trajan. It is situated at the base of the Capitoline hill, and extends toward the Palatine. It is said to have been the battle-field where the Romans under Romulus, and the Sabines under Tatius, fought each other. after the rape of the Sabine women, who acted as peacemakers, rushing in between the combatants and pleading that they preferred death to seeing either their husbands or their fathers slain. After the peaceful ending of the contest these tribes made the Forum their centre of common assemblage, increasing in importance under the Republic and Empire. Through the Forum the Via Sacra, passing under a number of triumphal arches, led to the Capitol. On account of extensive excavations the remnants of ancient grandeur in the Roman Forum are now revealed to the curious eyes of the nineteenth century; columns, altars, floors, and foundations of its numerous temples dedicated to the gods, touched by the finger of time or broken by the giants of war and devastation, are crumbling into dust, and strew the ground or raise their mutilated forms toward the sky. In the midst of this field of ruins stand the gray and venerable arches of triumph, erected by the pride of men, but telling a more important story than the record engraved on them of battles and victory, the vanity of human life and the emptiness of human greatness.

At one extremity of the Forum stand the vast, crumbling, but still magnificent ruins of the Colosseum. To this part of the city we paid more than an occasional visit. On one of these visits, having dwelt for some time in silent admiration on the forsaken centre of the life of ancient Rome, we retired into a church near at hand. It proved to be the church of St. Joseph, erected over the Mamertine prison, where St. Peter and St. Paul were confined before their martyrdom. In the church were a considerable number of persons praying. We descended into the lower dungeons where the two holy Apostles were imprisoned, and we had the privilege of kissing with pious veneration the place where they were fastened. We also saw the well which St. Peter caused to flow that he might have water with which to baptize his jailers, St. Processus and St. Martinianus, captains of the guard, together with forty others, who soon afterwards received the martyr's crown. In pagan times Jugurtha, the African king, after having adorned the triumph of his Roman conqueror, was cast into this prison and left without food, where in six days he died of starvation, B.C. 104. In this prison Lentulus and others, engaged in the conspiracy of the infamous Catiline, were strangled during the night. The Mamertine prison is one of the most ancient structures of Rome, which antedated even the Republic, and was built by Ancus Martius or Servius Tullius more than six centuries before the Christian era.

Several times we ascended the Capitoline hill and visited the church of Ara Cœli. The Franciscans of the Strict Observance have been connected with this church since 1251, almost from the foundation of the order of St. Francis, and the monastery adjoining has always been one of their most important houses. The church of Ara Cœli (Altar of Heaven) is one of the oldest churches in Rome. On the ancient Capitoline were two chief eminences, on one of which was the arx, or citadel, and on the other the magnificent temple of Jupiter. It has been disputed whether the temple was built on the northern or southern summit. It is known that the citadel occupied the other. Most modern critics agree that the church of Ara Cœli, which is on the northern eminence, stands on the site of the ancient citadel. It is said that on this place the pagan Emperor Augustus saw a vision of the Divine Child and Mother, according to an inscription in the chapel of St. Helena: "This chapel, which is called Ara Cœli, is believed to have been erected on the same spot where the most holy Virgin, Mother of God, revealed herself with her Son to Cæsar Augustus in a golden circle in the heavens." The emperor then built here an altar to the "First Born of God," which is enclosed within the present altar. In this church repose the ashes of the great empress, St. Helena. Without doubt a number of the pillars of the present structure of Ara Cœli once adorned the Capitoline temple of Jupiter. On our first visit, while we were viewing the church, a Franciscan father came forward, and, having addressed us in Latin, learned that we were from America. He then spoke in English, which was evidently his native tongue. He had been in America, even in our own city of Milwaukee, and knew one of our older priests. We did not inquire his name, but he gave us much serviceable information, for which we most sincerely thanked him.

We afterwards wandered over the Capitoline, and ascended and descended it from almost every direction, where there were streets and where there were none. Although the celebrated Tarpeian rock is pointed out, inasmuch as its exact locality is doubtful we gave our imagination freedom in the choice of places where the criminals of Rome were hurled down to death. In front of the Capitol is a remarkable equestrian statue of Marcus Aurelius, supposed by many to be in reality a statue of Constantine. The Capitoline is the least extended but the most important of the seven hills of Rome. Where Jupiter, king of the gods and chief of the devils, once held sway, Jesus Christ now rules, but never without a contest with His old pagan foe whom St. Michael cast out of heaven.

Between the Palatine hill and the Tiber, quite near the river, and not far from the ancient Circus Maximus, is an interesting locality which we twice visited, and which possesses some excellent specimens of pagan temples changed into Christian churches. One of these is the ancient temple of Fortuna Virilis, now the church of St. Mary of Egypt, probably the oldest temple in Rome, existing in the time of the Republic, and probably built more than five hundred years before Christ. It is in a good state of preservation, being surrounded by pillars, four at each end and seven at each side. We were unfortunate in not being able to find it open, although we made two journeys with the hope of gaining admittance, and passed it several times. But the exterior is said to be much more interesting than the inside. Near by is an old but elegant temple of Vesta, now the church of S. Maria del Sole. It is believed by many to have been built about seven hundred years before the time of Christ, by Numa Pompilius, the first king of Rome after Romulus, and who instituted vestals and pontiffs. By some it is thought to have been a temple of Hercules Victor. It is twenty-eight feet in diameter, circular in form, and surrounded by twenty Corinthian pillars of Parian marble, each thirty-two feet high. It is a very picturesque object, in the midst of a partially undisturbed quarter of ancient Rome. Across the street from this temple is the church of St. Mary in Cosmedin, probably the second church in Rome dedicated to the Blessed Virgin. It is built on the foundations of an old pagan temple, perhaps that of Pudicitia Patricia, where only noble unmarried females could enter; but by others it is considered a temple of Fortune, ascribed to Servius, sixth king of Rome, which would consequently make it very ancient. The church, though rebuilt in the year 772 A.D., dates from the third century, and contains some of the columns of the original temple. Here St. Augustine taught rhetoric, and here lie the relics of two hundred martyrs.\

Some distance north of the Colosseum, and on the Esquiline hill, is the church of St. Peter in Chains. It is said that on the spot where the church now stands St. Peter built an oratory. It was rebuilt 442 A.D., to receive the chains of St. Peter, those by which he was bound under Herod and also under Nero, which are miraculously united. We were aware of the fact that on account of certain regulations we should be unable to see them; but we desired to visit this ancient church, not only for its holy associations, but because it possesses the celebrated statue of Moses by Michael Angelo. This great work, chiselled by the hand of the great master, is considered by nearly all judges as the grandest and most perfect production, in sculpture, of Christian art. It was originally intended for St. Peter's basilica. In this church are the relics of many saints, among them the Machabean mother and her seven sons; and here St. Leo the Great preached his sermon on the "Festival and Martyrdom of the Machabees, and the Continual Conflict of Christians."

Our last Sunday in Rome was one of those days on which each of our number started out in a different direction from the others. Each of us had particular churches or other objects of interest which he had not yet seen, and he would not feel satisfied to leave Rome without seeing them. After I had said Mass in the

Crypt of St. Peter's, and had eaten my breakfast, I took a carriage and directed the driver to go first to the church of St. Pudentiana. This is probably the first and oldest Christian church in Rome. It is not the oldest edifice used as a Christian church, for some of the pagan temples are older; but it was the first place of prayer and sacrifice in the Eternal City, and has ever since been used as a church, and for three centuries was the cathedral of Rome. When St. Peter first came to the city he converted the Senator Pudens, Priscilla his mother, his two daughters Pudentiana and Praxedes, and his two sons Novatius and Timotheus. St. Peter took up his residence here—in the house of Pudens—where he celebrated the holy mysteries. Here he consecrated Linus and Cletus. What the Cœnaculum was to Jerusalem, this place was to Rome. It is situated between the Viminal and Esquiline hills, on the ancient Vicus Patricius, or Patrician Street. About the year 100 A.D. Pope St. Evaristus divided Rome into parishes and gave the name of "titles" to their churches; but this church, being the pontifical church, was left without a title until the middle of the second century, when Pope St. Pius I. added to it an oratory with the designation of the title of the Pastor, to which frequent reference is made by early Christian writers. When we arrived at the church it was closed, but the driver soon found the custodian, who unlocked it and pointed out to me its chief historic attractions. This church is specially rich in mosaics, and those in the choir are among the oldest and finest in Rome, dating not later than the fourth century, and representing our Lord with St. Pudentiana and St. Praxedes, and the holy Apostles, and the emblems of the Evangelists each side of the cross. In the aisles are also some very ancient mosaics; and the old pillars of the primitive church can still be seen. The custodian directed me up the left aisle to the altar of St. Peter, which contains the most venerable relic of the church—a portion of the wooden altar on which St. Peter was accustomed to offer up the Holy Sacrifice. The larger portion has been removed to the altar of St. John Lateran; but a large plank is preserved here with a glass covering before it, so that it can be clearly inspected.\

I knelt before that altar, and with deep reverence looked on that sacred wood consecrated by the Prince of the Apostles, and many thousand times consecrated by the Divine Offering of Calvary. How many saints of the "city and the world," in the different centuries from the time of St. Peter and the saintly family with whom he dwelt, have knelt before that altar! If, one after another, the whole number would pass in procession before it, and each for a moment would kneel and pray, what a long line of saints and martyrs we should behold, from every rank in life, from the canonized beggar to the canonized emperor and pontiff, and what a grand manifestation of devotion we should witness! My guide then lighted a taper attached to a long pole, and thrust it into a deep, dry well, in the bottom of which was revealed a large collection of human bones, which he told me were "the bones of the martyrs." The bodies of nearly three thousand martyrs, slain in the early persecutions, were buried beneath this church.

Leaving St. Pudentiana's with its holy memories, we drove to St. Maria Maggiore, on our way to the church of St. Praxedes, both of which were in the neighborhood. Although we had already visited St. Mary Major's, I stopped to see the picture of the Madonna by St. Luke, which is exposed on Sundays. It now appears very indistinct; but that matters not, for its antiquity and venerable associations render it far more attractive to the Christian heart than the grandest masterpieces that the world has ever produced. The very atmosphere surrounding it seems holy, not only on account of the hand of the artist who traced its lineaments before the living face of the Madonna herself, but also from the innumerable prayers that have risen in its presence from pure lips and saintly souls to the Mother and Son.\

Soon after we stood before the closed portal of the church of St. Praxedes. This church is, I believe, in the hands of the Olivetan monks. I was met by one of the monks at the door of an adjoining building, through which I was conducted into the church. It was dedicated as an oratory as early as the second century, but assumed its present noble proportions under Pope St. Paschal I. in the year 822. It is adorned with many beautiful mosaics of the ninth, tenth, and thirteenth centuries. The mosaic of the ninth century is an inspiring representation of heaven. In a side-chapel we were shown a large table of St. Charles Borromeo, which he frequently used. The church also contains a number of gifts presented by him, as this was his titular church. Near the opposite wall from the high altar is a slab with this inscription: "On this slab slept St. Praxedes." I was shown a well into which St. Praxedes and St. Pudentiana squeezed the blood of martyrs which they had gathered in sponges. I was then conducted to the chapel, on the right side of the church, which contains the portion of the pillar of scourging preserved in Rome. The other portion I had seen in the Chapel of the Apparition in Jerusalem. We entered the crypt under the high altar, where we saw and reverenced the tombs of the sister-saints, Pudentiana and Praxedes.\ .

Leaving the church, I directed the driver to convey me to the church of St. Agnes, outside the walls, erected over the tomb of the child virgin and martyr. We passed through the new part of the city, built up under the present administration. We passed out of the Porta Pia, the gate through which the Italian troops first entered Rome, under the present occupation. The ride into the country was a pleasant one. On either side of the road—the ancient Via Nomentana—were far-famed villas of noble and princely Romans, with extensive grounds and cultivated gardens surrounding them. On the left was an unobstructed view of the Sabine Mountains in the distance. Although it was a summer day, the description of the Nomentan villa of St. Agnes, and of the scenes on the Nomentan Way on the anniversary of the saint, as pictured by Cardinal Wiseman in his *Fabiola*, came touchingly to my mind. I seemed to live in the departed years, and the glory and pride of pagan Rome, and the humble lives of Christian saints and joys of Christian festivals, in turn passed before my eyes, and I beheld them as they reached the eternal gates of the city of the living God, where the long, glittering procession of human pride and worldly glory was turned back in confusion, and the chaste and radiant line of Christian souls entered in triumph under the white banner of the "Lamb that was slain."

A little more than a mile from the gate we came to the church of St. Agnes. The church was closed, but a monk put his head out of an upper window of the adjoining convent and said it would be opened immediately. We passed through an open court, and entered on a long, wide stairway of forty-five marble steps which descends to the church. On either side of the staircase on the walls are hundreds of primitive Christian symbols and inscriptions taken from the catacombs. In this church, on its patron feast, the Holy Father, or a cardinal appointed for the purpose, blesses the two lambs from the wool of which the palliums are woven for the archbishops throughout the world. Under the high altar rests the body of the saint. Here I knelt and prayed for my congregation and friends in my far-off home; for on Sunday more than on other days my mind was usually inclined to wander homeward. Having sufficiently observed the various parts of the church, I started back towards Rome. I had seen in a side-chapel a sweet picture of the Blessed Virgin and St. Agnes, painted by a modern Roman painter, and I began to feel a half-formed desire in my heart to be an artist. But as I did not see any strong probability of ever becoming very successful in that line, I concluded to confine my desire to words, and commenced to write a poem. As the road was rather rough, and writing consequently difficult, I finished only these two stanzas; the others exist in the dim, misty future:

> Would that I could paint a picture
>   Like the one that I saw there,
> With a face so sweet and holy,
>   And that wavy, golden hair;
>
> And with eyes so soft and tender—
>   Heaven's blue is not so mild,
> When they look upon the sinner,
>   Or turn pleading to the Child.

The time was drawing near when we must

leave Rome. Many of the rides and walks that we took together over the Pincian hill or to other pleasant but not remarkably interesting localities I will not take time to describe. In the immediate vicinity of our hotel nearly every building of importance became quite familiar to us—not alone the church of the Minerva, just across the street, but the Pantheon, the Roman College, the church of St. Ignatius, and the church of St. Mary in Via Lata; for we passed these several times each day. This was the region of the Septa Julia, founded by Cæsar, where the votes of the national assembly were taken, but which was turned into a market in the time of Tiberius. The church of St. Ignatius, adjoining the Roman College, belongs to the Jesuits, and contains the body of St. Aloysius. In visiting the Roman churches it is needless to say that we did not visit them "like the heathen that know not God." We did not kneel before all the altars, but before the chapel of the Blessed Sacrament we always knelt and prayed, and frequently before other altars in various chapels, especially those which contained particular objects of devotion. For this reason the churches of Rome did not seem like strange and unfamiliar places to us, as they must appear to those outside the household of faith. To us they appeared like home, the house of our Lord and Father, and a part of our own inheritance.\

In walking to the Corso, the principal street of Rome, only a short distance from the hotel, as we turned on the Corso was a church which I several times entered to offer a brief prayer. On one occasion the chapter were reciting the divine office. I was always interested in this church, for in some way it suited me, although at first I did not even know its name. I afterwards learned that it is the ancient church of St. Mary in Via Lata. The Via Lata—which was the Via Flaminia outside the city, and one of the chief streets of former times—very nearly corresponded with the present Corso. This church was first built by Constantine, over the place where St. Paul "remained over two years in his own hired lodging"; and it is believed that here St. Luke wrote the Acts of the Apostles. The present building was erected in the seventeenth century. We entered many other churches in different parts of the city, but in most cases their names are forgotten, and for the most part they did not make the same impression on my mind as those that I have remembered; perhaps in a few instances because we did not know at the time what churches they were.\

Before leaving Rome I wished to procure two relics for my church, and therefore went to the vicariate to procure those only that would be properly authenticated. I had to go several times on account of various delays, but finally obtained one of the Blessed Virgin Mary of the Holy House of Loretto, and another of St. Patrick, the patron of my church. During these errands I had the privilege of visiting the neighboring church of St. Augustine. It contains the body of St. Monica, mother of St. Augustine, a picture of the Madonna attributed to St. Luke, a miraculous statue of the divine Mother and Child, and many rare works of art. Among the last mentioned is a fresco of the prophet Isaias, by Raphael, who is said to have been influenced in its production by a desire to excel the "Prophets," by Michael Angelo, in the Sistine Chapel.\

We had arranged to leave Rome on Wednesday morning, but before leaving a few observations may not be out of place. The traveller from America, after passing through several countries of Europe having large standing armies, might not be surprised at the number of soldiers he would meet on the streets of Rome, for the agents of war would have become familiar sights; but to see so many priests, the messengers of peace, would be to him a new revelation, which, unless he were a Catholic, he might not quite understand. Priests are frequently met all over Italy, and in Rome you might meet one on almost every block, and sometimes in that distance, at certain hours of the day, a dozen or more. But Rome is the religious capital of the world. I was somewhat interested in observing the numerous clergy of the various cities and districts of Italy, because I had seen them so differently described by different writers. I can remember to have read only one Protestant author who has given them anything like justice. So far as good, priest-like appearances go, I have seen no other priesthood in the world who surpass them; nor have I seen any other class of men anywhere who even approach them. There is a look on their faces indicative of habitual moderation, abstemiousness, and virtue in their lives. Notwithstanding the slanders that I had read against them by non-Catholic authors, I had expected to meet a good priesthood, but they so far surpassed my expectations that I am ready to declare them to be at least equal to any body of clergy, and to excel—as a class—the men of any other profession or vocation in any country. I also made observation as to the temperate habits of the people. Nearly every one drinks wine, but I could hardly say—judging from my experience—that it is ever used to excess. During our sojourn of a month in Italy, travelling a good portion of the time, and frequently on the streets, I did not see one person drunk or laboring under the influence of drink. I believe that Catholic total-abstinence societies are beneficial in some countries, but not until the tastes of the people have become vitiated and their drinking customs uncatholic.

Another fact—to which I will merely allude, but which I will not explain—was noted by us which would indicate that, notwithstanding the corrupting influence of the present government, Rome is still the most moral large city in the world. Verily the influence of the Papacy has made a lasting impression on the Roman people.

As our time was quickly passing we concluded that we must miss either Florence or Loretto. It did not take us long to decide that to us Loretto was more attractive, although we very much disliked to leave out from our route beautiful Florence.

CHAPTER XXVI.

FROM ROME TO LORETTO.

On Wednesday morning, the 16th of July, we were leaving the walls of Rome behind us, as our railway train moved smoothly over the road towards Ancona. This road runs in a northeasterly direction, passing through the Umbrian Apennines of Central Italy, to the Adriatic coast, 184 miles distant, and continuous in the pontifical territory. For about fifty miles we rode through the wooded valley of old Tiber, the river being in sight—sometimes near at hand—during a good portion of the distance. For some time the railroad follows the direction of the ancient Via Salara, passing in sight of picturesque villages and towns, among them the old Sabine town Cures—the modern Correse—which was the birthplace of Numa Pompilius. To the left rose Mount Soracte, spoken of by Horace and Virgil.

Leaving the valley of the Tiber, we turned into the beautiful and fertile valley of the Nera, with its fine plantations of evergreen oaks. During the day we passed through many old cities, founded by Roman colonists before the Christian era, and noted as the birthplaces of many remarkable men, among others a number of pagan emperors and Christian pontiffs. Among these ancient towns was Spoleto, the Roman Spoletium, founded more than twenty-one centuries ago, and which within twenty-five years of its foundation courageously repulsed an attack by Hannibal. It was a Christian see as early as 50 A.D. Soon afterwards we passed through the charming vale of the Clitumnus, whose rich pastures and shady groves upon the sunny banks of the little river, and its temple of Jupiter, are described by Pliny; and whose snow-white herds of cattle are celebrated by Virgil, which with gilded horns and wreaths of flowers were adorned for sacrifice. Until this ride I had never looked upon the truly picturesque and attractive rural scenes of Italy.

I could trace with the eye the white, smooth road down the side of the hill, between stone walls and overhanging trees that enclosed the wayside vineyards, into some cozy little vale, and then up again, winding around the mountain side, descending into a more extended valley, over the gray arches of some old stone bridge, until it was lost sight of amidst the ancient streets of some venerable city whose buildings were already old centuries ago. The number of pleasant valleys in the Apennines seem countless. If a life on earth could anywhere be enjoyable it should be among a simple and pious peasantry, surrounded by all the charms of nature. These scenes of interior Italy only wanted a glimpse of the far-off blue sea, with its white, spreading sails, to make them perfect. We passed world-renowned Assisi on our left, but had not time to visit that celebrated sanctuary of St. Francis. About two hours before sundown we came in sight of the glistening waters of the Adriatic, and not long afterward we entered Ancona./

Ancona was founded by the Doric Greeks from Syracuse about four centuries before Christ, and is built on the slope of two hills, rising from the sea in the form of an amphitheatre. It contains a triumphal arch to Trajan, and several old churches, among them the cathedral, dedicated to St. Cyriacus, whose tomb it possesses, and built over a temple of Venus, mentioned by Juvenal, from which it has retained ten pillars. We entered only one church in Ancona, but as to the rest of the city and its churches we concluded to be satisfied with an inspection from the outside. So we took a carriage and directed the driver to drive through the principal parts of the city. On our way from the station we were stopped at the city gates by soldiers on guard, who demanded our passports. They were afraid that we might have come from some cholera-infected district. We had already been fumigated at the station. It is doubtful if one of us had his passport with him, as we never expected to be asked for them. But one of my friends, whose wits come to him quickest in an emergency, very coolly drew forth from his pocket a paper such as each of us had received from the Guardian of the Holy Land, stating that we had made the pilgrimage, and signed and sealed in Jerusalem. He pointed to the word Jerusalem, and said, Jerusalem; they repeated, Jerusalem, and said in the Italian equivalent: "All right; pass on." So far as most parts of Europe are concerned, a mortgage on one's house would answer all the purposes of a passport; and a policy from some of the fire-insurance companies would prove a flaming document that would insure the bearer every needed politeness and protection. /

We returned to the station in seasonable time to take the train for Loretto, only fifteen miles distant towards the south. The municipal council, or something of the kind, from some other city, had been visiting a similar body in Ancona. After a grand supper and the usual number of speeches, they were accompanied to the station by brass bands and silken banners, and the customary noise and ostentation./

In less than an hour we were in Loretto. We took an omnibus, which slowly climbed the hill on which the town is situated. We found a fairly good hotel, where having obtained rooms we immediately retired to rest, in order to rise early the next morning to say Mass in the Holy House. The next morning we were directed to the church, and soon found ourselves within the holy sanctuary which has made the name of Loretto familiar to the ears of the Christian world. Loretto is a small town, containing perhaps six thousand inhabitants. Along the street leading to the church are numerous venders of articles of devotion, and Loretto is also noted for the importunities of its beggars, who naturally collect here from different parts of Italy. At the season of the year when we were there they did not, however, prove to be very annoying. Having offered thanksgiving to God for His great kindness in permitting us to approach the sacred threshold of His house on earth, we went to the sacristy, where we obtained permission to offer up the Holy Sacrifice at the altar within its sacred walls, which contains the altar which came with the Holy House from Nazareth. My Mass was to come immediately after a High Mass celebrated—if I remember rightly—by a bishop. The chief sacristan was a Franciscan father whom I afterwards saw saying Mass at an altar immediately outside the Holy House, called the altar of the Annunciation. He asked me if there were any members of his order in my part of America. I informed him about the matter, and also told him that a Capuchin father had charge of my congregation during my absence. While waiting for my turn I had a good opportunity to look about me, not with the mere sense of curiosity, but with the more observant insight of faith and devotion./

The basilica erected over the Holy House is a magnificent structure, on which many eminent artists have been employed. The Holy House itself has been covered with marble, and adorned with reliefs and statues chiselled by the hands of eminent sculptors. The Holy House is constructed of a dark, reddish stone, proven by chemical analysis to be identical in chemical composition with the stone of Nazareth. It is about 31 feet 4 inches in length, 13 feet 4 inches in breadth, and—as well as I can judge—about 18 feet high, although I find that writers place its height all the way from 13½ to 28 feet. It has every mark of a former dwelling-house changed into a church, such as we know the Holy House of Nazareth to have been from the very time that it was last occupied by the Holy Family. A thorough investigation of the facts and miracles connected with its history, and finally the authority of the Church, leave no doubt that this House of Loretto is identical with the House of the Blessed Virgin in Nazareth, from which place it was translated nearly six hundred years ago.

I cannot do better, in relating the story of its miraculous translation, than to transcribe a portion of the Bull of Pius IX., which repeats the substance of what many pontiffs before him had written with reference to this fact: "Among all the temples consecrated to the Immaculate Mother of God, there is one which holds first rank. The most holy and august House of Loretto, consecrated by divine mysteries, ennobled by countless miracles, honored by multitudes of pious pilgrims, fills the whole Catholic universe with the glory of its title, and is the object of the devotion and veneration of all nations and races of mankind. It is at Loretto, this Holy House of Nazareth, cherished by the Eternal Father on account of the numerous circumstances and mysteries connected with it; first built in Galilee, then raised from its foundation by divine power, and transported by angels beyond the sea, first to Dalmatia, then to Italy. Happy and sacred House! where the Blessed Virgin, predestined from all eternity and exempt from the stain of original sin, was conceived and brought up; where the Angel Gabriel saluted her as blessed among women; where, filled with the grace of God, and by the operation of the Holy Ghost, without being deprived of her spotless virginity, she became the Mother of the only Son of God." In Nazareth I had already said Mass over the spot where the Annunciation took place, and now I was about to enjoy the same privilege within the walls where the great mystery of the Incarnation was accomplished./

I could not realize it; the very fact seemed to partake of the miraculous; and the holy mysteries of the Incarnation seemed to envelop me as in an atmosphere not of this world. One could afford to journey through strange lands, over rough and dangerous mountain roads to the extreme ends of the earth, in hunger and thirst, in heat and cold, until the final day of his life, if, on the last morning of that day whose setting sun should never rise again, he would be permitted to offer up the Holy Sacrifice in the House of Jesus, Mary, and Joseph. After Mass, and thanksgiving by attending the Mass of the venerable priest whom I had met in the sacristy, I started to return to our hotel. On the way back I bought some rosaries, and then walked slowly along until I came upon one of the finest views that I had ever enjoyed. Loretto is situated in the province of Ancona—the ancient Picenum—which is one of the most fertile and picturesque regions of Italy. Some of its most characteristic features could now be seen from where I stood, far below me on all sides, lying under the rich, bright glow of the summer sun To the west the Central Apennines rise to their highest elevation, and between them and the eminence on which I was standing reposed the smiling fields and pleasant valleys of the Marches of Italy. To the east, about three miles distant, the Adriatic sparkled in the sunlight. Although standing, as I was, under the oppressive heat of July, I remained for some time beholding this fair and tranquil scene.

During the forenoon we made one more visit to the Holy House, at a time when no others but ourselves within its walls whispered prayers to the Sacred Heart of Jesus and the Sweet Heart of Mary./

CHAPTER XXVII.

BOLOGNA, PADUA, AND VENICE.

About the middle of the afternoon we took the train for Bologna, by way of Ancona. During the late afternoon and early evening we passed through the "Five Maritime Cities," Ancona, Sinigaglia—the birthplace of Pius IX.—Fano, Pesano, and Rimini, all of which were founded before the beginning of the Christian era. Rimini, the northernmost of these cities, was the end of the ancient Flaminian Way, which here united with the Æmilian. As the shadows of evening lengthened over sea and land, and enveloped the whole earth, perhaps those last rays of light, straggling through the western mountains or dimly gilding the very tips of the topmost peaks, revealed to us the indistinct outlines of the liberty-loving little republic of San Marino, which was founded in those mountains a thousand and five hundred years ago by St. Marinus, and ever since has preserved its form of government and independence. It was only a few miles distant, but it would hardly be possible that we could distinguish it from the surrounding territory. We soon afterwards passed over the Rubicon of Cæsar.

About eleven o'clock we arrived in Bologna, and not long after, in our rooms in the hotel Brun, we had forgotten the events of the day; and, as often elsewhere when we awakened in the morning, we wondered where we were, for the room had a foreign look, unlike the one at home. As we were to take the train for Venice about noon, we started early to see the city. We directed the driver to convey us first to the church with which the convent of Poor Clares is connected; for it had been the chief motive of our visit to Bologna to see and pay reverence to the body of St. Catharine of Bologna.

Bologna is a walled city containing a population of more than one hundred thousand. About two centuries before the Christian era it became a Roman colony, but was already an old city, having been founded by the Celts about the fifth century before Christ. It contains about one hundred and thirty churches, some of which are quite remarkable for size, ornamentation, and antiquity. As we rode through the streets our attention was attracted to the wide and extensive covered porticos or arcades, in front of the buildings and over the sidewalks, protecting the foot-passengers from the hot rays of the sun and the inclemency of the elements. They were something new to us, which we had not seen elsewhere.

Arriving at the church, we entered, and, having met a priest, we told him the object of our visit. He was very kind in his manner, and rang a bell as a signal for the nuns to unlock a door leading into an adjoining room. This they did, but immediately retired. We passed through this room into another which contains the body of St. Catharine, who has been dead more than four hundred years, having died in the year 1463. St. Catharine is sitting in a chair, and the nuns have decorated her person with many ornaments of gold and precious jewels; but her face and hands are without covering. They have changed to a black color, except a spot on and near one of her lips, which is of a lighter hue, where it is related that on the holy festival of Christmas the Infant Jesus kissed her. After the death of St. Catharine, when it was found that her body had remained incorrupt, a chair was prepared for her, and, knowing that in life she had always been obedient, she was commanded to seat herself in it, which command she promptly obeyed. We knelt before her and prayed, requesting her to intercede for us with God. The father who accompanied us asked if we were priests, and, being told that we were, said that we might kiss her hand, which we did. Although black, it was as soft as my own living hand. We retired with praise in our hearts to God for His saints, for "God is wonderful in His saints"; and thanking Him that we "are fellow-citizens with the saints" and "partakers of the lot of the saints in light."/

Although we had become so accustomed to fine churches that it was difficult, at least in Italy, to find something new, several of the churches of Bologna occupied our well-rewarded attention during visits as long as our time permitted. The church dedicated to St. Petronio—who was bishop of the city in the fifth century, and is honored as its patron—is 385 feet long and 156 feet in breadth; although according to its original plan it was to have been 750 feet in length. The church of St. Dominic is also a grand edifice, and contains the tomb of St. Dominic, who died in Bologna. Among the other churches which we visited, the oldest foundation was evidently that of the cathedral church of St. Peter, founded by St. Zama in the third century. The church of St. Stefano—or the "Seven Churches"—over the site of a former temple of Isis, was founded in the fifth century by St. Petronius. Several other churches were founded by the same saint.

The university is perhaps the oldest in Italy, claimed by many to have been founded in the fifth century, and which in the middle ages often counted 10,000 students. It still continues to exist, but with enfeebled faculties and in a diminutive form. Bologna also possesses two leaning towers, one of which is only 163 feet in height, and is ten feet out of the perpendicular. Among the minor things for which the city is famous are its poodle-dogs, sausages, and modern radical opinions. We returned to our hotel, and from there went directly to the station, where we soon entered the train for Venice.

Our route led for the most part through a level, fertile, and well-cultivated country. Between

Ferrara and Rovigo we crossed the Po, and for some miles the railway extends along its banks. To us the most interesting city on the line was Padua, through which we twice journeyed, but only saw it as it is seen from the train. Its numerous high steeples and lofty domes were quite in contrast, and to me a pleasing one, with nearly all the towns of more southern Italy. Padua is one of the oldest cities of Italy, and is believed to have been founded by the Trojan prince Antenor after the destruction of Troy, more than three thousand years ago. It was an important town long before it passed under Roman power, and after that event it was, in the time of Augustus, the wealthiest city in northern Italy. It claims to be the birthplace of the historian Livy; he certainly was born in its vicinity. But during the whole time that my eyes rested on that attractive Italian town—and it makes a fine appearance from the railway—my mind seemed to dwell only on one personage connected with it, one whose name and spirit have rendered it illustrious, and whose ashes rest within the precincts of one of its grandest churches—St. Anthony of Padua. He was a native of Lisbon, in Portugal, but he so long resided in this city that its name is added to his as a distinctive title.

In about half an hour after leaving Padua the towers and domes of Venice rose in the distance against a blue horizon of sky and water; and in a short time we were passing over the waters of the lagoon in which Venice is situated, on a bridge more than two miles in length, and resting on 222 arches. A lagoon is a shallow lake formed by the sea, of which, strictly speaking, it is a part. The lagoon in which Venice is built is about nine miles in width and twenty-five miles in length, and is protected from the fury of the sea by islands of sand, which have been strengthened by solid and expensive bulwarks. Venice is built on three large and one hundred and fourteen small islands, but the land is entirely covered by buildings, piazzas, and streets —mostly narrow and next to some of the canals.

The "streets" are usually canals, or, correctly speaking, the shallow waters of the Adriatic. We did not stay long enough in Venice to find out the duties of their street commissioners, or to understand thoroughly their system of waterworks. We learned, however, that the drinking-water was not good, and that a new system of supply was soon to be introduced. On our arrival at the station gondolas were in waiting to convey passengers to the different hotels or to any part of the city. Every reader has seen pictures of these peculiar boats, and is therefore practically familiar with them. In all they number about four thousand within the limits of the city corporation. We entered one to convey us to the hotel Angleterre, on the Riva degli Schiavoni, a broad quay fronting one of the widest canals of the city, where a number of large vessels were always lying at anchor. It was only a short distance from the piazza of St. Mark, which is the centre of life and attraction in Venice. We arrived sufficiently early in the day to hire a gondola to carry us wherever the gondoliers fancied might please us. It was a pleasant, dreamy ride, full of romantic suggestions. Samuel Rogers well describes in oft-quoted lines the impressions of the traveller as he approaches and enters the city, or soon afterwards, in swan-shaped boat, glides through its silent streets:

> "There is a glorious City in the Sea.
>   The sea is in the broad, the narrow streets,
>   Ebbing and flowing ; and the salt sea-weed
>   Clings to the marble of her palaces.
>   No track of men, no footsteps to and fro,
>   Lead to her gates. The path lies o'er the sea,
>   Invisible ; and from the land we went,
>   As to a floating city—steering in,
>   And gliding up her streets as in a dream,
>   As smoothly, silently, by many a dome

>Mosque-like, and many a stately portico,
>The statues ranged along an azure sky ;
>By many a pile in more than Eastern splendor,
>Of old the residence of merchant kings ;
>The fronts of some, though Time had shattered them,
>Still glowing with the richest hues of art,
>As though the wealth within them had run o'er."

Our gondoliers first rowed to some islands opposite, where we entered different churches, among them S. Giorgio Maggiore and S. Maria della Salute. Connected with the latter is the Patriarchal Seminary. This church contains some of the masterpieces of Titian, who represents the highest excellence of Venetian art, which is quite distinct from that of the rest of Italy, and partakes liberally of Oriental richness. Our gondoliers next directed their boats through the Grand Canal, the entire length of which we had already seen on our way from the station, each time passing under the famous bridge of the Rialto. On either side of the canal rose the stately palaces of ancient Venice, for this is the aristocratic street of the city. They then turned into narrower ways, where we could see the different classes of people, and to a certain extent their modes of life.

Everywhere we saw people swimming in the streets, jumping into the water from their doorsteps. It occurred to me that in Venice a child should be taught to swim before it learns to walk or even to creep; for otherwise if it should manage to get out of any door of the house it would probably fall into the water and be drowned. I saw mothers teaching their infants to swim who could be scarcely two years of age. When they put them into the water they held them up by a rope, and the quickness with which they would learn the art of swimming might readily be to them a matter of life or death. Our boatmen brought us finally under the Bridge of Sighs, and soon afterwards landed us at the hotel. On the following days we often saw this celebrated bridge, as it was between our hotel and the piazza of St. Mark. It connects the palace of the Doges with the prison where criminals were executed, and when under sentence of death they went from the judgment-hall to their prison, they never returned; hence the name of the bridge over which they passed.

During the next day we spent most of our time in the church and around the square of St. Mark. To a traveller there are many attractive resorts in that vicinity. The piazzetta through which we had to pass on our way to the piazza and church is a pleasant place, where one can sit and enjoy the cool breezes from the water, with a good view of the lagoon and shipping; and several times we took advantage of the favorable situation, but not so often as we would have done had not our own rooms in the hotel commanded a finer view of the same scene. Next to the piazzetta on the one side, and the mole on the other, is the ancient and magnificent palace of the Doges. It is about 240 feet square. On two sides are double colonnades, one above the other, having 107 columns, whose capitals, mouldings, and traceries are rich in artistic designs executed in stone. This palace was founded in the year 800, but has been destroyed at different times, and each time rebuilt, until the present structure, which has been in existence about five centuries. It was, in one form or another, the palace of the republican doges for more than a thousand years; for Venice was a republic from the eighth century until its overthrow by Napoleon. If the republic of the United States of North America, or any other republic, had subsisted eleven centuries on the principles of mere secularism, or secularism mingled with some Christian principles, there might be a question as to whether secularism or the Catholic religion is more favorable to republican institutions. As the facts now stand, only republics founded on Catholic principles have on their side proofs from history. But had the republic of the United States existed for a thousand years, it would not be by any means a test of the principle of mere secularism in government, for her most important laws and articles of constitution are founded on the common law of Catholic times and on the principles of Magna Charta, which was simply the laws and customs for which the people of England always clamored; for their fathers had experienced their justice and protection under "good King Edward" the Confessor, their author and a canonized saint of the Catholic Church. It is not alone to republics that the principles of the Church are favorable, but they are the foundation and bulwark of every form of legitimate government.

Although for the present time the cry of Italian unity has captured the crowd—a cry which in some sense is an echo of Roman paganism and the apostasy of Julian, and a unity which has been acquired by tyranny and fraud—the grand genius of the Italian people will yet re-assert itself, and, under the fostering influence of Christian pontiffs, great Italian republics and freedom-loving kingdoms may again arise, and, with a milder spirit and more glorious destiny than the enterprising, giant republics of the middle ages, will outshine with beneficent rays upon the earth, and outrival in Christ-like deeds among men, any of their predecessors in the past. The enemies of Catholic Italy have tried to make little of the Italian name, and have slandered the Italian character. But Italy has furnished too many illustrious pontiffs and scholars, statesmen and literary men, painters and musicians, sculptors and architects, and men great in every vocation of life where genius and the more generous endowments of nature are required, to permit mal-conceived and low-born opinions to influence the judgment of fair-minded and intelligent men.

In the year 828 the body of St. Mark the Evangelist was brought from Alexandria—of which city he had been the first bishop—and the adjoining church, dedicated to his name, was built to receive it, where it now rests under the principal altar. It is believed by many —and the great veneration in which he has always been held by the Venetians would seem to add strength to the claim—that St. Mark established the see of Aquileia, a town about fifty or sixty miles northeast of Venice, and once a very important metropolis, from which

—their city having been destroyed by Attila in the year 452—the inhabitants fled to the lagoons of Venice, and became the founders of the city. The lion was the emblem of the evangelist Mark, similar to the likeness spoken of in the first chapter of the prophecy of Ezechiel. In Venice at almost every turn, on low pedestal or lofty pillar, is seen the winged lion, symbol of its patron saint, and also of the cherubim seen by the prophet Ezechiel before the throne of God. Meeting it so frequently, and knowing its meaning, it was to me one of the most inspiring emblems that I have ever seen. /

St. Mark's is a most wonderful church, of mixed Byzantine and Gothic style, and of oriental magnificence, on which the treasures of the East and West were lavished. It received presents from the wealthy and adventurous citizens of the republic which gold could not purchase. It is adorned by five hundred pillars of every variety of material and design, brought by ships of Venetian merchants from every region of the Orient, and among them are two, which help to support one of the altars, that are said to have belonged to the temple of Solomon in Jerusalem. St. Mark's is in the form of a Greek cross, and springing up from its walls and roof is a very forest of domes and pinnacles. At the entrance the eye is attracted by four gilded bronze horses, five feet in height, which even the man of uncultivated tastes will admire, but which the artist will at once recognize as among the choicest works of art. It is claimed by many that they are the productions of Roman skill in the time of Nero; by others it is thought that they were brought to Rome from Alexandria by Augustus Cæsar; while for a long time they were believed to be, and perhaps truly, the creations of the renowned Grecian Lysippus. In the interior the church is about 210 feet in width, by 260 feet in length. Its walls are covered with rich marbles and mosaics. How impossible it would be to give a brief and intelligible description of its remarkable mosaic pictures may be understood from the fact that they cover a surface of 45,790 square feet. When we entered the church we were somewhat surprised to find it full of people, but we immediately saw that preparations were being made for a solemn requiem Mass. The vast number of those present were standing, some were kneeling on the stone floors, while several long lines of aged men and women were occupying seats. They were dressed in uniform, the men having blue coats with brass buttons, and collars and facings like those worn by Americans in colonial days; the women were attired in a neat but more simple fashion. It was easy to see that a large number of those in attendance were not Catholics, but were drawn hither through curiosity. I approached as near to the altar as possible. Many priests were in the sanctuary, and after the Mass assisted at the absolution. A large choir occupied one gallery, and a full orchestra the other, both being just over the sanctuary on either side. The harmonious music of the two was very fine, and helped to raise my soul above the pleasures enjoyed by mere tourists, thankful that I was everywhere at home in God's Church; and for a time I forgot how hard the stone pavements are to the bended knee of the worshipper. For whom the Mass was offered I do not know, but I heard afterwards that one hundred Masses were said annually on that day for some person, who was a man of wealth and importance while he lived, and who had left a legacy to be applied in this manner for his soul.

At two o'clock in the afternoon we were waiting in the piazza to witness the feeding of the doves, which takes place daily at that hour, and has been a daily occurrence for nearly seven hundred years. Near the Church of St. Mark is a clock-tower, where two bronze Vulcans — called the "Moors" — strike the hours.

Other clocks from different towers struck the hour of two, and hardly a pigeon was seen, and none in flight; but the clock of St. Mark told us that hour had arrived, and hundreds of doves from every outside nook and corner of the great buildings around the square flew in flocks to the places where they are accustomed to be fed. Many strangers buy corn with which to feed them, and are quickly covered with the tame, confiding birds, which light upon their heads, shoulders, and hands, out of which they eat. They always know two o'clock, and wait for the right clock to strike it. /

In the evening we walked beside the harbor, and through the place of St. Mark, and observed the pleasure-seeking Venetians at their evening enjoyments. We afterwards returned to our hotel, and each chose his own method of passing the remaining two hours before retiring. I enjoyed myself at my room window, overlooking the lively street and harbor. It seems that on that particular Saturday night the inhabitants were celebrating some special event or festival, and they made a great deal of noise, with gay spirits and happy voices. But notwithstanding the more endurable temperature of the evening, and the faint breath that came over the waters from the sea, I began to long for the cooling breezes of more northern climes. The next morning was Sunday, and we attended early Mass at St. Mark's. /

CHAPTER XXVIII.

NORTHERN ITALY AND SOUTHERN SWITZERLAND.

THE early forenoon found us at the railway station, and soon after we were moving behind the iron horse over the waters that separate Venice from the mainland, on our way to Milan. We went back to Padua over the same road by which we came, but beyond that city we continued in a westerly direction, passing through Vicenza — ancient Vicetia — Verona, and Brescia—Brixia of the ancients. Many of these northern Italian cities were founded or occupied by the Celts before the Christian era, and centuries ago were towns of great wealth and importance. Brescia was once the rival of Milan, and Verona was the residence of the Ostrogoth, Theodoric the Great, and of other notable monarchs. It was also the native place of several of the classic authors. We rode along the southern shores of Lake Garda, the largest lake of Upper Italy—the Lacus Benacus of the Romans, and whose tempestuous waves are spoken of by Virgil, who was born in these northern regions, near Mantua, not far south of the place which we were now passing. It seems that the milder clime and dreamier days of the southern peninsula were more congenial to his poetic nature than the more inclement seasons of his northern home. But without doubt the more vigorous blood of his youth infused strength and energy into the warmer and more passionate life-glow of his maturer years. Our eyes rested with pleasure on the well cultivated southern borders of the lake, and penetrated as far as they were able into the wilder recesses of its northern shores, where the mountains of Tyrol raised their rugged outlines against the northern sky. I had always desired to visit the country of the devout Tyrolese, but want of time, added to the inconvenience of the route that we should have to take, discouraged the fulfilment of our first plans in that direction. We saw its mountains from the south and north, and passed nearly around its borders, but like Moses, who beheld the promised land from afar, we did not enter into it. /

/ We were now in Lombardy, a country rich in the products of nature, and in the physical and intellectual qualities of its manhood and womanhood. Rows of trees, which to my eyes resembled those familiar to us in many parts of our own land, and called by us Lombardy poplars, reminded us of home; and in other respects different regions of northern Italy were not dissimilar in appearance to parts of our own country. The country and people of Northern Italy appeared to me to differ in many of their characteristics from those of Southern Italy, and both of these from those of Central Italy; although the inhabitants of some of the seaport towns in the northern and central provinces seemed to a greater extent than the others to resemble the people of the more southern latitude. |

About the middle of the afternoon the city of St. Ambrose and St. Charles Borromeo came in sight, and soon afterward the railway guards shouted "Milano!" But the train guards of northern Italy, however robust in other respects, will never be able to sound the musical names of even their grandest cities with the lung-power and noise with which the southern

Italian guard shouts the name of his favorite "Napoli!" Milan, the Mediolanum of the Romans, is situated in the centre of Lombardy, and has always been an enterprising and wealthy city. In the earliest times known to history the surrounding country was inhabited by the Etruscans, until about the sixth century before Christ, when they were driven out by the Celts, who then founded the city of Milan, which in the third century B.C. came under the power of Rome. We directed our driver to convey us to the hotel Roma, which was some distance from the station, but near Milan's celebrated cathedral. As we rode through the city all the signs of a vigorous population were evident at first sight. The city and suburbs possess frequent and extensive lines of tramways, and we saw a number of their cars, especially in the suburbs, making fast time behind locomotives, puffing clouds of black, dirty smoke, and making their usual noise and bluster. /

When we arrived in Milan we had become wearied with much sightseeing. Sometimes for days we might recover our old enthusiasm, and then it would die out again. I think if any one of us had been asked why he came to Milan, he would have answered: To see its great cathedral; and there just before us it now appeared. No one could mistake it who has ever seen its picture; and who has not seen it many times? It seemed like an old, familiar sight, as if we had seen it in our youth, and now returned to it once more. It sometimes happens that you wish to leave on your mind the impress chiefly of one object alone. This was the case with me both in Milan and Cologne; and in each place the object was its grand, magnificent cathedral. We drove through the city of Milan, and were most favorably impressed with its appearance and people. We entered several churches, but I could hardly name them. I now wish that we had cared to observe something more of two which we passed than the mere outside. One of these was the Church of St. Ambrose, whose body lies beneath the high altar, and where the saintly bishop rebuked the Emperor Theodosius, and where he preached those learned and eloquent homilies which accomplished the conversion of St. Augustine. The other church — or rather convent adjoining — was that of St. Mary of Grace, which contains the world-renowned painting of the Last Supper by Leonardo da Vinci. We saw a fine statue of the artist in one of the public places; and during our ride, after the first visit to the cathedral, we saw the outside of the principal public buildings, places, and monuments of Milan. But having seen them we were attracted back to the great cathedral church, and were best satisfied when we could sit or stand where we could enjoy a new view of its grandeur and beauty. /

After engaging rooms at the hotel, and before our jaunt through the city, we started out to pay our first visit to that temple whose shining walls we had seen only from the outside and in the distance. When we entered, an afternoon service, that did not seem to be Vespers, was just terminating, which was followed by a sermon delivered with life and energy, and, if I remember rightly, was concluded with the Benediction of the Most Holy Sacrament. We afterwards had an opportunity of viewing the church. The present edifice was commenced in the fourteenth century, and was consecrated about two hundred years afterwards by St. Charles Borromeo; and beneath its dome, in a subterranean chapel richly ornamented with gold and silver and precious stones, his body rests. St. Charles became Archbishop of Milan at the age of twenty-three, and ruled the see half his life, dying at the age of forty-six. It is said that the church of Milan was planted by St. Barnabas the Apostle. Besides St. Ambrose and St. Charles, thirty-one of its bishops have been canonized saints. The present cathedral edifice was built on the site of the ancient episcopal basilica of the city. Its length is 486 feet; its width in the transepts, 288 feet; the highest point in the arching of the nave, 155 feet; the height of its highest tower, which is surmounted by a statue of the Blessed Virgin, 360 feet; and, next to St. Peter's in Rome, it is the largest church in the world. It is built almost entirely of white marble, which has become tinged with a color more or less yellowish, according to its exposure to the weather. Springing from its walls and roof are 135 pinnacles and spires, and it contains about three thousand statues in its niches or rising from the topmost points of its spires and turrets. Many niches are yet vacant, and when they are occupied the total number of statues will be 4,500. In the interior of the structure are 52 pillars, each 12 feet in diameter and 80 feet in height. Instead of the foliated capitals usual to columns in Gothic churches, their summits or capitals, which are 18½ feet in length, although not lacking in foliations, are encircled and adorned with canopied niches in which are placed statues of the saints. Nearly every reader is already acquainted with its lavish ornamentation, rich emblematic windows of stained glass, and the numerous works of art that adorn its altars. We saw and appreciated this great church as only a Catholic can see and appreciate the temple which he knows was built for the tabernacle and has become the dwelling-place of the Incarnate God./

Towards evening we seated ourselves in a pleasant place, not far distant from the church, where we could enjoy the golden light of the departing day and quietly contemplate a scene truly Milanese. Throngs of people of both sexes, on foot and in carriages, were constantly passing. More than half the females wore black lace veils instead of bonnets for a head-covering. We sat and watched the happy faces, and listened to the merry voices of the passers-by, which with a large number were without doubt the reflections of the bright sunlight of peace and love, and echoes of the rippling music of joy which the Lord's Day brings to the hearts of many. We lingered while the resplendent sunbeams climbed higher and higher up the walls of Milan's great cathedral, until its forest of spires and statues, turrets and towers, was bathed in an ethereal sea of splendor which the rising or setting sun alone is able to pour out upon this world of ours. We did not depart until the last rays of the orb of day had crept to the very brow of the statue of the Queen of Heaven that adorns the highest tower, and had encircled its head with a halo of glory, which slowly melted away into twilight./

Early the next morning we were already settled in a railway carriage, with tickets for Lucerne, in Switzerland. The ride for the first few miles was not very interesting, but we knew that before we reached the end of the day's journey our eyes and hearts would be delighted with probably the finest and grandest scenery of Europe. While the country was yet Italian, with most of the characteristics that belong to the name, it became more and more distinctively marked as northern Italian. The Alpine Mountains gradually appeared more clearly defined, and we could see that we were approaching a region in many respects different from any that we had before seen. The clear, blue waters of Lake Como soon came in sight, surrounded by their lofty mountain shores. This lake is considered one of the most beautiful in the world, lying in the midst of a fertile district, which is inhabited by an intelligent and prosperous people. Lake Como was the Lacus Larius of the Romans, and Virgil sings its praises. The town of Como is claimed to have been the birthplace of the elder and younger Pliny, and of other distinguished men. At stations like that of Como our train usually stopped five or ten minutes. For a short distance after leaving the station the railroad ran along the borders of the lake, and I tried to get a good view of every changing scene, to see if there was any that I remembered ever to have seen in pictures. In about half an hour we reached the shores of Lake Lugano, along which we rode for nearly half the way from Como to Lugano, a succession of views appearing as delightful as any that I have ever seen. I am unable to express my full admiration for this country, so beautiful and grand, so rich and rare in all the resources of nature.

At Lugano our baggage was examined and we were fumigated. It was lucky for us that we were travelling north instead of south, for the Italian authorities had proclaimed a quarantine of five days. The next year Italy got the cholera, and Switzerland escaped it. We passed through the charming valleys of Ticino, the Italian canton of Switzerland. We traversed almost the entire length of the valley of the river Ticino, and at length began gradually to ascend the Alps. The road would pass through a tunnel, and then curve around the mountain and into another tunnel, until finally, with Alpine peaks half-surrounding us, we could look down the mountain-side into a wide-extended valley spread out far below us, with its farms, villages, and cities, and its river like a thread of shining silver winding through a green velvet ground. We passed over rushing torrents and through many quiet Alpine hamlets, reposing in the silence and solitude of the mountains, where even the noisy, hastening train hardly seemed to disturb them for a moment in their dreamy existence. I began to feel a desire to live in one of those mountain hamlets, far away from the noise, business, and molestations of the world. I began a poem, which I intend to finish on some future occasion, as an expression of my feelings at that time:

> Oh! in the Swiss mountains would I might dwell,
>   With a few loved friends around me,
> While none but those bound by love's mystic spell
>   Should in my hamlet surround me.

After a while we were entirely surrounded by the grand, glorious mountains. Sometimes on both sides were mountain heights; at other times on one side would be a deep, wild chasm, and looking down into its depths the brain would grow dizzy; on the other side, thousands of feet above us, giant peaks raised their crested heads into the regions of perpetual snow, and seemed almost to touch the sky. In places the snow did not appear to be far above us, while in others it was more distant, and, melting under the heat of a July sun, sent down the rocky steeps cascades white-foaming and bright-shining in the sunlight, which, as well as I could judge, fell down in an almost perpendicular line two thousand feet. When not entirely occupied with outside scenery we found a number of things inside the car to invite our attention, and, when the train would go slow or stop, the conversation was not altogether uninteresting. Our car was modelled partly after the American style, and I must acknowledge that this fact—because there was a larger and more diversified company—added in some ways to the pleasure of the journey. As we began to leave the valley and ascend the mountain, I made closer observations of my immediate surroundings. I found that the more dogmatic of my two friends was crowded into rather close quarters in the neighborhood of an English lady, who, finding that he spoke English, and seeing a number of wayside shrines along the mountain road, unhappily for herself had made a bigoted remark about them. He was engaged in telling her some salutary truths which probably she never before had heard. My other friend, who rather prides himself on business matters, was explaining to the lady's brother how it happens that English stockholders do not always realize as large a percentage on their American railroad stocks as they had anticipated. Just in front of me, on a seat facing mine, were a bride and bridegroom. She was a good-looking country girl, but there was no great attraction in that; it was the old-fashioned bridal costume she wore that interested me. If I remember rightly, she wore a colored skirt, with a white and colored bodice, while silver chains and ornaments, fastening the various parts, were skilfully arranged to produce a pleasing effect. Her mother and her grandmother, and perhaps her ancestors in the female line for centuries, wore a bridal dress like the one in which she was now adorned. I like old fashions, for they have a memory and a history attached to them. I like those people who cling to the customs and costumes, and who have a love for the traditions of their forefathers. /

The train had at length climbed the mountains until we were nearly four thousand feet above the level of the sea, and about to enter the tunnel of St. Gothard, which is the longest in the world. It is nine and one-half miles in length, and it took the train twenty-five minutes to pass through it. The highest summit of the mountain through which the tunnel is made rises to the height of about eleven thousand feet. We were now in the vicinity of the sources of the rivers Rhine, Rhone, and Ticino, whose respective waters flow into the German, Mediterranean, and Adriatic seas. At the next station after our exit from the tunnel we took dinner. Although in the valleys below the day had been quite warm, we were here surrounded by thick mists, and it was so chilly that we were thankful to have our overcoats to wear on leaving the train. /

CHAPTER XXIX.

THE HOME OF WILLIAM TELL AND THE FOUR FOREST CANTONS.

The descent had already commenced, and was a reversed repetition of the ascent, although the northern side is not so steep as the southern, and in some other respects the nature of the country had changed; the southern side of the mountains being the land of the vine and yellow sunshine, and the northern side a land of lowing herds and green pastures. We had now entered the region where Swiss independence had its birth. We passed through Bürglen, the birthplace of William Tell, and soon after through Altdorf, the place where Tell is said to have shot the apple from his son's head, although this story is probably a fable. The next station was Flüelen, where the beautiful waters of Lake Lucerne, "the lake of the four forest cantons," lay calmly in the midst of the grand Swiss mountains, whose rocky heights so often echoed to the shouts of heroes in their battles for liberty. Many of the passengers here left the train to take the boat for Lucerne, as that is considered the most interesting route. We were doubtful whether to throw away our railway tickets and go by steamboat, or continue by land. We decided to go by rail, and I, for one, was not sorry. Probably the water route was to be preferred, but we should have missed so many charming views, where mountain scenery, glimpses of the bright waters of the lake, green pastures and meadows, grazing flocks and herds, large, comfortable Swiss farmhouses and pleasant and picturesque villages, commingled in ever-recurring scenes of delight, that I am well satisfied with our choice. If we had not chosen as we did, no other part of Europe that we saw could have taken the place of that journey of an hour.

The "four forest cantons," Lucerne, Schwytz, Uri, and Unterwalden, which surround the Lake of Lucerne, three of which formed the original Swiss league of the thirteenth century, which the fourth soon afterward joined, are the strongholds of Swiss freedom, as Switzerland is the keystone of civil liberty in Europe. Sometimes Switzerland forgets her traditions, and by a bare majority overrides the rights of those of her citizens to whose ancestors she owes whatever of liberty she possesses. The inhabitants of these four cantons are almost entirely German, and have retained that ancient faith which their forefathers held when the morning sun which ushered in the day of Swiss national independence shone with a new light over their mountains, lakes, and valleys./

About the middle of the afternoon we arrived in Lucerne. The situation of the city, humanly speaking, is perfect. On the banks of the Reuss, on the shores of the lake of Lucerne, it reposes like a picture encircled in a frame of mountains. Before sin and its effects entered into the world, Switzerland was an earthly paradise; and so far as the mere charms of nature are concerned, the curse of God fell lightly on it. He evidently wished to preserve some spots of earth as only partially disfigured patterns of the first beauties of His creation. Probably not every one would enjoy Swiss scenery as I did, but, next to God and faith, and the objects they present to my devotion, nature and nationalities have always held one of the most sacred places in my heart. And it is possible that the spirit of freedom, which so often dwells in the fastnesses of mountains, may have enhanced in my eyes the natural charms of Switzerland.

I was born under a democratic government, and the first banner that pleased my childish eyes was the flag of a republic; it is therefore but natural that wherever in the Old World I found republics, past or present, which had exalted the name, and where the home was loved and the family honored, I experienced a feeling of gratification. Yet I have a no less sincere admiration for those kingdoms and empires that have fulfilled the true destiny of civil government towards the people and towards God. But in Switzerland the angel of liberty that first floated on the light of the morning had around her brow not alone a garland of all that is beautiful in nature, but a nimbus of all that is radiant in grace divine.

We went to the hotel which we had selected, the name of which I have forgotten, but it proved to be an excellent one. Lucerne has so many good hotels, so pleasantly located, that it would hardly be necessary to mention the name of any one in particular. After we had been shown our rooms we started out for a long stroll through the town, visiting several churches, in which there were monuments and decorations quaint and old, and where we were glad once more to see pews. In my mind pews or well-arranged chairs are in some way closely associated with proper Christian instruction. We passed over the different bridges with their legendary paintings, and saw whatever else was curious or interesting. We bought a number of articles, and were always pleased with the honest habits of the people. When we entered one of the stores, the English lady whom we had met on the train was trying to make a bargain, speaking German with a decided English accent, which seemed very much to puzzle the saleswoman. One of my friends made proper explanation of what she wanted to say, and the parties came to an understanding. Towards evening and again the next morning we spent our time sitting in some quiet place enjoying the scenes surrounding us. We thought of making an excursion on the lake. A ride on the lake would have been pleasant, and a visit to the Rigi, which appeared in the near distance, would have been inspiring; but we finally concluded that we enjoyed ourselves full as well where we were.

Towards noon on the day after our arrival we took the train for Rorschach, on the lake of Constance. Early in the journey we passed through the two old cities of Zug and Zurich, situated on lakes of the same name. At Winterthur we could have made connection with a train which passed through St. Gall, but we did not know it in time, and had bought tickets by way of Romanshorn. From this last place the railway ran by the side of the lake until we reached our destination, where we arrived about three hours before dark. During the day we had passed through a fertile and prosperous country, and had the opportunity of testing the truthfulness of the statement of some Protestant travellers, that one can readily discern when he passes from a Catholic to a Protestant canton by the signs of superior industry in the latter. I had supposed it hardly possible that imagination and bigotry could so prejudice the judgment of man, for it is impossible to tell the difference between them. The scenery of most of the Catholic cantons that we saw during the ride pleased me better, but yet I could not in honesty affirm that in them the farms were better cultivated or the farm-buildings better than those of their Protestant neighbors. They seem to learn good farming and habits of industry from each other without regard to the religion that they profess. I am sure that I am not at all prejudiced in this matter, for the neat hedges and well-kept farms of England delighted my eyes just the same as if they had not been owned and cultivated by Protestant farmers. How such fictions can be related by honest men is inconceivable. But bigotry usually makes men dishonest and incapable of truthful statements on any matter even remotely connected with religion. We had partly expected to meet in Rorschach an honored priest and professor of our Provincial Seminary, who was visiting his native place, and who had requested us to notify him of our coming, which we had failed to do. We were informed by his brother that the doctor had been absent for several days on a visit to Lucerne, the city which we had just left. We enjoyed ourselves until dark strolling through the quiet town, refreshed by the breezes that were wafted over the land from the cool surface of the Boden See.

CHAPTER XXX.

FROM LAKE CONSTANCE TO THE CITY OF THE APOSTLE OF GERMANY, BY WAY OF MUNICH.

The next morning we took the boat for Lindau, in Bavaria, on our way to Munich. The lake of Constance, which we were now crossing, is about forty-five miles long and nine miles wide. Its shores belong to the territory of Baden, Würtemberg, Bavaria, Austria, and Switzerland.

It was a beautiful morning, and as we floated out over the waters of the lake the receding shores of Switzerland rose into higher uplands at the south, and towards the north settled into a level, fertile plain with farm-houses and villages. Toward the southeast the snow-capped mountains of Tyrol shone in the morning sunlight, while close to the water, but near to the mountains, reposed the fair Austrian town of Bregenz. We were sorry that we could not set our feet on Austrian soil, but were glad that under such favorable circumstances our eyes rested on so pleasant a corner of the Austrian domain. I have a very friendly feeling toward Austria, because it is a land that has probably been least harmed by irreligious liberalism of any country of national importance in Europe. Before us was the Catholic land of Bavaria; and probably that low-lying line of blue between the lake and sky, darker than either, away to the northwest, belonged to Würtemberg and Baden. To the true German heart this must be one of the central places of interest in the Fatherland. No one of us had any German blood in his veins, but we all appreciated that calm morning when a loving sky smiled upon a region of the earth so fair.

In about an hour we landed at Lindau, which is built on an island, where we were to take the train for Munich. It would not start for more than an hour, so we concluded in the meantime to ramble through the city. The streets were quiet, and the inhabitants had evidently begun the day with the intention of keeping as cool as the weather would allow. By a few purchases we got our first experience of the cheapness of articles of food and drink in Bavaria and some other parts of southern Germany. Nearly everything in that line costs only about half what it does in other parts of Europe, and for those having incomes from other countries, it must be a very economical place of residence./

We returned to the station in time for the train to Munich. The country through which we passed was comparatively level, and seemed to be chiefly agricultural. The towns were not large, but were well built, and always possessed a substantial church, of the plain, German style, and which was usually the principal edifice of the place. During nearly the entire ride the Bavarian Alps presented an uneven chain of rocky heights and snow-capped peaks along the southern horizon. We were now passing through Catholic Bavaria. The population of Bavaria is almost entirely of the Germanic race, and about three-fourths of its inhabitants are Catholics. Near the middle of the afternoon we arrived in Munich, and having chosen a hotel not far from the railroad station, and having secured rooms, we started out to see the city. Munich, which was originally a monastic town, is not a city of great antiquity in the European sense, although if it were in America it would be considered a very old city, having been a place of considerable importance for about seven centuries. Looked on from a modern standpoint, it is one of the most attractive cities of Europe. It is situated on the river Isar, and contains a population of more than 230,000. It is stated by good authorities that the excellent qualities of the water from the Isar, coming as it does with quick flow from the mountains of Tyrol, have much to do in making Munich beer celebrated throughout the world. Whether this peculiar quality was discovered by the people of Munich from chemical analysis, or whether they actually drank some of the water, I was not informed. In other countries of Europe Vienna beer appears to be more popular; but when we consider the size of an ordinary measure of beer according to the Munich standard, its low price, and the natural patriotism of any people which influences them to patronize home institutions, we can readily surmise why so little Munich beer ever gets outside of Bavaria. It has been noticed that the many foreigners who live in Munich become quickly attached to the native habits of the people, and it is not an uncommon sight to see a stranger from foreign lands sitting in some public resort with a half-gallon beer-mug before him, trying to look like a native of the place; and oftentimes he would not be detected if he did not drink his beer in about half the time taken by one to the manner born. /

We went to Munich to see the manner of life of its inhabitants as they appeared in the churches, on the streets, in the parks, and wherever we might meet them. Among the first objects that I wanted to see was the Isar. We took a street-car—whose passengers to some extent made me think of Milwaukee—and rode until we had crossed the swift-flowing stream, where we alighted just at the entrance into an extensive park. Here we had full freedom to wander up and down the river-bank, amid the shady groves and grassy dells, where we could get a brief rest from the scenes and noise of cities and railway trains. Snatches of Munich stories of artist and student life floated on dreamy wings through my memory, and communicated a poetic atmosphere and spirit to Munich life and scenes.\

The next day we started out at rather an early hour to get a sight of the people and streets in the morning; for we had found from experience that the morning hour presents another view of the people than midday or afternoon. We walked a part of the time, and then would rest ourselves in some place favorable for observation. At length we reached the cathedral church, which is a venerable edifice, containing a large number of finely adorned altars. Near the door through which we entered was a notice, printed in different languages, forbidding tourists and others during the morning hours to walk about the church inspecting the paintings and other works of art. This did not apply to us, for we united some devotion with our curiosity, and knelt for a short time before making an inspection of each altar and its adornment. In this way we better appreciated what we saw ; for when with reverential spirit one visits the different parts of a church on which much labor and art have been bestowed, he gets a better conception of the fitness of the work for the special objects of devotion. We learned that in a few hours afterwards the archbishop would bless two handsome bells which were mounted near the front entrance. We determined to return at the time appointed, more than anything else to see the archbishop and clergy. There were but few present when the hour arrived. The archbishop with the clergy soon appeared, and began the long ceremony of benediction. We also visited the church of St. Michael, which is decorated in the style usually adopted by the Jesuits. We entered several other churches, the names of which I have forgotten. Some were rich in the material and style of architecture employed in their construction, and one was chiefly noticeable for its ancient appearance. We took the tram-cars and rode through the streets containing the principal public buildings; we also made a hasty visit to the University, and then passed under a triumphal arch into a country-like district. Having taken a long walk, we again entered the street-cars to return to the more central portion of the city. I have since wondered why I did not visit some of the celebrated Munich art-galleries. But at that time I was impressed with the idea that, for a while at least, I had seen enough of picture-galleries, and wanted to see more of the people and out-door life and characteristics of Europe. Not that I was weary of the works of the great masters, but, outside of those that I might meet in the churches, I did not wish to put myself to the inconvenience of going to the places where they were exhibited. We took two of our meals in restaurants. The second place we visited for that purpose appeared to be a favorite resort of students and young artists. Next to German, English was the language oftenest heard among them.

When evening came two of our number sought our rooms for rest, but our companion declared that evening was the best time to enjoy Munich life and to witness her people in their gayest mood. During the night it commenced to rain, and when I looked out of my window in the morning it appeared very much like the first day of the Deluge. I love a rainy day when I can remain in-doors, and under almost any circumstances I do not dislike it. The streets and city had wonderfully changed, under the dark shadows of the storm, from what they were on the bright day preceding, but I enjoyed them almost better.

Towards noon we were passing out of the city on the train for Ulm. The country was drenched by the rain, which still continued. As a consequence, nature was clothed in a clean, fresh mantle of beauty, which needed only the bright rays of the sun to make it a smiling green. We passed through Augsburg, which is one of the oldest cities of Germany, colonized by the Emperor Augustus on a site already inhabited, and called Damasia. The country through which we passed was more pleasing to my eyes than that from Lindau to Munich.

Early in the afternoon we crossed the Danube and arrived in Ulm, where we had concluded to spend the remainder of the day and the night. We rarely travelled by night, as we wished to see the whole country through which we journeyed. We selected a hotel near the station. There were only a few other guests, but among them was a priest from Switzerland, who was much interested in the narrations of one of my companions about the Holy Land. After making all necessary arrangements we started out to take a stroll through the city. The rain had almost entirely ceased, although at times we found it convenient to make use of our umbrellas. Ulm is a quaint old Swabian town, and its buildings are stately and old-fashioned. The waters of its various streams were rushing past its picturesque old mills and under its venerable bridges, soon to join the deeper waters of the Danube. From this point the Danube becomes fully navigable, and in consequence Ulm has always been an important commercial centre.

The chief object of interest in the city is the "cathedral," which is more than five hundred years old. It is now in the hands of the Protestants, and is one of the largest Protestant churches in Germany, being 420 feet in length and 165 feet in width. If it had been built by them it would not have been so large. Notwithstanding some late efforts at restoration, it continues to appear very dilapidated. A feeling of sorrow entered my heart when I considered that it is of so little use to them, and how much labor and self-sacrifice it cost those who built it in the spirit of faith, with full confidence that so long as it would exist it should be the temple of sacrifice and the habitation of the sacrificial Victim. In the large sacristy we were shown, as curiosities, the ancient adornments of the altars and church: an old crucifix, some sacred paintings and metal reliefs, and other objects once held in veneration, a part of them preserved for their intrinsic value, and others because they were presented by kings and emperors. When it was late in the afternoon we returned to our hotel for dinner. The proprietor, who was a Catholic, tried to make us feel quite at home, in which he was very successful. \

The next morning we took the train for Mainz, and during the forenoon passed through the fertile kingdom of Würtemberg. We enjoyed the fine country, the well-cultivated fields, and the cities and villages along the line of road, surrounded by their gardens and park-like suburbs. But we were not specially interested until we began to approach the region of Heidelberg. It is an ancient university town, now belonging to Baden, situated on the river Neckar, amidst hills whose sloping sides are covered with vineyards. For fully an hour, including the stop at the station, we enjoyed its romantic surroundings. Yet, after all, its scenery could not compare with that of scores of other places which we saw. But to me there was a poetic enchantment of my youth spread over the scene. It was like the remembrance of something humanly sacred, almost forgotten and suddenly revived; or, if it were possible, the memory of something never experienced, but so vividly hoped for that it had become a partaker of some of the attributes of actual existence; or like something that had been realized in another state of existence, and now remembered as if a dream. When I was a Protestant student in college I had asked my father to let me finish my studies in Heidelberg. He did not then consent, because it was so far away from home. But when the time came that my desire might have been gratified, God's providence had changed the whole direction of my life. When I looked out over the place that might have been my home for years, and saw the scenes that might have become familiar to my eyes, it made a sad, strange impression, like, if it could be so, the loving remembrance of a place that had reflected its image in my soul, but which I had never seen. Heidelberg soon disappeared, and the imagination of youth and the vision of an hour now stand side by side in fancy, and the one does not seem much less real than the other. For a considerable distance the train ran by the side of the Neckar, which we at length crossed, and shortly after entered Hesse-Darmstadt. About four o'clock in the afternoon we reached Mainz, the city of St. Boniface, Apostle of Germany.

CHAPTER XXXI.

FROM MAINZ TO COLOGNE—THE VINE-CLAD AND CASTLE-CROWNED RHINE.

MAINZ, or Mayence—the ancient Roman Moguntiacum—is a fortified town situated on the Rhine in Hesse-Darmstadt opposite Nassau. It was a Roman camp in the time of the empire, and contains many remnants of the occupation of the Consul Drusus, who died just before the beginning of the Christian era. St. Boniface chose Mainz for his archiepiscopal see about the middle of the eighth century, and ever since it has been an ecclesiastical centre of great influence. Having taken rooms in the hotel which we had chosen, we rambled about the city until near dark. Some kind of musical festival was in progress, and the streets had put on a holiday appearance. Our first visit was to the cathedral, the erection of which was commenced in the tenth century. It is a venerable building with imposing battlements and towers, and many times popes and emperors have passed under its portals within its walls. It has pews, like most of the German churches which we entered. In some churches of Europe chairs—having kneeling-stools—were so well arranged in rows that they answered all the purposes of pews. In the Guttenberg Place we saw the statue of Guttenberg, the inventor of printing, who was a native of the city.

Towards evening we wandered into the suburbs to an eminence overlooking the town and commanding a fine view of the Rhine and surrounding country. And when the dark shadows of coming night enveloped the earth, and the lights appeared in the city and on the river, we conversed in lower tones, and I at least felt our solitude, but with a vivid consciousness that we were near one of the great arteries of the world's life, so near that we could feel a tremulous movement from its pulsation; and so powerful was the mysterious influence of the time and place that, if I had my friends around me, here would I be content to dwell in the land of the stranger.

The next morning, which was Sunday, we attended Mass in the cathedral, preparatory to taking the boat at nine o'clock. At that hour we went on board a pleasant Rhine steamer, which soon after swung out into the stream. The voyage before us was the one so much praised by all who have ever made it; for we were about to pass through the most interesting scenery of the celebrated river whose mountainous banks are vine-clad and castle-crowned. It would be useless to attempt to describe the towns, the castles, and places of historic name, or to recite the innumerable legends connected with this romantic "Paradise of Germany." During the first and last part of the journey the country on either side was comparatively level, but during the greater portion of the voyage it presented a series of rocky heights and luxuriant undulations, marked by the ruins of Roman occupation, and adorned with the castellated strongholds and picturesque towns of the middle ages.

The castle of Johannisberg, on its vine-covered hill, founded as a priory in the year 1006, appeared upon our right, and, after a while, Bingen on our left, at the entrance of the fair valley of the Nahe, surrounded by its vineyards, and Rüdesheim on the opposite side of the river, above which, on a high slope of the Niederwald, the statue of Germania raised its colossal form. It was a beautiful day, and our boat glided over the waters of the romantic stream, between its historic banks, with their ever-changing scenery, until it had borne us into the very midst of that region where the fancies of dream-land, the fairy scenes of legendary stories, and the grand dramas of history exert a mysterious influence upon the thoughts of men who wander within their realms. The appropriate lines of an English poet of the last century could well be applied to our summer-day voyage and the scenes that we saw:

> "Twas morn, and beautiful the mountain's brow—
> Hung with the clusters of the bending vine—
> Shone in the early light, when on the Rhine
> We sailed and heard the waters round the prow
> In murmurs parting; varying as we go,
> Rocks after rocks come forward and retire,
> As some gray convent wall or sunlit spire
> Starts up along the banks, unfolding slow.
> Here castles, like the prisons of despair,
> Frown as we pass!—there, on the vineyard's side,
> The bursting sunshine pours its streaming tide;
> While grief, forgetful amid scenes so fair,
> Counts not the hours of a long summer's day,
> Nor heeds how fast the prospect winds away."

Among the many places that attracted our attention, either in themselves or because we already had some knowledge of their legends and history, I will only mention a few: Sonneck castle; Lorch, one of the oldest of the Rhenish towns, at the entrance of a beautiful valley rich in fairy legends; Bacharach, which derives its name from a rock in the river called the "Bacchi-Ara"—altar of Bacchus; Caub, with a palatine castle in the centre of the stream, and the castle of Gutenfels above the town; the castle of Rheinstein; the pleasantly situated town of Oberwesel and Schönberg castle; the rugged and steep Loreley rock, where the Siren sits with the golden harp, and which returns fifteen echoes and has a legend connected with it—which last is also true of the rocks a little higher up the river in mid channel and called the Seven Sisters; Stolzenfels, a fine castle of the Middle Ages; St. Goar and the Rheinfels, a strong robber castle of the thirteenth century; the castles called the "Cat" and the "Mouse"; Lahneck castle, built in the year 900; the Brothers, Sternberg and Liebenstein, the subject of a legend; the fine old castles of Braubach and Marksburg; the city of Coblence, the Roman Confluentia, where the Emperor Caligula was born, and which possesses the church of St. Castor, easily recognized by its four towers, and built in the year 836; the White Tower, where Julius Cæsar crossed the Rhine on a bridge described in his *Commentaries;* the fine modern, Gothic Apollinaris church, built by the renowned

Zwirner, the restorer of the cathedral of Cologne; Roland's rock, the beautiful island of Nonnenwerth, and "the castled crag of Drachenfels," the most celebrated of the Seven Mountains, where the dragon was slain by the hero Siegfried of the old German epic poem, *Nibelungenlied;* and, not far distant across the river, Godesberg with its stately old castle on the hill.

We left the grander region of the Rhine when we passed the university city of Bonn —the Roman Bonna—which ancient town is said to have embraced Christianity within the first century of the Christian era, and which contains a minster built by the Empress St. Helena, which was founded by her in the year 320. In a short time the glorious spires of the cathedral of Cologne appeared in the distance. No one who has seen their picture could mistake the edifice to which they belong. Like the cathedral of Milan, that of Cologne is familiar to the eyes of the civilized world. In half an hour our boat had reached its landing, and we took a conveyance to a hotel in the immediate vicinity of the cathedral.

Cologne was founded by the Roman Emperor Claudius, A.D. 51, and named Colonia

Agrippina in honor of his wife, Agrippina, who was born in Cologne when it was a Roman camp, and who was the daughter of Germanicus, and sister of Caligula, and the mother of Nero. It is claimed that even to this day many of the citizens of Cologne have much of the old Roman blood coursing through their veins, and some pretend to see in their features and complexions traces of their Roman descent. I went to Cologne to see the cathedral, and whenever I left the hotel I directed my steps thitherward, and spent nearly all my time in and around it. There are other grand old churches in Cologne, but I did not visit them, for I wanted to leave the city with one lasting impression on my memory. As soon as we had arranged matters at the hotel and our baggage had arrived we went to the cathedral. The first Christian church was established here during the time of the Roman occupation, but the old cathedral was founded early in the ninth century on the site of the ancient citadel. The present edifice was begun about the middle of the thirteenth century; it is dedicated to St. Peter, and is frequently called St. Peter's of the North. It is often styled the "queen of cathedrals and the pearl of Gothic churches," which designation is altogether fitting. When we entered the church the people were beginning to assemble for afternoon services. We had time, before they commenced, to walk through the different parts of the vast edifice, and then went outside to get a look at its external proportions and beauty. When we re-entered we found that a large audience was listening to a sermon which was delivered with much spirit and animation.

When the sermon was ended many left the church, while the larger number removed to another part of the church where Benediction of the Most Holy Sacrament was to be given. The music, as near as I can remember, was first a beautiful solo by a female voice, which under the circumstances I never like—or it may have been a piece by a select choir with that one voice chiefly prominent—and afterwards singing by the whole congregation, which I always like. When Benediction was over I had more liberty to walk through the church and admire its exquisite architecture. It springs up from the strong foundations of faith on which it was begun into the ten thousand enduring graces and beauties of love and devotion in which it abounds, on the inside of its sacred walls catching the prismatic colors of heaven, and on the outside, on its flying buttresses and forests of pinnacles and traceries, and on its spires reaching towards the sky, the golden sunlight of God's countenance. I went outside and walked around it different times, often standing for a while to see it more perfectly, and delighted with every point of view. For several hours I looked on the interior and exterior of this marvellous creation of genius and religion, which ravishes the eye but far more expands the soul, and admired ; but how in so short a time could I properly appreciate Cologne's cathedral?

It contains the entire relics—bones and skulls—of the three Wise Men from the East who came to Bethlehem to adore the Infant Saviour, whose names are handed down by tradition as Melchior, Caspar, and Balthasar. These relics formerly belonged to the cathedral of Milan, but were transferred to her Gothic sister by the Emperor Frederick Barbarossa.

CHAPTER XXXII.

FROM THE BANKS OF THE RHINE TO BELGIUM'S AND HOLLAND'S CAPITALS.

The next morning we took the train for Brussels, intending to break our journey for a few hours at Aix-la-Chapelle. The part of the country through which we first passed was flat and level, but fertile and well cultivated. In less than two hours we had arrived at the last-named city, and alighted from the train to spend a brief and pleasant time in that interesting town where Charlemagne fixed his residence, where he was buried, and which he made second city of his empire.

We decided to walk leisurely through the streets of this historic old place on our way to the cathedral, which was the principal object of our visit. A church comparatively new, built in the Gothic style, attracted our attention and we entered. It was a real modern gem of architectural beauty. When we reached the cathedral Mass was being offered, and a large number of worshippers were present. After Mass was finished we found ourselves at full liberty to go through the many different parts of the church, which is filled with relics and antiquities. It was built by Charlemagne, and was consecrated in the year 804 by Pope St. Leo III., who came all the way from Rome for the occasion. There were present at the ceremony many princes and cardinals and three hundred and sixty-three bishops. Thirty-seven emperors and eleven empresses have been crowned within its walls. It possesses many remarkable relics, presented to Charlemagne by different kings and pontiffs. Among them are the dress of the Blessed Virgin, the swaddling-clothes of the Infant Jesus in Bethlehem, the cloth which encircled the loins of our Lord on the cross, the cloth which enveloped the head of St. John the Baptist after his death, the cincture of the Blessed Virgin, the leathern belt of our Lord, a piece of the cord with which the hands of our Lord were bound during His Passion, a portion of the sponge that was dipped in vinegar and gall and presented to Him, a rib of St. Stephen, and many other relics of great importance. A few of the greatest are exposed publicly only once in seven years. We were admitted to the treasury and were permitted to venerate its sacred treasures, whether all of them—there are so many—I cannot well remember. They are kept in strong iron safes —which were opened for us—and many of them are preserved in costly reliquaries. We also saw the throne of Charlemagne, and his empty sarcophagus, in which, long before his time, one of the greatest Roman emperors had likewise been buried. The other historical objects which were pointed out to us were so many that, although interesting in themselves, their list would be long and tedious.

In due time we took the train for Brussels. It was not long before we passed out of German territory into Belgium. Our first experience of the Belgian land was most agreeable, for we were traversing the most picturesque region which that country affords. Our road ran through a continual succession of beautiful valleys, crossing and recrossing the charming river Vesdre, past delightful villages under the protecting shelter of rugged and well-wooded hills; and the green, well-watered pastures, adjoining luxuriant meadows, were stocked with plentiful herds of sleek, noble-looking cattle. Every farm seemed to be a perfect rural picture in itself, on the banks of the rushing river, adorned with trees, where the eye could rest on pleasant, comfortable farm houses and nestling villages, and the landscape encircled by a rustic frame of romantic hills.\

After more than an hour we passed through Liège, the industrious capital of the Walloon district. The Walloons are of Celtic race, and have ever enjoyed the distinction of being a hardy, hard-working, and brave people. Their Flemish fellow-countrymen on the west in Brabant, of which Brussels is the centre, and in other provinces, are of Germanic origin, and in the whole country are in a small majority over their Walloon compatriots. The remainder of the journey to Brussels was at first through a district of industrial activity, and for two hours afterwards through a level, well-cultivated country, passing on our way the university town of Louvain. In Rome and southern Italy high silk hats are extremely rare. As one goes farther north they become more frequent, and in France and England, especially in Paris and London, they are the stylish hats; but Belgium and Holland seem to be their own country, and they are seen everywhere on the heads of two-thirds of all well-dressed gentlemen. In our compartment besides ourselves were five gentlemen, of whom four wore high silk hats, and the other one looked lonesome. Our fellow-travellers were speaking a language which to us was altogether strange; whether it was Walloon or Flemish I am unable to decide; and the printed words that we saw, often occupying places of prominence, were a wonder to the eye, and, when spoken, a mystery to the ear.

About four o'clock we reached the Station du Nord, and for our sojourn we chose the Grand Hotel Gernay, because it was near the station where we arrived and from which we would take our departure. Brussels dates back to the eighth century, when it was a town of but little importance. At the present time, including its extensive suburbs, its population is nearly 400,000, but the city proper does not contain half that number of inhabitants. It is a finely built city, with many wide and splendid streets, and is often called "Paris in miniature," which city it pretends to rival, but with the magnificence of which it can never hope to compare. We strolled through the streets during the remainder of the afternoon and early evening; and on the following day we visited those parts of the city that might prove to be of special interest.

The cathedral of St. Gudule and St. Michael is a grand Gothic building, 354 feet long by 165 feet wide. It was built in the thirteenth century on the site of a former church erected in the eleventh century. It contains some of the finest painted windows in Europe, and its pulpit is considered one of the great masterpieces of carving, representing the expulsion of Adam and Eve from the Garden of Eden, and the redemption of Christ. St. Gudule, to whom the cathedral is dedicated, is patroness of Brussels. The Gothic structure called the Hôtel de Ville, or city hall, is also a noble edifice, which was begun at the opening of the fifteenth century. It is claimed that the Place in front is one of the finest and most picturesque mediæval squares in existence. On our way to the cathedral of St. Gudule we saw a hearse standing in front of a church, and we knew that a funeral was being solemnized. We entered, and saw at least one ceremony that we had never before seen: a large number of men were advancing to the altar, and in turn kissed the paten held by the celebrant. At the time we did not know the meaning of the custom, but afterwards a Belgian priest in America explained to me its significance, which is by no means inappropriate. We visited the cathedral more than once, and admired the many works of art with which it is enriched. Chairs with kneeling-stools were well arranged for worshippers, many of which were finely cushioned. We received many invitations from agents to visit manufactories of the celebrated Brussels lace, none of which I accepted. In all Belgium about 130,000 women are employed in this industry. Across the street from St. Gudule's I entered a church-goods store, attracted by a picture of Louise Lateau. I found the proprietor very polite, and, although he knew that I did not intend to buy, he showed me many rich, hand-worked vestments of correct ecclesiastical style. He also showed me many orders for his goods from America, and I learned that he was president of a society for the production of all kinds of church goods according to strict rubrical patterns. We wandered through the boulevards and parks in a leisurely manner, and entered the churches, and saw all we could see of the life and habits of the people. In some of the older parts of the city, where the people retain their old Flemish customs, these walks were specially interesting. One of my companions went out of town to see the battle-field of Waterloo. It had been our intention to return to Paris and visit Lourdes. But as our time was limited, and as the cholera was raging in a portion of southern France, and the consequent excitement was extending throughout the country, we feared that we might be somewhere delayed by an unexpected quarantine, and therefore reluctantly abandoned our journey to that celebrated shrine of Our Blessed Lady.\

The next morning we took the train for Rotterdam, in Holland. The first and last part of the journey was through an interesting country. In a short time we reached Mechlin, or Malines, an archiepiscopal see, and within an hour Antwerp came in sight, which is the principal seaport town of Belgium, and one of the strongest fortresses on the Continent. It was founded in the seventh century, and at one time was considered the wealthiest city in Europe. The high tower of its famous cathedral rose in the distance, which is the largest and is considered the finest Gothic church in the Netherlands, and is enriched with the masterpieces of Rubens and others of the Antwerpian school of artists. We saw some Belgian priests leaving the train, who were the last of the priests of Europe whom we saw dressed in the full clerical habit: cassock, cincture, clerical hat, and mantle. This is the dress, with some slight variations, of all clergymen in Italy, France and Belgium, and most other Catholic countries of Europe. Why it is not worn in some other countries which we visited, which in every sense are Catholic, I do not pretend to understand.

Leaving Antwerp we passed over the moorlands of northern Belgium and southern Holland. Our baggage had to suffer an examination by the Dutch custom-house officials at Roosendaal, which is a few miles inside the limits of Dutch territory. When we passed over an arm of the sea, called Hollandsch Diep, on a bridge which cost more than two million dollars and is one and five-eighths of a mile long, we began to realize that we were indeed in the Low Countries. We passed the city of Dort, and over another bridge, the scenery becoming more and more characteristic of Holland. Almost continually before our eyes was some scene that would have answered admirably for a Dutch landscape in painting: a low, flat plain, intersected by canals with trees on their borders, farm-houses with quaint gables, and numerous wind-mills, some standing still and others waving their long, gigantic arms.

About noon we arrived in Rotterdam. Having secured rooms at the Hotel Weimar, and as we should have all the following day to remain in Rotterdam, we determined to take the next train, at about two o'clock, to make an afternoon visit to The Hague, which is not quite fifteen miles distant. The name of the railroad is "Hollandsche Spoorweg." The country is the same flat expanse everywhere. The canals take the place of roads, fences, and hedges in other lands.; and it was a peculiar sight to see the masts and sails of a vessel rising in the midst of fields and farms. Two rather important towns, of a little more than 20,000 population each, are on the line between the two larger cities; they are Schiedam and Delft, the former boasting of 230 distilleries, which manufacture the famous "Hollands," or "Schiedam schnapps," and the latter was celebrated in former times for its pottery and porcelain works, and is a pleasant town, one-third of whose population is Catholic./

We soon alighted from the train at The Hague, which is the capital of Holland and residence of the king. It is a city of 123,000 inhabitants, one third of whom are Catholics. Although Holland is a Protestant country, two-fifths of its people are Catholics, a fact which a large number of writers, when they have spoken of Protestant Holland, probably never mistrusted. The Hague is considered the finest city of Holland, having broad streets, spacious squares and parks, and substantial and imposing edifices.

I was agreeably surprised at one thing in Holland—that such a large number of the people have remained so old-fashioned. In many other parts of Europe I was very much disappointed in this regard, but in Holland I could not complain at least of the female attire. Their costumes, head-dresses, and ornaments were very attractive to one like me, whose poetic fancy revels in the romantic days and scenes of long ago.

The following day was spent in Rotterdam, a town of 157,000 population—one-sixth of which is Catholic—and the second city of the kingdom. It is intersected in every direction by canals, which are spanned by numerous draw-bridges. In Rotterdam I never succeeded in getting any idea of the cardinal points, and I am not at all sure that I did not think that north was south and east was west. Early in the morning we started out to see the "sights," which include the whole town rather than anything in particular. The houses are often four, five, and six stories high, and are usually very much out of the perpendicular. One might easily imagine that he had discovered a city of leaning towers, which had been built only one-third their intended height when work on them had been stopped through fear that they might topple over; or he might suppose that an earthquake had shaken the city, and had skilfully twisted it out of shape, but in every part had left it standing. This peculiarity is due to the soft, swampy nature of the ground, which prevents a firm foundation.

I crossed over bridges and wandered through shady streets which run by the side of the great water thoroughfares of the city, which are able to float the largest East-Indiamen. I strolled down the broad, busy quay called the Boompjes, where the Dutch East India Company's house was located, but which is now turned into colonial warehouses, and imagined that I saw its daily scenes in the time of Holland's commercial greatness, when so many Hollanders acquired those fortunes which have left their results to the present generation, and which have made their impress on the manners and appearance of the moneyed aristocracy of Holland of the present day. After inquiry I found my way to one of the Catholic churches, which possessed a number of paintings of some merit. As preparations were being made for Mass, I waited. For a weekday there was a generous attendance, and I noticed that there were present a large number of men of the more comfortable classes, judging from their dress and respectable appearance. They nearly all carried in their hands on entering the church the ever-popular high silk hat. A very respectable-appearing, portly gentleman, past the middle age, entered the pew where I was kneeling. He proceeded to unlock a drawer under the pew in front, taking from it his prayer-book and two very soft kneeling-cushions, one of which he offered to me. This drew my attention to the fact that nearly every pew was supplied with the same convenience, which—let alone the cushions—seemed to me to be a very useful contrivance; nor could I help admire the old gentleman's sincere politeness.

After Mass I again wandered leisurely through the streets, enjoying the people and houses, and in a little while met one of my companions; we were both beginning to get lonesome, and were glad to continue our rambles together. In Holland, August is one of the most pleasant months of the year, and the day was a brief interval of sunshiny existence. We entered one other church, which appeared to belong to the Jesuits, where a priest was instructing a class in catechism. Several times we passed through the square in which stands the bronze statue of the erudite and distinguished Erasmus of Rotterdam. As we had sufficient free time, I had once thought of visiting the museum, which contains some good paintings by eminent Dutch artists; but I finally concluded to let the visit go, on account of my usual reason, that I preferred the living scenes around me in a strange land. At the hotel I found a description of one of the wonders of the museum, which was supposed to have been written in our mother tongue, and was the most ridiculous and amusing specimen of English that I remember ever to have read; yet it was meant in all earnestness to be a very brilliant production./

CHAPTER XXXIII.

RETURN TO ENGLAND, AND A TRIP TO SCOTLAND.

/Towards evening we went aboard the steamer for Harwich, where we should connect with the train for London. We sailed down the wide river, meeting and passing many vessels of different kinds which were hurrying, by quick stroke of wheel or under full sail, towards their various destinations. When the day began to show signs that its departure was near, the broad waters of the North Sea spread out before us, and as we floated out upon their bosom, the low lines of the Holland coast gradually receded from our sight. And when they seemed submerged beneath the wave, the giant windmills swung their huge arms, as if waving an adieu to the white-winged ships and smoky steamers leaving their shores; and we, turning our faces towards the land, bid farewell to the Continent of Europe./

The next morning, soon after we had risen, our steamer entered the beautiful harbor of Harwich, which indents the eastern shore of England, and whose calm surface shone in the morning sun like a sea of crystal, bearing on its waveless waters a large number of vessels at anchor. The extensive shipping which some of those small, sea-girt countries possess is something wonderful. It seemed strange and pleasant to hear once more the English language spoken everywhere around us.

In about half an hour the railway train moved out of the station for London. We passed from corner to corner through the fertile county of Essex, whose farms are classed among the best in England. The morning was foggy, but it did not prevent a partial view of the clumps of magnificent trees, green hedges, grassy fields, herds of fine cattle, and comfortable farm-houses, which form such striking features of the rural districts of England. It was yet morning when we arrived in London. We directed our driver to convey us to the neighborhood of Charing Cross, where we engaged rooms at the hotel of the Golden Cross. On account of language and familiar objects on the streets, before the bustle of the day began we felt a kind of feeling of "home again," which was quickly dispelled when we left the vicinity of the Strand and the streets which are a continuation of it on either end. During the day we visited some other parts of the city, especially Kensington, but the most of our time was spent in the district between Charing Cross and St. Paul's. In the afternoon we took a ride on the Thames from London Bridge to Battersea and return, in order to see the city from the river. It would be a useless task to attempt to describe what we saw in London, but our second visit was spent in quietly observing the people and characteristics of the city, in such a manner that some particular impression might be left in the mind, rather than have it filled with a confused mass of many things seen and only half-remembered.

The following day one of my companions and myself determined to make a visit to Oxford, although we should have only two hours to remain in that old university town. Our companion preferred to remain in the city, as he wished to see the inside of the Tower of London, which we often saw in the distance, but had not visited. The journey to Oxford was a pleasant one, occasionally revealing choice views of English country scenery. In about two hours the spires of Oxford came in sight.

The university was founded by King Alfred the Great in the year 872, and has already celebrated its millennial anniversary. In the Middle Ages it was sometimes attended by as many as thirty thousand students. At the present time it consists of twenty colleges, with an attendance of about two thousand. We told the driver to drive to every college in the city, although we did not enter them, but when he came to each he told us its name. These ancient piles of masonry, with their fine old towers, and niches, and statues of mediæval bishops, in many respects have a Catholic appearance on the outside, and one could readily imagine that he is in a venerable Catholic city of an old Catholic land. It is not strange that the great traditions of the past should sometimes exert their influence on the minds of the students and professors within these college walls; it is stranger that the spirits of the old abbots and bishops who made Oxford illustrious do not move before the astonished eyes of the modern occupants of their ancient foundations, and demand their own again. It is stranger how men can resist that appeal to return to the bosom and life of the Church which every stone in each gray edifice, and every memory of Oxford's glorious days, and every noble spirit of her saintly sons, is constantly making. The very stones in her walls cry out, Return! and a hundred thousand souls, for ever dear to God, make intercession with Him that Oxford may find the old paths from which she has strayed. I am glad that I did not enter any of those ancient cloisters of devotion and learning, to sadden my soul with the sight of "desolation standing in the holy place."

We returned to the station in time to take the one o'clock train back to London. After some distance the line diverged from the one on which we came, and thus we enjoyed the pleasure of another route. We passed in sight of Windsor Castle, the principal residence of the kings and queens of England. It covers twelve acres of ground, and from the railway presents a majestic appearance. The present edifice was founded by William the Conqueror, but Windsor was the residence of the old Saxon kings. Across the Thames is the town of Eton, chiefly noted for its college.

We had decided to take each his own course, during the coming days, until Monday evening, when we would meet in Liverpool. My route lay to the north, for I had determined to see York, with its old cathedral, and to climb the hills of Edinburgh. The train which I took left London soon after five o'clock.

For several hours the journey led through a fine agricultural region, mostly set apart for pastures and meadows. My heart is delighted more than my eyes with the quiet scenes of the country in a tastefully-kept and well-cultivated land. Even the uneducated, but, in this matter, not altogether uncultivated human heart possesses many of the feelings of nature's artist, by which the green fields, the sunny dales, the sheltering trees, the greensward on the sloping hills, the curling smoke rising from the hearth-fires of faithful neighbors, seen in the innocent days of youth, in the stronger and deeper life of manhood, and in the declining years of old age, are the sources of a purer and more exquisite joy than anything else on earth, next to the unselfish love of friends and family and the consolations of religion. I am glad to say that in Europe and the British Isles I did not see in the fields many reaping or harvesting machines. They serve to advantage in America, where laborers are scarcer, but in Europe every such machine takes the bread from the mouths of the hungry poor; and I will go farther and state my belief that it becomes another instrument of tyranny in the hands of the rich for the oppression of the poor. We passed through many busy towns, among them the old episcopal cities of Peterborough and Lincoln. The former possesses a fine cathedral church of early English and Norman architecture, with three broad, lofty arches in a row over its front entrance, and which was founded in the year 655, but was afterwards destroyed and rebuilt. The Lincoln cathedral is one of the finest in England, and was built in the eleventh century, and rebuilt in the following century, and was consecrated to the Mother of God in those ages when England bore the sweet title of "Dowry of Mary."

It was some time after dark—which in summer-time in England is rather late—before we arrived in York. I took a carriage and was driven to the "Black Swan," one of the oldest hotels in the city. York is the Eboracum of the Romans, and is one of the oldest, if not the oldest of the cities in England, whose existence dates back a thousand years before the coming of Christ. It became an important town under the Romans, and was the British residence of the Roman emperors; where Septimius Severus and Constantius Chlorus died, and where Constantine was proclaimed emperor, and which many claim to have been his native place. It is surrounded by ancient walls which had their origin in the time of the Roman dominion.

The next day was Sunday. I inquired for a Catholic church, to which I was easily directed. The church, which was a sightly, substantial edifice, was in the immediate neighborhood of York minster, the ancient cathedral of the archiepiscopal see of York, over whose destinies so many saints in former times presided; among whom were St. Wilfrid, St. Oswald, and St. John of Beverly. Cardinal Wolsey was also archbishop of York./

After attending Mass I directed my steps to the cathedral. By many it is considered the finest church in England. Before the conversion of the people to Christianity a pagan temple stood on its site, where in the seventh century a noble Christian church was raised to the honor of Christ. The present edifice was begun in the twelfth century on the ruins of a grand church built in the preceding century, but it was not completed until after the lapse of three hundred years. It was dedicated to St. Peter, Prince of the Apostles. It is 524 feet in length and 249 feet in breadth. It has a peal of twelve bells, one of which is the largest in Great Britain. The cathedral windows are among the largest and most beautiful in the world. The great east window is 78 feet high and 32 feet wide, and its traceries, carved in stone, appear like delicate lace-work, and are filled with admirable stained glass, making it an open book treating of sacred historic subjects, which even they who know not letters are able to read. This window has been declared by artists and architects to be the finest of its kind in existence. The large window over the central front entrance is also considered to be without a rival elsewhere in England.

I walked beneath the lofty arches of this stately minster, over the pavements trod in former centuries by the feet of Catholic multitudes, and beheld the walls yet grand, although deprived of many of their adornments which made them attractive in the ages of faith, and thought of the scenes, the processions, and the solemn services that they had witnessed in the old times when England was Catholic.

I wandered among the tombs of those buried here, some modern and others ancient, with reclining effigies carved in stone upon them. The old tombs alone represent *the faith, the piety, and the genius that raised this wonderful monument to the glory of God. In a short time the people began to pass through the church for ten o'clock service. They all entered the place which was once the sanctuary, and, although the number appeared respectable, only a part of the reserved space was occupied. When services commenced they closed the doors and shut off from the rest of the great cathedral their little corner, which was once so bright with the Presence of the Glorious King. About twenty like myself stayed outside in the church, who, rather than "fain fill themselves" with the dry moral husks which would be offered for spiritual sustenance, preferred to revel in the grand banquet of the soul's aspirations, symbolized in material forms and pictured rays of beauty created to a new image and likeness by the heart and hand of religion./

There was one thing about their service that was not dreary when heard from the place where I was sitting. The music was stately and solemn, and when the rich, deep voices of the male singers resounded through the arches I gave myself up to my imagination, and the olden times of Catholic devotion had returned, and the cathedral chapter, assisted by a pious clergy, were chanting the praises of God in the sublime language of the Divine Office. But if the door between us had opened, my eyesight would have quickly dispelled the illusion.

It was a bright, sunshiny day—supposed to be rare in England—and the golden light that came through the fine old windows in so many rich and delicate shades and forms of color beautified everything on which it rested with that ethereal tint or brighter hue that none but an angel's hand could paint or gild.

After some time I went out to take a better view of the exterior of the church and its surroundings. I made the circuit of the building and saw it from every side, until at length I found a convenient seat under a widebranching, grand old tree, which cast its welcome shade on the smooth greensward that extended a considerable distance from the church in that direction. I sat and mused, while I selected different parts of the grand edifice for closer inspection, and then traced their relation to the general plan, until the whole symmetrical ideal stood realized before my eyes.

Returning to my hotel, which I had a little difficulty in finding, I passed my time in reading and conversation until the hour in the afternoon when the "Salvation Army" would parade, which the landlord of the Black Swan desired me to see, as I had never yet seen that newest form of fanaticism, the off-spring of ignorance of the nature of true religion. There were several separate divisions on exhibition, each having a different kind of music. Bands and banners, street prayers and exhortations, composed their doubtful stock in trade. Their methods seem to move the lower rather than the higher nature of man, and those who once enlist in their ranks will probably remain loyal to their flag so long as excitement, profit, or the shame of desertion are able to keep them./

Afterwards I took a walk through the city, which has many picturesque and venerable buildings. I again visited the Catholic church, and took another look at York minster. I returned to the hotel in time for a late dinner, which was specially prepared for me. A young officer of the British army had not yet finished his dinner when I commenced mine. We soon got into an interesting conversation, and he remained until I also had finished. He had never met any Americans, and expected, from what he had heard, that my accent in speaking the mother-tongue would be entirely different. We talked over matters pertaining to the army, certain rules of honor among gentlemen, national characteristics, and religion.

After dinner I took another long walk. When night was coming on, and the rays of the sun no longer lingered, but the day was yet clear, the magnificent cathedral of York stood in bold form against the sky, but softened into milder lines in the mellower light nearer the earth. How many grand cathedrals and fine churches, built in the ages of faith, remain in every part of England as enduring monuments of her ancient religion! "Behold your house shall be left to you desolate." "Many pastors have destroyed my vineyard; they have trodden my portion under foot; they have changed my delightful portion into a desolate wilderness. They have laid it waste, and it hath mourned for me. With desolation is all the land made desolate" (Jeremias xii. 10, 11). Will the time ever come when the light will once more burn before the altars of these ancient churches of England, proclaiming the return of the Lamb that was slain, and will the Divine Office once more be heard in their sanctuaries—in a word, will they ever again become the temples where the Incarnate God dwells and receives due worship from His creatures? "O our God, hear the supplication of Thy servant and his prayers, and show Thy face upon Thy sanctuary which is desolate."

Late that night I left York on the train for Edinburgh. When morning dawned, I looked out of the window and found that we were in the hilly country of northern England. The most part of our journey afterwards was through a region of hills, which in Scotland — passing on our way through the hills of Lammermoor—became more and more rugged until we reached Edinburgh. But in their midst were frequent dimpled dales, where sometimes fields of grain appeared, but which more commonly were devoted to pasturage and meadow. This district of northern England and southern Scotland through which we passed is famous the world over for its sheep and cattle.

Crossing the Tweed, we were in Scotland. The morning was chilly, but one is always interested when he enters a country for the first time; and hardly a hill, or valley, or farm-house was passed without my observation. On our entrance into Edinburgh we passed the abbey and palace of Holyrood. The town of Edinburgh was first called Edwin's burgh in the seventh century, after Edwin, King of Northumbria, who resided there. We arrived at the station at about five o'clock in the morning, and as it was my intention to walk about the city until the departure of the train for Liverpool, which would leave about noon, I took a cab and left my baggage at the station from which the train would depart. I walked along Prince's Street, on which is located the rather ornate monument of Sir Walter Scott, to a high eminence towards the east, which I learned was Calton Hill. It was my desire to view the city at early morn from an elevated position. When I had reached the summit of the hill a fine panorama stretched out before my eyes on every side, slightly obscured by the mists of the morning, which were gradually disappearing before the risen sun. Below me in the valleys, and on sloping ridges and rugged heights, lay the city, awakening to the life and activities of another day. Towards the north the pale blue waters of the Frith of Forth were seen dimly in the hazy distance. Near me on the hill were various monuments erected to Scotch celebrities, and below in the city were numerous monuments to the memory of men of every kind of distinction. When a city once determines to ride a hobby in any particular direction, it usually succeeds. The good people of Edinburgh seem to have directed considerable attention to the building of monuments, for which purpose their city offers many natural advantages. Across the valley, at the extremity of the ridge on the opposite side, rose from its rocky foundations the battlemented walls and broad, strong towers of Edinburgh castle. The hour that I spent on Calton Hill was the most pleasant of my brief stay in the city.

I walked across the bridge to the old town, and loitered through some of its streets, finally going around one side of the castle into the valley below. I did not have time to enter castles, palaces, or other historic buildings, nor had I much desire left for such visits, and the only public buildings which I entered were railway stations and restaurants. Out-door life and views pleased me better. Their churches—as I did not happen to find those that were Catholic—had for me but very little attraction. I then took a long walk through the new portion of the town, which is much the finest part of the city.

I spent the last two hours of my visit in the beautiful valley below Edinburgh castle. It is divided into gardens, extensive greensward, and shady groves, through which runs a small but sparkling river. The long beds of foliage plants and flowers were arranged with almost perfect taste, and kept with most scrupulous care. I sat down on one of the numerous seats under the shade-trees, and tried to compare the past and present. High above me the great, gray old castle, standing on its almost perpendicular, dizzy heights, frowned upon the smiling valley. It is said that the daughters of the Pictish kings once resided there, and that it was called the "castrum puellarum." But in those ancient times, when the fair eye of beauty looked in joy or sadness o'er the scene, it rested not upon the sylvan valley, but on a silver lake whose dreamy waters rippled with low, sweet sounds against its high, overhanging shores, and dimpled with smiles in the happy sunshine of heaven. The lake of former times, which was called North Loch, was drained in 1763 and changed into a park and gardens. I walked over the bridge and through the valley, and took different views of the same surroundings, and enjoyed my own reflections on the days gone by and the days that are ours, until it was time to go to the station. I was not sorry that I should so soon meet the two companions of my journey, for one is inclined to get lonesome in a foreign land. Our route by railroad led down through the centre of Mid-Lothian—now called Edinburghshire—and other southern counties of Scotland. We passed through several ranges of hills, and even when we traversed wide, level plains, low lines of hills were always visible in the distance.

The first English city of any importance which we reached was Carlisle. We passed through those counties of northeast England that compose the lake district, which is looked on by the English as a very charming region. I did not get sufficient knowledge of the country, from those parts of the counties through which the railroad ran, to form a judgment as to the merits of the claim. The western part of England, as seen from the train, presents a very different appearance from the eastern portion of the country. During nearly the whole distance a long, low range of hills stretched along the eastern horizon; and the towns through which we passed during the last part of the journey were dirty, smoky, and noisy from the vast manufacturing establishments which they contain. At one of the stations on the route a gentleman with two or three friends entered the compartment in which I rode. He was very much interested in telling his friends of the flattering reception given him by a certain club, and of several other honors of a similar nature which he had enjoyed during that or the preceding day. He seemed to be swelling very big with local importance, and the thought came to me: A conceited man is the same in every land. But, after all, he may have been a good-hearted and simple man, easily pleased with the baubles of life, who did not appear to his usual advantage, at least in the eyes of a perhaps too critical stranger. Late in the afternoon we reached Liverpool, the greatest seaport town of England. Noise and business reigned supreme within its confines.

To a certain class of men, whose minds are filled with industrial and commercial enterprise, Liverpool would probably be one of the most attractive cities on the globe; to me it was the exact opposite. Without doubt it possesses many pleasant localities, but I did not care to hunt them out; and Liverpool is one of the cities of the Old World where I should not care to live. I engaged a carriage and drove to the hotel where we had agreed to meet.

My companions had arrived before me, and one of them had already seen a considerable portion of the city. The next day we made the final arrangements for our return voyage across the Atlantic, and we would start from Queenstown one week from the following Friday. In the evening two of our number went on board the night steamer for Dublin. Our companion had concluded to make Liverpool the starting point for a trip to Scotland.

Without doubt a good view of Liverpool Harbor, with its immense shipping, would be an interesting scene; but this we missed on account of the darkness.

CHAPTER XXXIV.

THE EMERALD GEM OF THE OCEAN.

WHEN we rose in the morning we were entering Dublin Bay. As we were very much fatigued by our travels, and had not slept well during the night, we concluded to set apart the forenoon and a part of the afternoon for a quiet rest. Towards evening we enjoyed a stroll, directing our steps to the attractive walks and retreats of St. Stephen's Green. It is one of the largest city parks of Europe, and in all things is true to nature, even in its most lavish artificial adornments, and contains a lakelet—on which float great white swans—a cliff with waterfalls, sylvan shades, and a fine, grassy expanse beside the cool waters and under the pleasant trees.

Early the next morning we were at the station to take the train for Rathdrum, in the County Wicklow, from which place we should visit Glendalough and the ruins of the Seven Churches. For the greater part of the way the morning ride extended along the sea-coast; and the still waters of a sheltered bay, or the wide extended waters of the sea which united with the blue sky at the horizon, afforded us many enjoyable views on that fair August morning, when the golden rays of the sun gilded the emerald landscape with a mild brightness, and, while each color retained its own rare beauty, the two were so commingled and combined that each was made more beautiful by the presence of the other.

It was yet early when we reached Rathdrum, and we immediately took a jaunting-car for Glendalough, which was a little more than eight miles distant. As a number of tourists were going over the same way, every car was fully occupied, and some of them were crowded. A young gentleman and lady from England, who were born in Ireland, were on the car with us, and we kept together during the day.

Nearly the whole distance our road ran by the side of the river Avonmore, and at nearly every turn or eminence on the way we came upon some new prospect of grand natural scenery, or some charming rural retreat, the most delightful of which was the lovely Vale of Clara, embosomed in green. And as it lay below us in the soft light of a sunshiny Irish day, it seemed as if the pure angel of the vale, living in the light of heaven and catching its radiance, reflected its beauties in mildness o'er the sweet, dimpled face of the valley.

In due time we reached the small village of Glendalough, composed of perhaps a dozen houses. We preferred to make the remainder of our excursion on foot and by boat. The most important ruins of the churches, together with St. Kevin's Kitchen, were near at hand. Several guides offered their services, with some of whom we were not favorably impressed. They were probably good persons, but, as we did not want "smartness" instead of knowledge, we chose an old woman of simple pretensions who could point out to us the different places of legend and history.\

We soon reached the first and most important ruins. A splendid specimen of the ancient round tower stood at the entrance to the cemetery and ruins. At its base we found some sod thick with shamrocks. With our knives we cut loose several pieces—each one being a few inches square—to plant in American soil. Mine lived nearly two years and then died. The American climate did not prove altogether congenial to their nature. We then wandered among tombs and crumbling walls where the religious and saints of centuries lived, and where they are buried,

These ruins mark the site and are the remnants of an ancient monastic city whose walls were laid thirteen hundred years ago, and which became one of the most flourishing holy cities of Ireland, with a long line of saintly and learned abbots, from its founder, St. Kevin, to St. Lawrence O'Toole, who was abbot here before he became archbishop of Dublin.

A writer has well described the place in these words: "The long, continuous shadow of the lofty and slender round tower moves slowly from morn till eve over wasted churches, crumbling oratories, shattered crosses, scattered yew-trees, and tombs, now undistinguishable, of bishops, abbots, and anchorites." When St. Kevin founded this great monastic establishment in the sixth century, it was soon after the beginning of the golden age of Irish learning and devotion.

To-day you will find in Ireland grander ruins than those of St. Kevin's time, and which represent religion in the middle ages, but they belong to a period, however notable, six centuries after the era of Ireland's most glorious religious annals. There is probably not a county in Ireland that does not possess ruins of the fifth, sixth, or seventh centuries, and in some counties a large number of such ruins mark the places where history tells us once stood those monastic towns within whose walls were gathered thousands of monks, and to which students flocked from nearly every country of Europe, where they learned music, architecture, carving, metallurgy, and the classic languages Greek and Latin. The monks themselves were diligent copyists of the Holy Scriptures and works of the classic authors, and whose ancient manuscripts are found in many European libraries. They also preserved to the world, in their immortal *Annals*, a record of the important events, as well as a mirror of the age in which they lived. These monks were men whose fathers were pagan warriors who had worshipped according to the religious rites of the Druids, and whose blood, in the desire of battle and in the fight, had often burned with the fierce fires of revenge. Such men, having become Christians, had reared sons and daughters who became saints by thousands \

In that age St. Kevin founded Glendalough, St. Kieran founded Clonmacnoise, St. Finian founded Innisfallen, another St. Finian founded Clonard, St. Bute founded Monasterboice, St. Carthagh founded Lismore, St. Enda founded the monasteries of Arran, St. Bridget, the great convent of Kildare, and a hundred other saints founded monastic houses over the length and breadth of Ireland, whose wonderful religious life and influence continued in the following centuries. As a fair illustration of the greatness of many of those foundations, I will mention Bangor, founded by St. Comgall in the sixth century, which is said to have had at one time no less than three thousand monks, who were divided into seven choirs of three hundred singers each, who day and night continually sung the praises of God. The great Montalembert in his immortal work, *Monks of the West*, speaking of Ireland, states that "the number of 3,000 monks is constantly met with in the records of the great monasteries"; and farther affirms: "It has been said, and cannot be sufficiently repeated, that Ireland was then regarded by all Christian Europe as the principal centre of knowledge and piety."

We walked by the shores of one of the two lakes, and crossing a bridge over the stream that unites them, we soon reached other ruins near a large pool and rushing stream, where the old woman kindly pointed out to us a great rock "split in twain by the giant

Finn Mac Cumal" (Finn Mac Cool). Near this spot we took a boat on the upper lake, to visit "St. Kevin's Bed." This part of the glen is wilder and more sombre than the scenery of the lower lake, and even to this day, if it were not for its numerous visitors, would be a fit place for deep religious solitude. We soon reached the cave,

> "By that lake whose gloomy shore
> Skylark never warbles o'er." /

The "bed" is about twenty-five feet above the surface of the lake, almost directly overhanging it. For this reason we had first to climb an inclined rocky shore to a narrow ledge, from which, by putting our hands and feet in small openings, we made our way around the almost perpendicular side of the rock into the cave. I am easily made dizzy, but I thought that if I fell into the water it could not do much more harm than to wet me. As an example of the mistakes sometimes made by even learned writers I will quote from a note in *Butler's Lives of the Saints*, taken by him from another author: "It is a cave hewed in the solid rock on the side of the mountain, exceeding difficult in the ascent and terrible in prospect; for it hangs almost perpendicular over the lough about three hundred feet above the surface of the water, says Harris." I entered it alone, and had a short time for contemplation. Its walls are smooth and there is sufficient room for two persons. At one end is a slight elevation of stone for a pillow, and at the other is the mouth of the cave, which looks out over the silent waters, darkened by the deep shadows of the desolate surrounding mountains. In this grotto St. Kevin spent many days and nights in holy retreat and penance; and here St. Lawrence O'Toole passed much time in prayer and spiritual exercises. I was surprised to see the names of many titled and literary gentlemen of the British Isles carved in the sides of the cave. It is a vulgarism that I had not expected to find among that class of people, and even if it had been perpetrated by the class of wealthy, upstart Americans of vulgar manners who sometimes travel abroad, I should have been ashamed of them.

By boat and on foot we returned to the hamlet of Glendalough. As we walked down the road by the side of the lake, farmers were working in the adjoining fields on the sloping hillsides, and I almost envied them their constant enjoyment of the wild but beautiful scenery of the "Glen of the Lakes."

After a short delay we returned to Rathdrum over the same road by which we came. We concluded to remain over-night in that village, at "Crowley's" neat and comfortable hotel. The next morning my companion returned to Dublin, and I took the southern train for Enniscorthy, in the county of Wexford. Before starting we had sufficient time to take a walk in the suburbs of that quiet country village, which possesses an abundance of grand shade-trees.

Our train towards the south passed down through the "Sweet Vale of Avoca."

> "There is not in this wide world a valley so sweet
> As the vale in whose bosom the bright waters meet;
> Oh! the last rays of feeling and life must depart
> Ere the bloom of that valley shall fade from my heart."

On entering the County Wexford we passed through several towns, among which one of the smallest but most ancient was Ferns, which gives its name to the episcopal see of the county, although the bishop resides in Enniscorthy. The see of Ferns was established in the sixth century by St. Mogue, and in this ancient town stood the castle and principal residence of the famous MacMurrogh, King of Leinster. I arrived in Enniscorthy soon after nine o'clock, and, as I should return to Dublin that day, I immediately hired a jaunting-car for my trip through the county, going to the sea-coast, near which my route lay for about nine miles, and taking a late afternoon train at Gorey, which is fifteen miles by rail north of Enniscorthy.

It was a warm day, considering the usual mild climate of Ireland, and as we rode out of Enniscorthy the sun darted down on us some of his most fervent rays. Vinegar Hill, which became noted in the Irish rebellion of 1798, appeared for some time on our right. There was nothing specially interesting during the first half of the journey, except that to me rural scenes in a pleasant country are always enjoyable. In outward appearance Wexford seems to be one of the most prosperous counties in Ireland, although it is said that the soil is not so fertile as in some other parts. The farm-houses, taken in general, were among the best that I saw in the country. Towards noon we entered the village of Kilmucridge, where the parish church of Litter is located.

The next village where there is a parish church is Ballygarrett, about four miles distant, which I was anxious to see, as I had once written a poem describing it and the country through which I should pass in going there from Litter. As I had never seen the place when the poem was written, I was desirous to know if my description had been true to the reality. I can now state that if I were to write it again I would not change one word. In order that the reader may travel over the road with me, and in the distance see with my eyes the village and church for the first time, I will here transcribe my poem, which was entitled:

MEMORIES OF AN IRISH EXILE.

Oh! I love thee, Ballygarrett!
   As I loved thee when a child,
Love thy chapel and thy altar,
   With a love still undefiled.

O the innocence of childhood!
   O the purity of love!
In my native home in Ireland,
   Its pure symbol, whitest dove.

All the memories of childhood,
   All that joy and love impart,
Are a portion of my being,
   And the chords that thrill my heart.

Sweet and tender are these memories,
  Dearest part of all my life;
Stronger, purer do they make me
  In the battle-field of strife.

Birds are sweetly to me singing,
  Flowers entice of every hue,
Fields of green and joy around me,
  And above me heaven's blue.

And the friends of youth surround me,
  Father, mother, kindred, kind;
Holy scenes before the altar
  Fill and sanctify my mind.

Little, quiet Irish village,
  With thy houses thatched and gray,
I have never met thy equal
  All the years I've been away.

And thou bright, green Irish landscape,
  Where my own home smiling lay,
In my many years of absence
  I have thought of thee each day.

On the charming road to Litter,
  Near the bridge that you cross o'er,
In my own dear Ballywater,
  You would pass our cottage-door.

Dear old home of youth and kindred,
   Where my father's race was born,
Dear old house that saw my childhood,
   And where first I saw the morn;

Where I saw the morning breaking
   Of a life that soon is o'er,
Home from which we sadly parted,
   To return, oh! nevermore.

Not a place so brightly smiling,
   Not a corner of the earth,
As the home of early childhood,
   And the place that saw my birth.

Other lands true friends have given,
   Who have shown me loving care,
But the love and joys of childhood
   I have never found elsewhere.

There the blackbird whistled gaily,
   And the thrush was singing nigh,
And the skylark, lightly rising,
   Sung his matins in the sky;

Birds were singing in the hedges,
   And in trees above our door;
Oh! their notes they will be singing
   In my heart for evermore.

While the voice of Irish songsters
    Nevermore will please my ear,
Yet the captive bird, sad singing,
    Will the exile's spirits cheer;

And each note it sings in sadness
    I will treasure in my breast,
For I know 'twas sung in gladness
    O'er its dear old Irish nest.

In those days of purest childhood
    One thought hallowed all the rest:
Day of joy or day of sorrow,
    Peace of God dwelt in my breast.

Joys of faith and thoughts of heaven
    Erin's children treasure up,
And the smile of Christ and Mary
    Sweeten sorrow's bitter cup.

And the priesthood and the altar
    Have made light the heavy rod,
When the sorrows of the people
    Left to them no hope but God.

Once there came to us a Curate,
    Entered in the peasant's door,
Pale and thin, and poor in raiment,
    Whom we loved as none before;

Served his God and loved his people
  Offered up the Sacrifice,
Gave to us the Bread of Angels,
  Gave us hope of paradise;

Heard the tale of sin and sorrow,
  Calmed with holy words our fears,
Knelt beside the dying Christian,
  And brought sunshine to our tears.

Yes, the priest was with his people,
  Holding out the saving hand,
And in pity felt their sorrows
  And the sorrows of his land;

Felt their sorrows more than human,
  Changed dark sorrows into joy,
By the thought and hope of heaven,
  Which no tyrant could destroy.

He is now the royal shepherd
  Of the ancient see of Ferns,*
But I love him as I loved him,
  And my heart in exile turns

---

* The late Dr. Warren, Bishop of Ferns, was once curate of Ballygarrett, County Wexford. Very Rev. Canon Furlong informed the writer that this poem, which the bishop received in his last illness, gave him the greatest consolation, for which I am thankful.

To the angel of my childhood,
  To that holy priest of God,
Who traced out for me the pathway
  In which once my Saviour trod.

And my feet have kept that pathway,
  While that gentle voice I hear
Sounding in my heart for ever,
  As it sounded in my ear.

Oh! the thoughts that throng my memory
  Of those now departed years,
How they stir deep sorrow's fountain,
  How they fill my eyes with tears!

But I left thee, Ballygarrett,
  Turned my face away from thee,
Left my friends and home and kindred,
  Found a home beyond the sea.

I remember, when we parted,
  All the thoughts I left unsaid,
Looked upon thee in my silence,
  As one looketh on the dead;

Took one long look in my anguish,
  Ere I went from thee away;
O my God! it is heart-breaking
  When I think of thee that day.

Oh! I lingered at the doorway,
  And I lingered at the gate,
Then I took one last look backward,
  And I yielded to my fate.

But I love thee, Ballygarrett,
  With a love that ne'er grows cold,
And I'll love thee e'en in heaven,
  Where the streets are paved with gold.

"Near the bridge that you cross o'er" I gathered some flowers, and dug up some soil with shamrocks for a friend in America, to whom they would bring back all the memories of childhood and early years, described by me in poetical verse.\

Arriving in the village, I first entered the church for a few minutes, and then called on the parish priest, the Very Rev. Canon Furlong, at the parochial residence, who received me warmly. He kindly and cordially invited me to stay several days; but I was able to spend in his agreeable and intelligent company only a brief hour, when I bid him good-by and continued my journey. Since my visit to Ballygarrett, Canon Furlong has been promoted to the more important parish of Gorey. As he had requested me to go by way of Courtown Harbor, to see the new Riverchapel which he had just built, I took that route. I found the chapel to be a very neat, substantial structure, in good architectural taste, and an ornament to the quiet, beautiful village and neighborhood in which it is situated.

At Gorey I entered the train for Dublin, where I arrived some time after dark. Each time that we returned to Dublin its streets and buildings became more familiar objects to our eyes, but I should hardly dare to enter into any farther description of the city through fear of becoming tedious./

The next day one of my companions and myself took the early afternoon train for Galway, "the city of the tribes." On our way we passed through the six counties of Dublin, Kildare, Meath, West Meath, Roscommon, and Galway, and the towns of Mullingar, Athlone, and Athenry. We saw the fine, collegiate-appearing buildings of Maynooth; and we passed near a number of ruined castles and ecclesiastical edifices of various kinds, among them the church-tower of Clonard, where once stood the celebrated monastery of that name, founded by one of the several saints who bore the name of Finian.\

During the journey we enjoyed the sight of some fine stretches of country, with gently undulating and well-watered pasturage, where fleecy flocks and fat cattle grazed in fields of green by the side of silver streams reflecting the summer sky, or lay lazily under the shade of grand old trees, half-lulled to sleep by the whispering breezes among the leaves or the low musical sounds of the waters.

At Athlone we crossed the river Shannon. From the bridge a good view was obtained of the river, and of the lower part of Lough Ree, whose waters expand in the distance. Athlone is well situated, and when we first saw it, and also on our return, it presented an agreeable picture. We arrived in Galway after dark, so that we could not see anything of the city until the following morning.

The next day was Sunday. We took an early morning walk, which well repaid the trouble. The poorer classes of people are very old-fashioned, and appeared to good advantage on the streets and about their homes during the morning hours. In the middle ages Galway enjoyed a monopoly of the trade with Spain, and probably many of the inhabitants of modern Galway have a considerable mixture of Spanish blood in their veins, and possess many Spanish characteristics, because of the close and long-continued intermingling of the two peoples. We entered almost every church in the city, and finally remained in one to hear Mass. After breakfast we took the tram-car and rode some distance along the bay. We took a seat on top of the car, from which we got a good prospect of the city and harbor. At the end of the line we alighted, and continued on foot some distance farther. The view was somewhat obscured by mists, which indicated a rain-storm later in the day. The harbor is really a fine one, and it is a pity that its advantages are not more generally turned to use; but the hope is entertained that when through Home Rule prosperity returns to the island, Galway will take its place among the most important maritime cities of the British Isles./

Across the bay through the misty distance rose the indistinct outlines of hills and mountains, which we would gladly have seen under a clearer sky; but sea and land, over which hovered the spirit of the storm, presented a greater attractiveness and more characteristic wildness of nature to the western coast of Ireland than would have been afforded under a brighter sun. The western shores of Erin are regions of romantic interest, where, on the extreme coast-line of Europe, they present their great rocky sea-wall to the mists and storms and wild billows of the northern Atlantic. /

Having seen the town to our satisfaction, we returned to our hotel, and soon after hired a jaunting-car to convey us to Tuam on our way to the village and chapel of Knock. The first part of the journey was pleasant, as the rain-storm threatening us had not yet arrived. One feature of this and adjoining parts of Connaught was new to us; instead of the green hedges which are seen in all directions elsewhere in Ireland, here their places are taken by gray stone walls, which, so far as the eye can see, checker the landscape. This part of Connaught was much better in soil and appearance than I had expected to find it. When we had gone several miles into the country we began to meet men and women returning from Mass, and, having passed the church, we overtook many on the road. They were a healthy, robust-looking people, with whom hardships and poverty—endured with a good conscience, in the mild, healthy climate of their native land—seemed to agree. Yet there are so-called statesmen who are narrow enough and hard-hearted enough to advocate driving such people into exile—which they call assisted emigration—where, even though they get a more generous diet, their bright, happy looks and rosy cheeks are retained only for a few years.

Soon afterwards we passed an old castle in ruins, close to the banks of a winding stream, where a goodly number of young men had gathered and were engaged in youthful sports. The rain, which for some distance back had only been drizzling, now became drenching. During the remainder of our journey we met but few passengers on the road, and persons for the most part kept within their houses, looking out of the windows and open doors at the rain—an old, dear, familiar acquaintance. In seasons too wet they probably forget to love their old-time companion, but without doubt they would be lonesome without him. We met one carriage—with a liveried driver —hurrying along. We covered ourselves from the rain as closely as possible, and with the aid of our umbrellas kept almost dry.

About four o'clock in the afternoon we attained an eminence which overlooked a fresh, green, undulating expanse of country, in the midst of which lay the white and gray walls of the houses of Tuam, above which, here and there, its church-steeples uplifted their crosses towards the sky. St. Jarlath established a see in Tuam early in the sixth century, and founded a famous school in its vicinity, where St. Brendan, abbot of Clonfert, and St. Colman, first bishop of Cloyne, received their saintly training. When we had arrived in the town we drove to Daly's hotel, which, for an inland country town, proved to be among the best that we found in Ireland. As it continued to rain I did not venture out, but my companion took a little out-door exercise on the soaked streets.

Towards evening, when the weather had returned to a drizzly state, we went out together to visit the cathedral, which is a large, substantial structure, rather commodious than ornate.\

The next morning we took passage on a mail-car for Claremorris. On the car with us were a sick girl and her mother, who had come some distance to see a priest who lived between Tuam and Claremorris who had acquired a reputation for curing the sick; an Irish nationalist, who could give us information on every imaginable subject connected with the country, and who, considering his education, was a clever talker; and an old Irish gentleman of the old stock, the most characteristic portions of whose dress were leggins and a high hat which had long served to establish the respectability of its owner. Judging from the inquiring glances cast at him by several female passengers whenever a particularly strong national sentiment was uttered, I concluded that he owned perhaps a few more acres than somebody else.

Early in the afternoon we entered Claremorris and drove to a hotel for dinner. After we had dined we hired a jaunting-car to convey us to Knock. A part of our ride was through a pleasant country, while a portion of it led through a bleak and desolate district, where we saw a number of half-ruined and tenantless cabins. We asked about them, and were informed that this was the scene of some of the late evictions. I know nothing more of this particular case, but this I do know, that many of the heart-rending scenes of eviction in Ireland take place in the poorest and most desolate parts of the country, and the poor victims who are driven out of their homes are unable to pay the extortionate rent demanded of them, even though they have gone from place to place working for others, in order to remain in the poor little cabins where they were born or where they began their wedded life. Without doubt there are many kind-hearted and noble-minded landlords in Ireland who possess all the qualities of true Christian gentlemen, and against such I have not one word to write; but probably a larger number, in proportion, of Irish landlords have been unchristian, unjust, and hard-hearted towards their tenants than of any other landlords in any civilized country on the face of the globe.\

That such men should call themselves either true gentlemen or true Christians is an inconsistency; for the true gentleman has gentle feelings, manifested externally in gentle manners in all his relations and dealings with his fellowmen, whether they are his superiors, equals, or those in a more humble condition of life. Yet these tyrannical landlords—frequently absentees—who compose a numerous class of Irish landed proprietors, have subjected to rack-rents and harsh treatment one of the poorest and most patient tenantries of the world, and when tenants refuse to pay their unjust demands they have a great deal to say in hypocritical tones about their dishonesty. A true Christian must be just in all things, even though the civil law might permit injustice. But many Irish landlords have formed their conscience according to other standards than those of Catholic moral theology, otherwise they would not dare to demand a higher price for the use of their land than it is worth. These men have often collected double the rent that their land was really worth, and for so many years that, were they to make restitution, the half-starved victims of their oppression, instead of being evicted from their holdings, would own them in fee-simple.

Knock was not more than one hour's ride from Claremorris, and soon the thatched hamlet, with its chapel of world-wide reputation, appeared before us. We first visited the chapel and said some prayers, and then called on the parish priest, Archdeacon Kavanagh, by whom we were kindly received. He told us that our other companion had left the village that morning after celebrating Mass.

There is only one hotel in Knock, which is about a half-mile or more distant from the church. We found it to be a retired and pleasant place. It was formerly the most respectable private residence in the neighborhood, where the proprietor yet lives, although he has set apart a portion of his house for the uses of a hotel, and has hired persons to conduct it. It is situated in a grove of fine trees which extend down the avenue to the road. Having made all necessary arrangements, we walked through the fields to the chapel. It was near sunset, and as we loitered on the way, with the grove of stately trees behind us—and forming a pleasant feature of the landscape—and the little, silent village before us, we began to enjoy in their fulness the peaceful happiness and quiet contentment of the Irish country districts, and caught a glimpse of every-day rural life in Ireland when far removed from the highways of traffic.

The church has been much improved in size and appearance since the concourse of visitors to Knock. I will abstain from any opinion with reference to the supernatural manifestations or apparitions said to have been witnessed here, as ecclesiastical authority has not yet pronounced as to their truth or nature. One fact is certain, that every visitor in Knock will see perhaps a hundred canes and crutches hung up against the outside walls of the chapel, left there by the infirm and cripples as proof of their cure.

The next morning we said Mass at the principal altar of the church, after which Archdeacon Kavanagh showed us many presents received from different persons, one of the finest coming, as a token of gratitude, from the bishop of Toronto, in Canada.

After breakfast we started on a jaunting-car

for Ballyhaunis, where we would take the train back to Dublin. The morning was bright and warm. The road led through a country district that seemed never to have been entered by the pleasure-seeking tourist. I do not remember that we met even one wheeled vehicle for many miles. Large girls from fourteen to eighteen years of age were frequently met on foot, driving donkeys with creels of turf upon their backs, which was being stored for winter fuel, and which was heaped up in piles near their dwellings. We also met and overtook so many children—some of them barefooted—on their way to school that we could hardly see how the school-house could contain them. Some of them—small children, too—must have walked several miles. There was a cheerful, earnest look on their faces which I always like to see with school children. It is an indication of that eagerness for book-learning which has always characterized the Celtic Irish child. I am convinced that no children in the world are more ready to embrace every opportunity to acquire learning than Irish children in Ireland, and their readiness amounts to a genuine eagerness.

When we arrived in Ballyhaunis the streets were alive with people, and, from the number of cattle, sheep, and pigs that were gathered in many of the public places of the village, we concluded that it must be some kind of market-day. We entered the church, but remained only a few minutes, and then took a stroll through the streets, and tried to imbibe, with as little effort as possible, the spirit of a market-day morning in an Irish country town. On a knoll at the end of the village towards the railway station were the ruins of an old monastery, which must have been merely ruins for a century at least. It is doubtful if any of the monks, who dwelt within those walls laid low, were remembered even in the childhood memories of the grandfathers of the gray-haired men of the present generation. I did not inquire nor have I read about them, for sometimes I prefer to fill into the framework which I know to be real, pictures of the imagination.\

At the station we met an excellent young man who had crossed the ocean with us, and who had soon become intimate with my companion, whose brother lived in his neighborhood in Pennsylvania. While we were travelling on different continents, he had been enjoying the well-remembered scenes of his native land. How many exiled hearts long for that privilege, but almost fear to attain it on account of the disappointments that must necessarily come through the changes of years! He had just returned from Lough Derg, in Donegal, where he had made the Stations of St. Patrick's Purgatory. We had intended to go there, but it was now Tuesday, and our steamer would sail from Queenstown on Friday afternoon, and we had yet to see the Rock of Cashel and the lakes of Killarney./

The railroad towards Dublin passed down through the entire length of the County Roscommon and through the city of Roscommon, which is famous as having once been the seat of the royal house of O'Connor. For some time before reaching Athlone the bright waters of Lough Ree amid shores of emerald delighted the eye. From Athlone we returned to Dublin over the same route by which we came. In the compartment with us was a gentleman with his mother. I should judge that he belonged to the middle class, but he was a person of much more than ordinary intelligence, and had lived for some years in Richmond, Virginia, although he had returned to live in Ireland. As we were passing a workhouse he told us the number of paupers in all the workhouses of Ireland. I have forgotten the exact number, but it was surprisingly large. When we consider how adverse the Irish are to becoming paupers—probably the proudest, in this matter, of any race in existence—these figures show, as plainly as they can prove anything, the terrible misgovernment of the country.\

When we reached Dublin we were joined by the third member of our party, who had just returned from Belfast. Dublin now began to seem to us like home, and the persons in our hotels like familiar acquaintances, to which and whom we should bid good-by on the morrow, probably for ever. My two friends declare that in five years they will return to Europe; but as for myself, I so much dread the Atlantic, if I ever return it will be that my last sigh on earth may be breathed forth in the land in which the Son of God and the Son of Mary commended His spirit into the hands of his Eternal Father.\

CHAPTER XXXV.

CASHEL OF THE KINGS AND THE LAKES OF KILLARNEY.

The next morning we left Dublin by the same railway by which we entered it nearly four months before. We intended to reach Killarney that evening, but on the way we would stop over at Goold's Cross station, from which we would visit Cashel—"Cashel of the Kings." The round tower at Kildare, Slieve Bloom Mountains, and the "Devil's Bit" looked slightly more familiar than they did on our upward journey. At the station in Thurles we bought some blackthorn sticks. At Goold's Cross station we took a jaunting-car for Cashel, which was distant, through a fine, undulating country, about five or six miles. Before we reached Cashel the majestic, ruin-crowned Rock raised its sublime head amidst the fertile plain.

The ruins and Rock of Cashel are without doubt the most historic combination in Ireland. The earliest legendary history of this celebrated Rock relates that the devil was once making an excursion over this part of

Ireland, and, feeling hungry, took a bite out of the mountain at the place called the Devil's Bit; but finding it gritty and unpalatable, he let it fall in the plain, where it remains the Rock of Cashel. On this Rock the ancient kings of Munster were crowned and had their palace. On this Rock Ængus, king of Munster, was baptized by the hand of St. Patrick. At the opening of the ninth century Cormac Mac Cullinan, the bishop-king, founded a church on its heights, which in the tenth century were fortified by Brian Boru. In the twelfth century Cormac's chapel was built by Cormac Mac Carthy, and in the same century the cathedral of St. Patrick was erected by Donald O'Brien, king of Munster. These two structures are among the most important and best preserved ruins of the royal Rock. Near the cathedral stands a massive square tower or castle. Not far distant is a large Celtic cross of grit stone, supposed to date from the time of Cormac's chapel. The ancient round tower, which here, as elsewhere in Ireland, adds such enchantment to historic ruins, and so much picturesqueness to their pictures, is about twenty feet in diameter at its base, and ninety feet in height.

When the traveller looks up at this Rock,

whose great stone temples and strongholds are crumbling into pieces under the touch of the finger of time, he cannot realize the remarkable events that have taken place on those heights and in the surrounding plain below, nor the scenes of pageantry and splendor that have been a thousand times witnessed in the pagan and Christian ages of the past. Chieftains, prelates, and kings have ascended the rocky paths that led to the sanctuaries of religion and strongholds of power and influence, for purposes of devotion or consultation, and oftentimes to make preparations for battle or long-continued wars, from which they would return with the waving plumes and banners and tumultuous noise of victory, or lifeless, with cold, white face upturned, as they were borne on their shields by their warlike retainers, marching with steady step and muffled sounds. And then again hostile armies bearing hostile flags have swarmed around the base of Cashel's Rock, while out of its castellated ramparts its brave defenders have poured forth, and halfway down its heights have met their foes in deadly conflict. Beneath its broken arches kings and bishops sleep their last sleep, waiting the final summons; but before that day comes will there be a resurrection of Cashel's ancient glory? Kings may never rule there again, but let us live in hope that the time is not far distant when on the summit of Cashel's historic Rock a new cathedral shall rise from the ruins of its ancient temples, and that on its consecration-day a long line of Ireland's bishops will join in a grand religious procession, symbolical of a full return to the inheritance of their fathers. May the poetic spirit of the closing lines of a poem that I once wrote become prophetic—but in a more peaceful way:

> Behold ye Cashel's Rock o'erhead!
> I see strange visions of the dead,
> Which fill my soul with mighty dread;
>   I see from out historic graves
> Strange visions rise and disappear,
>   And Cashel's ancient banner waves,
> And sounds of triumph reach my ear.
>
> I see the king, and bard, and priest,
> In grand procession like a feast,
> Come forth and hail the sunlit east;
> And crumbling bones take flesh again,
>   A mighty army is revealed,
> Which nerves the arms of living men,
>   And fights with golden sword and shield;
> And Ireland wins, as win she must,
> For God has always been her trust,
> And God is true, and God is just.

After we had driven to a hotel and had made

arrangements for dinner, we returned to the Rock. We were admitted by the custodian through the walls which enclose the summit. We then wandered about at will, climbing to some of the higher windows, where we enjoyed a very extensive view, both near and far, of the fertile Golden Vale of Munster. Having sufficiently satisfied our laudable curiosity, we returned to the hotel, and soon afterwards to the railway station in time for the afternoon train south, which would connect at Mallow with the train for Killarney. The ride back to the station on that bright afternoon was very pleasant.

It was quite dark when we arrived in Killarney. Jaunting-cars were waiting at the station to convey passengers to the various hotels. We chose the Lake hotel, which is pleasantly situated on the shores of the lower lake. In the morning we looked out of the window over the lake, with its craggy rocks and sylvan islands, while near at hand and stretching away in the distance green, blue, and purple mountains reflected the morning sunlight. The lake district of Killarney has not inaptly been entitled "the Mecca of every pilgrim in search of the sublime and beautiful in nature, the mountain Paradise of the West."

After breakfast we started on a jaunting-car through Killarney, and around the lakes to the entrance of the Gap of Dunloe. This brought us to the very opposite extremity of the lakes from that on which our hotel was situated. On our way we stopped at the cathedral in Killarney, which was designed by one of the Pugins. In the morning we began to discover, what the day fully disclosed to us, that the region of Killarney possesses some of the most magnificent trees in Ireland, and the lawns and greensward spreading out from the highway as far as the eye can reach are as delightful as any that I have ever seen. The ride to the "Gap," in the balmy morning air and mild sunshine, would tend, if too often indulged in, to make romantic dreamers of the least poetic. Very near the opening to the Gap we visited the "cottage of Kate Kearney"—now occupied by a descendant of the original Kate Kearney, made famous in song by Thomas Moore—where you can take your choice of goat's milk or "mountain dew"; and you will get the same choice of "good or evil" at short intervals all the way through this famous mountain defile. The "Gap" extends about four miles between Toomies Mountain and the Macgillicuddy Range, the heights on either side being lofty and wild in appearance. On the way through some of the more rugged and romantic parts of the glen several men made themselves generally but picturesquely useless by firing old anvils, in order to awaken the echoes of the mountains and the generous spirit of the tourist. A stream flows through the entire defile, at times widening into small mountain lakes. When we had made about half of this part of our trip, which had to be accomplished on horseback, a blind fiddler and his wife, standing under a sheltering rock, attracted our attention. He played for our benefit with vigor and spirit, and his airs were full of patriotism, for he seemed unmindful or regardless of the fact that any one would ever pass that way except men of the strongest Irish national sentiments.\

The principal attractions of Killarney have been described so many times that it would hardly interest but would rather confuse the reader to give a new and extended description of such well-known objects as the Toomies Mountain, the Macgillicuddy Range, Mangerton, Devil's Punch-Bowl, Glen of the Horse, Purple Mountain, Torc Mountain, Carran Tual, Loch Dubh, Eagle's Nest, Old Wier Bridge, Meeting of the Waters, Dinis Island, and

Glena Bay. Our exit from the Gap was near the head of Upper Lake, where the boats were waiting for us. We enjoyed a delightful ride through Upper and Middle Lakes and out upon the waters of Lower Lake, which had become somewhat rough under a stiff breeze that had sprung up since morning.

The boatmen were hardly satisfied to row us to the island of Innisfallen, as it was considerably out of their way; but as I cared more to see that island than everything else in Killarney, I insisted, and they yielded. As they had to row against the waves, it must have been nearly a half-hour before we reached a landing. This island, which is called the "Gem of Killarney," contains about twenty-one acres. When we had landed, each took his own course. I wandered about in search of the ruins of the ancient monastery founded by St. Finian in the sixth century, and on account of which the island became so celebrated. Here the *Annals of Innisfallen* were written, which are so often quoted by historians. The ruins are overgrown with trees and vines, which hold them together. It is said that the wide-spreading ash-trees which overshadow them are among the largest and finest in Ireland. In fact, magnificent groves of ash, holly, beech, yew, and other trees are seen on every part of the island, between which are green lawns and sunny glades, which look out upon the waters of the beautiful lake and its numerous isles. Standing on some spot where we could get glimpses, in places, of the bright water, and on other sides a more extended view of the bosom of the lake, and through the branches of the trees the irregular outlines of the blue mountains, Innisfallen seemed to us to be one of the most favored places on earth for poetic musing or heavenly contemplation.

Innisfallen is one of the few places in the world where I would willingly spend a lifetime. It is now the property of the Earl of Kenmare, whose new and splendid residence appears on the mainland in full view of the island. On leaving its shores we appreciated the lines of Thomas Moore:

> "Sweet Innisfallen, fare thee well;
> May calm and sunshine long be thine!
> How fair thou art let others tell—
> To feel how fair thou art is mine.
>
> "Sweet Innisfallen, long shall dwell
> In memory's dream that sunny smile,
> Which o'er thee on that evening fell,
> When first I saw that fairy isle.

"Weeping or smiling, lovely isle!
  And all the lovelier for thy tears;
  For though but rare thy sunny smile,
    'Tis heav'n's own glance when it appears.

"Like feeling hearts whose joys are few,
  But when indeed they come, divine,
  The brightest light the sun e'er threw
    Is lifeless to one gleam of thine!"/

After our return to the hotel we drove to Muckross Abbey, which is considered one of the most venerable and perfect middle-age ruins in Ireland, mantled with ivy, and surrounded by one of the most beautiful demesnes in the British Isles. An aged yew-tree, said to be as old as the abbey itself, stands in the centre of the ancient enclosure. The immediate grounds are used as a burial-place, and beneath the pavements of Muckross lie the mortal remains of several of the celebrated kings of Munster.\

At six o'clock we left the station at Killarney on our way to Cork and Queenstown, at which latter place we arrived late in the evening. Early the next forenoon we saw the vessel which was to bear us to New York riding at anchor in the harbor. Early in the afternoon we went aboard the tender which brought us alongside the great Atlantic steamer, and soon after we were on deck ready to commence the voyage across the vast expanse of waters.

To me the voyage was a dreary one, although the thought of home lighted up the inner temple of my soul, where the gloom of nature could cast no shadows. Thirteen priests were among the passengers. On the second Sunday morning after leaving Queenstown our vessel was steaming past Staten Island into New York Bay, and I recognized the fact that we had enjoyed but few brighter or more beautiful scenes in the bays and harbors of the Old World than the one now presented to our eyes. On landing we drove to the hotel; and we arrived at St. Patrick's Cathedral in time for ten o'clock Mass.

A few days afterwards and I was at home again. A few days more passed by, and I was hardly able to realize that I had been away from home, and the scenes which we beheld in foreign lands seemed to exist only in the enchanted realms of dream-land.

FINIS.

www.ingramcontent.com/pod-product-compliance
Lightning Source LLC
Chambersburg PA
CBHW051852300426
44117CB00006B/360